Southern SEAFOOD Classics

The Official Cookbook of
The Southeastern Fisheries Association

PEACHTREE PUBLISHERS, LTD.

Published by
PEACHTREE PUBLISHERS, LTD.
494 Armour Circle, N.E.
Atlanta, Georgia 30324

Manufactured in the United States of America

Design by Paulette L. Lambert

10 9 8 7 6 5 4 3 2 1

Library of Congress Catalog Card Number 88-60000

ISBN 0-934601-43-7

C O N T E N T S

F O R E W O R D

Seafood has been available for millions of years. Ancient cave drawings depict fish-like creatures, and history is full of legends and myths associated with the sea.

Seafood heritage is strong throughout coastal America but is particularly strong in the Southeast. Important fisheries including shrimp, mullet, blue crab, stone crab, spiny lobster, snapper, grouper, oyster, clam and calico scallop were discovered in the southeastern part of the country some time during the era of the Spanish, English and French explorers in the late 1500s.

Discovery continues to this day—discovery of new ways to prepare the delicacies of the deep, discovery of healthful ingredients in seafood, such as omega-3 oils, which are important in reducing cholesterol.

The Southeastern Fisheries Association and the Florida Department of Natural Resources Bureau of Marketing and Extension have been in the seafood recipe business for over two decades. This partnership has made possible the development of the recipes found in *Southern Seafood Classics*. They have all been tested many times and in many parts of the world. We hope that within these pages you will find recipes that will broaden your experience with seafood.

Southern Seafood Classics opens with a section called "The Basics" to give every cook the confidence to purchase and handle the many species of fish found in southeastern waters. Next come chapters on hors d'oeuvres; brunch; soups, salads and sandwiches; entrees; and sauces. Scattered throughout are full-color pictures of many of the dishes. After the recipes are a brief history of southeastern fishing, with photos, and appendices on availability and nutrition, charts on smoking fish and timetables for other cooking methods.

Our goal in developing this book was to provide cooks with a complete and practical guide to using seafood as an integral part of the daily diet. The recipes are designed to make family dining as enjoyable as a special event and to give special occasions a simple elegance.

Our organizations would like to dedicate this book to the memory of H. Heber Bell, who was recognized as the father of the Florida Seafood Marketing Program, and to Janas Taylor Ware, home economist for the Florida Department of Natural Resources, who, during her short time on Earth, dedicated a major portion of her life to the enhancement of the seafood industry.

On behalf of all the members of the Southeastern Fisheries Association, we invite you to read this book from cover to cover and to enjoy seafood for a long time to come.

Bob Jones
Executive Director
Southeastern Fisheries Association

Carol Harrison
Chairman
SFA Cookbook Committee

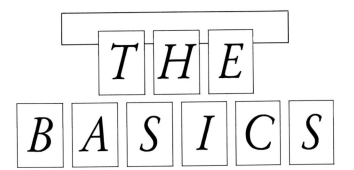

THE BASICS

Common Name	Flesh/Taste	Substitute Species	Preparation	Serving Tips

Clams

Hard Clam, Southern Quahog	Chewy texture, more strongly flavored	Oysters in certain preparations	Steam, stew, fry, simmer in own juice, fry or serve raw on half-shell	Grind clams for use in fritters and stuffed clams; use in choice of chowders. Use clam juice with seasonings.

Blue Crab

	Distinctive crab flavor, sweet, delicate meat available in 3 forms: lump, special, or flake, and claw meat.	Shrimp or Lobster may be substituted in some preparations	Simmer or steam hard-shell crabs; soft-shell crabs may be fried or grilled	Lump: cocktails and salads. Flake: salads, dips and spreads. Claw: stuffing deviled crab, casseroles.

Stone Crab Claws

	Claw meat is rich, sweet and firm in texture.	Blue Crab Claws	Always sold precooked; they can be served cold or steam just long enough to heat	Serve hot or cold with butter or mustard sauce.

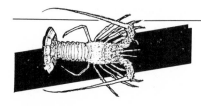

Spiny Lobster

Florida Lobster, Rock Lobster	Texture more coarse than American lobster, but flavor is similar.	Rock Shrimp in certain preparations	Boil, broil, steam or bake	Small tails can be split, battered and deep-fat fried similar to tempura shrimp.

Oysters

Atlantic Oyster, Eastern Oyster	Firm yet tender, flavor ranges from neutral to sweet to slightly salty.	Clams in certain preparations	Bake, broil, steam, fry, stew, roast, smoke or serve raw	Raw on the half-shell with cocktail sauce; baked as Oysters Rockefeller and Oysters Bienville.

* "Lean Fish" is a designation given to fish species with a fat content of not more than 5 percent.
"Fat Fish" are those fish with a fat content of more than 5 percent.

Common Name	Flesh/Taste	Substitute Species	Preparation	Serving Tips

Scallops

Calico, Bay	Firm with a sweet, delicate flavor, meat is creamy white to light tan to pink.	Calico, Sea or Bay Scallops	Bake, broil, poach, sauté or pan-fry	Use in crepes or salads or add pea pods and tomatoes for an Oriental stir-fry.

Rock Shrimp

	Texture is similar to lobster, flavor between shrimp and lobster	Shrimp, Lobster	Broil, bake, simmer, fry, sauté	Broil with garlic and butter, serve with green vegetables and rice. Note: Rock Shrimp require less cooking time than other shrimp.

Shrimp

White, Pink, Brown	Distinctive sweet flavor, crisp texture.	Rock Shrimp	Broil, bake, steam, simmer, grill, deep-fat fry, sauté	Large shrimp: use in entrées prepared in seasoned butter or sauce. Medium shrimp: shrimp cocktail, gumbo and curry. Small shrimp: dips and spreads, salads, soups.

Black Sea Bass

Blackfish, Southern Sea Bass, Rock Bass	Firm white meat, light, delicate flavor. Lean fish.*	Sea Trout, Snapper, Flounder	Steam, bake, broil, deep-fat fry	Combine with tomatoes and seasonings for a hearty chowder, or deep-fat fry, and serve with a sweet and sour sauce.

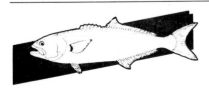

Bluefish

Blue Snapper, Tailor, Skipjack, Skip Mackerel	Moist, soft-textured with long flake, darker meat with more pronounced fish flavor. Fat fish.*	Spanish Mackerel, King Mackerel, Mullet	Bake, broil, grill, smoke	Broil with lemon or lime and butter, or bake Mediterranean-style with tomato, onion, oregano, garlic and olive oil.

9

Common Name	Flesh/Taste	Substitute Species	Preparation	Serving Tips

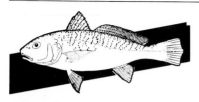

Croaker

Atlantic Croaker, Hardhead, Golden Croaker, Drum	Firm flesh, light meat, light to moderate flavor. Fat fish.*	Mullet, Pompano	Pan-fry, bake, grill, poach	Delicious in stew, serve with light lemon sauce to bring out flavor.

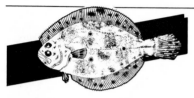

Flounder

Gulf Flounder, Southern Flounder, Southern Fluke, Summer Flounder	Firm white meat, delicate flake, fine texture, mild flavor. Lean fish.*	Sea Bass, Sheepshead, Sea Trout	Bake, broil, pan-fry	Bake and stuff whole with crab meat stuffing, or serve with light wine or cream sauce accompanied by a leafy green vegetable.

Grouper

Red, Black, Yellowfin, Nassau, Gag Scamp, Rock Hind	Firm white meat, heavy flake, mild flavor. Lean fish.*	Tilefish, Sea Bass	Poach, deep-fat fry, broil, bake	Makes excellent chowder or stock for bouillabaisse. Cubed or cut into fingers, battered and deep-fat fried is most popular.

King Mackerel

Kingfish, "King's" Cero, Cavalla, Sierra	Firm texture, darker flesh with more pronounced flavor. Fat fish.*	Spanish Mackerel, Bluefish	Broil, bake, steam, grill or smoke	Marinate steaks in lime juice or with herbs and spices before grilling. Excellent smoked for use in salads and dips.

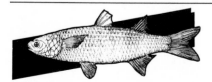

Mullet

Black, Striped, Jumping Mullet	Firm texture, light-colored flesh, moderate nut-like flavor. Fat fish.*	Croaker, Pompano	Bake, broil, oven-fry, deep-fat fry, pan fry, smoke	Fresh mullet is a favorite fried, or smoke it for fabulous dips, spreads or salads.

Common Name	Flesh/Taste	Substitute Species	Preparation	Serving Tips

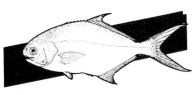

Pompano

Cobblerfish, Butterfish, Palmenta	Firm texture, light-colored flesh, moderate flavor. Fat fish.*	Croaker, Mullet	Broil, bake, plank, grill, pan-fry or deep-fat fry	Most famous preparation is pompano en papillote, or simply sprinkle with lemon juice and broil over charcoal.

Redfish

Sea Bass, Red Drum, Channel Bass, Red Sea Bass	Firm texture, moist, white and heavy flaked, mild flavor. Lean fish.*	Grouper, Tilefish	Bake, broil, poach, deep-fat fry	Stuff with an herb and lemon rice stuffing and bake, or use in hearty fish chowder.

Red Snapper

Gulf Snapper, Pensacola Red Snapper	Tender, moist white meat, delicate, sweet flavor. Lean fish.*	Flounder, Sea Bass, Sea Trout	Broil, bake, steam, poach, fry, grill	Baste with combination of orange juice, butter and soy sauce and broil, garnish with orange slices.

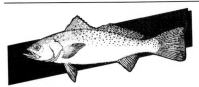

Sea Trout

Weakfish, Speckled Trout, Gray, Spotted, "Specks"	Finely textured white flesh, mild, sweet flavor. Lean fish.*	Flounder, Sea Bass, Redfish	Bake, broil, poach, sauté, pan-fry	Sauté sea trout fillets with almonds for delicious Fish Almandine.

Sheepshead

Convict Fish, Fathead	Light-colored meat, light to moderate flavor. Lean fish.*	Sea Trout, Redfish	Bake, broil, poach, pan-fry	Prepare simply with a seasoned butter sauce and broil.

Common Name	Flesh/Taste	Substitute Species	Preparation	Serving Tips

Shark

Mako, Blue, Blacktip, Angel, Hammerhead	Firm texture, white meat with very mild flavor, no bones. Lean fish.*	Grouper, Redfish, Tilefish	Deep-fat fry, bake, broil, smoke, grill, poach	Marinate in teriyaki sauce, grill over charcoal and serve with sautéed vegetables.

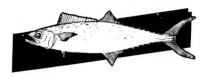

Spanish Mackerel

American, Atlantic Blue	Darker meat, more delicately flavored than other mackerels. Fat fish.*	Mullet, Pompano, King Mackerel	Broil, bake, smoke	Smoke and serve bite-sized pieces with mustard or dill sauce.

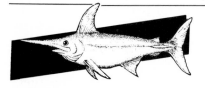

Swordfish

Billfish, Broadbill Swordfish	Firm flesh, light meat, light to moderate flavor. Lean fish.*	Shark	Oven-broil, grill, bake, poach	Marinate and grill over hot coals, serve with baked potato and salad for a uniquely different steak dinner.

Tilefish

Golden, Grey, Blueline	Firm yet tender flesh, comparable to lobster or scallop, mild, sweet flavor. Lean fish.*	Grouper, Redfish	Bake, broil, poach, deep-fat fry	Combine cooked, flaked fish with citrus fruit to make a low-calorie salad.

Purchasing and Handling Seafood

Of all the species in the sea, only a small percentage of edible products are harvested. The seafood industry is continually seeking new and better ways of harvesting, processing and preparing fish and of increasing consumption of under-utilized species. With so many choices available, consumers need the best information possible to make wise decisions about seafood purchases and preparation.

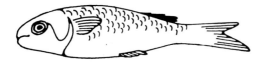

Fish

When selecting a whole fish (just as it comes from the water) or drawn fish (eviscerated only), look for these signs of freshness: **eyes**—bright, clear and bulging; **gills**—bright red in color and free of slime; **flesh**—firm and elastic, fresh-cut with no traces of browning or drying out; **skin**—iridescent and unfaded characteristic markings and colors of that species; **odor**—fresh and mild, with no disagreeable "fishy" smell. Judge fresh steaks and fillets on the basis of flesh, skin and color.

Fresh fish may be frozen at home in a block of ice or by glazing, both of which prevent moisture loss. To freeze fish or shrimp in a solid block of ice, put the seafood in a container, fill the container with water and place it in the freezer.

Glazing is as effective as block freezing and takes less freezer space. To glaze fish, dress it and steak or fillet it if desired. Place the fish in a single layer on a tray, wrap and freeze. As soon as the fish is solidly frozen, remove it from the freezer and

unwrap and dip it quickly into ice cold water. A glaze will form immediately. Repeat the dipping process three or four times. A thin coat of ice will result from each dipping. It may be necessary to return the fish to the freezer between dippings if the glaze does not continue to build up. Handle carefully to avoid breaking the glaze. Wrap the fish tightly in freezer paper or aluminum foil and return it to the freezer. Glazing may need to be repeated if fish is not used within one to two months.

Thaw frozen fish by placing it in the refrigerator, allowing eighteen to twenty-four hours for a one-pound package to thaw. For a quicker method of thawing, place fish under cold running water. *Never* thaw fish at room temperature and *never* refreeze.

To dress a whole or round fish:

1) Lay the fish on a board and grasp the head firmly. Using a scaler or a large tablespoon, scrape the scales off, working from the tail to the head.

2) Make a cut the entire length of the belly and remove the entrails and the pelvic fins.

3) Using a sharp knife, remove the head and the pectoral fins by making a cut just in front of the collarbone. If the backbone is large, cut down to it on either side and snap the head off.

4) Remove the dorsal fin by cutting along each side with a sharp knife. Then grasp the end near the tail with one hand and give a quick pull toward the head. Clean and rinse the fish thoroughly. The fish is now dressed or pan-dressed.

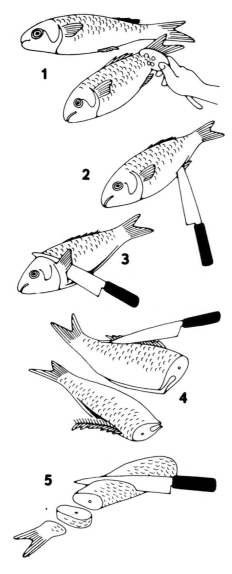

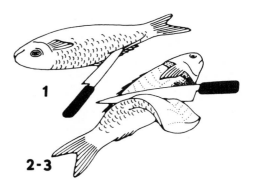

3) Turn the knife flat and slide along the rib bones to the tail, cutting the flesh away from the backbone. Turn the fish over and repeat the procedure.

To skin a fillet:

1) Do not scale the fish. Lay the fillet, skin side down, on a cutting board. Hold the tail end of the fillet with the fingers of one hand. With a sharp knife at an angle, make a cut about half an inch from the fingers through the flesh to the skin, being careful not to cut through the skin.

2) Lay the knife blade flat against the skin and push the knife forward along the skin while holding the free end of the skin firmly with the fingers.

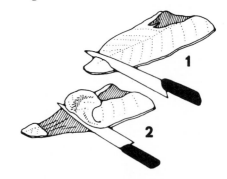

5) With one additional step, a large dressed fish can be steaked by cutting across the backbone with a sharp knife at approximately one- to one and a quarter-inch intervals.

When purchasing fish, allow one pound of whole or drawn fish per serving, one-half pound dressed fish and one-third pound of steaks or fillets.

For cooking and freezing instructions, fish are loosely grouped

To fillet a fish:

1) It is not necessary to dress the fish completely. Scale the fish, unless the fillet is to be skinned. With a sharp knife, cut through the flesh along the backbone from the tail to just behind the head.

2) Cut down to the backbone just behind the collarbone.

into two categories—fat and lean, based on the type and amount of oil found in the fish and the fish's flavor. Although these groupings are generally accepted, the amount of oil will vary according to the time of year, and some fish fluctuate from fat to lean.

"Lean" fish is a designation given to species with a fat content ranging from 0.5 percent to not more than 5 percent, with the oil in these fish characteristically concentrated in the liver. Weakfish or sea trout, sheepshead, grouper, black drum, flounder, snapper, whiting, spot, jewfish and tilefish are among the more common commercial southeastern species in this category. Due to low oil content, these fish maintain quality during freezing up to six months and the very leanest can be held in the freezer up to one year.

"Fat" fish is the general name given to those species which have an oil content of more than 5 percent. Since the oil is distributed throughout the flesh of the fish, the flesh color of the fat fish tends to be darker than that of the leaner species. The exact percentage of oil in the fish flesh depends on such variables as species, season of the year, and the water depth from which the fish is taken. Spanish mackerel, king mackerel, mullet, bluefish, croaker and pompano are among the species that should be handled as fat fish. These fish do not freeze as well as some lean fish, and it is recommended that they be used within three months.

Keep these general hints in mind when selecting a fish for recipe preparation:

1) As a general rule, the species which contain higher percentages of oil have a stronger flavor. Lean fish may be substituted for fat fish in a recipe, but the flavor of the fish may be masked and more frequent basting may be required due to the low oil content. (For a guide to substitutions, see the chart on pages 8-12.)

2) If recipe preparation requires frequent handling of the fish, as in chowders, soups or pickling, a firm-textured fish (grouper, shark, jewfish, tilefish) will retain its shape and have a more pleasing finished appearance.

3) Cooking time will vary according to the thickness and the size of the fish. To prevent overcooking, the fish should be tested about halfway through the recommended cooking time and frequently thereafter until it flakes easily when tested with a fork.

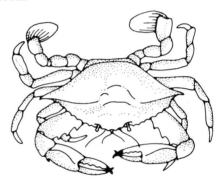

Blue Crab

Blue crab, like other crab, possess five pairs of legs with the first pair always equipped with pincers. When fully grown, a blue crab averages five to seven inches across the shell from tip to tip.

Blue crab are caught and marketed in both the hard-shell and soft-shell stages. Soft-shell crabs are available fresh or frozen, and soft-shell blue crabs should be *solidly* frozen when purchased. Hard-shelled crabs are sold either alive or as cooked meat—fresh or pasteurized. Fresh or pasteurized cooked crab meat is usually available in the following forms:

1) cocktail claws (exposed claw meat attached to pincer);

2) lump meat (solid lumps of white meat from the back fin of the body);

3) special or flake meat (small pieces of white meat from the body);

4) claw meat (a brownish meat from the claws, used in recipes where appearance is not important as it is generally more economical than the other forms).

Since blue crab meat does not freeze well, pasteurization was developed to prolong the shelf life of fresh crab meat. This process involves hermetically sealing the packed cans and immersing them in a hot water bath. Pasteurization does not alter the taste or texture of the crab meat, but simply prolongs the shelf life, if the can is not opened, for up to six months under refrigeration.

If crabs are to be purchased live, make sure they show movement. Fresh or pasteurized crab meat has a very mild odor. Since crab meat is sealed when purchased, if it should have a disagreeable odor when you open it, return it to the market along with the ticket from the day of purchase, or at least call the market to report the problem. Fresh crab meat is best if used within one to two days of purchase and maintains quality better if it is packed in ice in the refrigerator. Pasteurized crab meat must be kept under refrigeration.

When purchasing live crabs, allow three hard-shell crabs per serving. One pound of lump, special or claw meat is enough to make approximately six servings.

People who catch their own crab sometimes wish to freeze the meat. Since pasteurization is a commercial process and freezing cooked crab meat is unsuccessful, the next best way to preserve crab meat for approximately one to two months is to freeze it raw. It is best to remove the claws and the inner pod of cartilage containing the body meat and to discard the rest of the crab. Freeze the uncracked claws and

unpicked pod of meat whole in a block of ice.

Laws in some states make it illegal to take egg-bearing females, easily recognized by the large orange mass of eggs protruding from beneath the apron. Be sure to throw these back to protect the species and insure future blue crab populations.

To clean a blue crab:

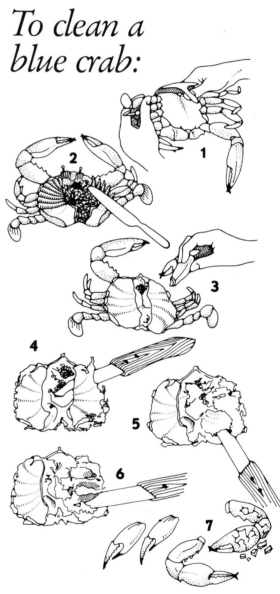

1) With the crab upside down, grasp the legs on one side firmly with one hand, and with the other hand lift the flap (apron) and pull back and down to remove the top shell.

2) Turn the crab right side up, remove the gills and wash out the intestines and spongy material.

3) With a twisting motion, pull the legs loose from the body. Remove any meat that adheres to the legs. Break off the claws.

4) Slice off the top of the inner skeleton and remove all exposed meat on this slice.

5) At the back of the crab, on each side, lies a large lump of meat. With a very careful U-shaped motion of the knife, remove this back fin lump.

6) Remove the white flake meat from the other pockets with the point of the knife.

7) Crack the claw shell and remove the shell along with the moveable pincer. This will expose the claw meat and, if meat is left attached to the remaining pincer, it will make a delicious crab finger hors d'oeuvre. Or the dark meat can be removed and used in soups, casseroles or salads.

Crab fingers can also be breaded (using the breading instructions on page 137) and deep-fat fried for thirty to forty-five seconds or until golden brown or batter-fried (using batter instructions on page 137) and deep-fat fried for eight to ten seconds or until golden brown. Plain or fried, crab fingers and a seafood sauce make a delicious main dish or hors d'oeuvre.

Stone Crab

Crab have the unusual ability to cast off their legs or pincers if they are caught by one leg or experience changes in temperature. The separation always occurs at one of the joints to protect the crab from bleeding. During the life of a crab, the same appendage may be regenerated three or four times. Florida law takes advantage of this ability by making it illegal to harvest whole stone crabs. One or both of the very powerful black-tipped claws may be removed, provided the length of the forearm measures two and three-quarter inches. If not, the claw must be left on the crab and the live stone crab returned to the water.

Although stone crabs are found along the coast from North Carolina to Mexico, they are commercially landed only in Florida. Since Florida law forbids the taking of whole stone crab, only the claws are marketed. Freezing or icing raw stone crab claws causes the meat to stick to the inside of the shell. For this reason, they are cooked immediately on landing and sold cooked.

Cooked stone crab claws, unlike blue crab meat, freeze beautifully in the shell, making it possible to purchase cooked stone crab claws refrigerated or frozen. When purchasing cooked stone crab claws, freshness can be judged only on the basis of a mild odor.

Store cooked stone crab claws, like other cooked seafood, in the refrigerator at thirty-two degrees to thirty-five degrees or packed in ice for no longer than two to three days. If the claws are purchased freshly cooked and frozen in the shell the same day, the shelf life of the claw is about six months. Shelf life will be reduced if the claws are improperly handled or not of good quality when frozen. Always examine cooked claws for broken joints or cracks in the shell before freezing. The shell protects the meat during freezing and eliminates the necessity of block freezing or glazing. Freeze only claws that are completely intact. Frozen stone crab claws are best when thawed in the refrigerator for twelve to eighteen hours. Quality is lost if the claws are thawed under cold running water or at room temperature.

To serve stone crab claws:

Crack all the sections of shell with a hammer or nutcracker and let people pick the meat out themselves. The claw portion makes an attractive hors d'oeuvre or appetizer. To serve crab this way, crack the claw and remove the shell and moveable pincer, leaving the meat attached to the remaining pincer. The cooked meat can also be picked from the shell and used in any recipe calling for cooked crab meat or lobster. Approximately two and one-half pounds of cooked stone crab claws are required to yield one pound of crab meat. Most people are purists when it comes to stone crab and prefer it cold or steamed only long enough to heat it and served with clarified butter or warm lemon butter. The delicately flavored meat of Florida stone crab is considered one of the Southeast's finest seafoods.

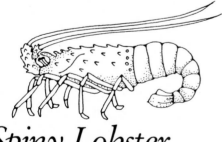

Spiny Lobster

The spiny lobster, also called Florida lobster, sea crawfish or crayfish, is a beautifully colored crustacean mottled with brown, green and blue and dotted with light yellow or white spots on the tail sections.

The meat of the spiny lobster comes primarily from the smooth tail section since this species does not have the large, meat-filled claws characteristic of the northern lobster.

During the harvesting season and shortly thereafter, spiny lobster is available live or frozen "green," either as whole lobster or lobster tails. Like other shellfish, if purchased live, the lobster must show movement. After the harvesting season is closed, it is difficult sometimes to find the frozen "green" form since most of the lobster is cooked and marketed as frozen cooked whole lobster or lobster tails. Cooked lobster can easily be recognized because the shell turns bright red-orange in color and the meat is snowy white with tinges of red on the membrane surrounding the meat. This reddish membrane sometimes becomes tough when a cooked lobster is frozen and may need to be removed before serving.

When purchasing lobster, allow a one-pound green whole lobster per serving. However, when used in combination with other ingredients, one pound of cooked lobster meat will make approximately six servings. It is helpful to know when purchasing a lobster that a one-pound green lobster will yield approximately one-third pound cooked lobster meat.

Lobster must be handled with care to preserve quality after purchase. Freeze green lobster live for the best quality. Since the shell protects the meat from drying out, no glazing or block freezing is necessary unless it is to be kept longer than four months. If the lobster is purchased frozen, make sure it is completely frozen; then return it to the freezer as quickly as possible after purchase to prevent thawing. If thawing does occur, cook right away. Cooked lobster will maintain quality in the refrigerator for two to three days. If frozen green, lobster in the shell wrapped in freezer paper will maintain quality at zero degrees or below for four months. Frozen cooked lobster in the shell is best if used within two months. Thaw frozen lobster in the refrigerator for twelve to twenty-four hours or under cold running water. Lobster which is partially frozen, as well as other partially frozen seafood, can be prepared but will require a little longer cooking time.

Cleaning boiled lobster and preparing green lobster for baking are the same process.

To prepare boiled or green lobster:

1) With a sharp knife cut lobster in half lengthwise.

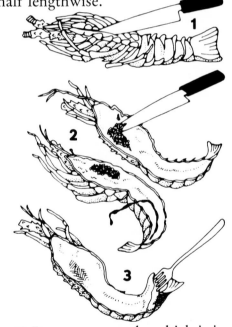

2) Remove stomach, which is in the body section, and intestinal vein, which runs from the stomach to the tip of the tail. Rinse and clean body cavity thoroughly. The green lobster is ready for baking.

3) If the lobster is boiled and the meat needs to be removed from the shell, use a sharp knife to loosen meat from the edges. With a fork, pierce the meat at the tip of the tail, lift upward and pull the meat toward the head and away from the shell.

Oysters

One of nature's richest sources of iron is the succulent oyster. Women require more iron each day than men, and only six select oysters provide enough iron to meet a woman's daily iron requirement. Oysters are also rich in other minerals, contain most of the essential vitamins and supply protein as well.

Eastern oysters found along the Gulf and Atlantic coasts can be marketed live in the shell, fresh and frozen shucked, breaded and frozen, and canned. Oysters must be alive when purchased in the shell—shells that close tightly when handled are the sign of a live oyster. Fresh oysters are sold by the dozen or by bags, which contain approximately one bushel. They will remain alive from seven to ten days if stored un-iced in the refrigerator at thirty-five to forty degrees. Shucked oysters are graded and sold according to size, usually in pints or gallons. The largest shucked oysters are marketed as *select*, while the average size are marketed as *standard*. Only on rare occasions will a smaller size (stewing oyster) or a larger size (count) be available.

Fresh shucked oysters are plump and have a natural creamy color and clear liquid. If properly handled and packed in ice in the refrigerator, freshly shucked oysters will maintain quality for about a week. Oysters lose considerable quality during home freezing and should be used in casseroles or fried upon thawing. Although home freezing of oysters is not recommended, commercially frozen oysters are fine. The difference is quick freezing, which is not possible with a home freezer. If necessary, freshly shucked oysters can be frozen in the commercially packed can in which they are purchased or frozen in their own liquor in a container that will leave very little airspace when sealed. Use frozen oysters within two months and sooner if possible. Thawing in the refrigerator or in an airtight container under cold running water is acceptable.

One pint of shucked oysters will yield six servings. Some oyster lovers will eat more when the oysters are fried or served on the half shell.

To shuck oysters:

Cotton gloves and an oyster knife are essential. An oyster knife is a heavy piece of metal with a wedge-shaped blade and handle in one piece, designed to withstand the pressure required to open oysters. Never use a sharp knife. Rinse the oyster thoroughly. The cleanest way to open oysters is to grasp each oyster securely by the thin end or "bill," leaving the hinge (thicker portion) exposed toward the other hand. Usually there is a small crevice at the hinge.

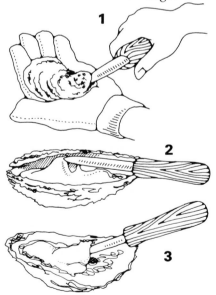

1) Insert the oyster knife in this crevice between the shells; twist the knife while pushing it firmly into the opening to sever the hinge.

2) Once the hinge is broken, before pulling the shell apart, slide the knife

along the inside of the top shell and cut the adductor muscle loose from the shell.

3) Remove the top shell and again slip the knife under the oyster, being careful not to mutilate it, and cut the muscle away from the bottom shell. Remove any remaining shell particles that may be attached to the oyster.

Most oysters, except the very largest, can be opened by this method. Larger oysters can be opened by breaking part of the shell on the

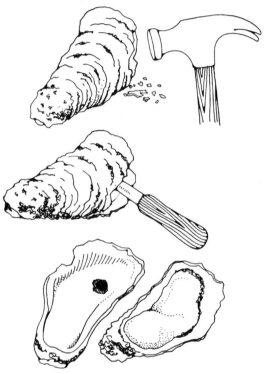

thin end with a hammer to make an opening. Insert the knife in this opening and slide it along the inside of the top shell to cut the adductor muscle and then cut the oyster away from remaining shell. This method tends to leave more shell particles on the oyster. Be careful not to mutilate it.

Oysters are easy to prepare, entirely edible and delicious raw or cooked in a variety of recipes. To retain the delicate, distinctive flavor of oysters, cook them only long enough to heat them thoroughly. They should maintain their natural plumpness and tender quality.

Scallops

The scallop, like the oyster, is a bivalve mollusk, but, unlike the oyster, the scallop is a very active swimmer. By snapping its shells together, the scallop expels a jet of water that acts as a means of propulsion. The adductor muscle of the scallop thus becomes oversized. It is this muscle that furnishes a lean, light, firm meat with a delicate, sweet flavor.

The Southeast produces two scallop species commercially—the bay scallop and the calico scallop. Calico scallop meat size compares to the size of bay scallop meat in diameter (approximately one-half to three-quarter inches) but is longer than the bay scallop.

Scallops are unable to close their shells tightly and consequently die soon after being taken from the water. For this reason the scallop is always shucked immediately after being harvested, and the meat is iced. Since only the adductor muscle is eaten, the name *scallop* has generally come to mean the adductor muscle when used to describe shucked meat. The word *scallop*, when used in *Southern Seafood Classics* in reference to purchasing or cooking, refers to shucked scallop meat, which is what is generally available on the market.

In choosing fresh scallops, examine the product for a creamy white, light tan or pinkish color and a mild, slightly sweet odor. When purchased in packages, fresh or frozen scallops should be practically free of liquid. Fresh scallops should be stored on ice in a refrigerator at a temperature between thirty-five and forty degrees. They are best used the day of purchase but can be held on ice for two days with little flavor or texture change. Raw frozen scallops can be held at zero degrees or below for three to four months. Like most other seafood products, scallops retain quality better if frozen in the raw state. Cooked scallops lose moisture, texture and flavor during freezing. Thaw frozen scallops in the refrigerator or under cold running water. After thawing, raw scallops should have the mild, slightly sweet odor characteristic of the fresh product.

To shuck a scallop:

1) Holding the scallop in the palm of one hand with the shell's hinge against the palm, insert a slender, strong knife, not sharp (a dinner knife will do) between the halves of the shell near the hinge. Then twist to give access to the inside. Do not force the shell open as this will tear the scallop muscle.

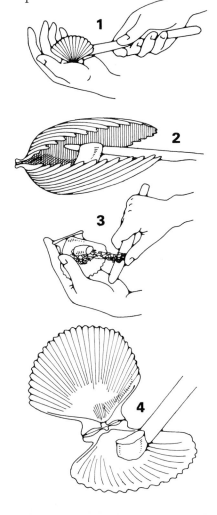

2) Lift the top side of the shell far enough to insert the knife point and sever the muscle from the top shell. Remove the top shell. Leave the muscle attached to the bottom shell until all viscera is removed.

3) To remove the viscera, grip the dark portion of the scallop firmly between the thumb and knife blade and pull gently. This should remove everything but the edible white scallop muscle.

4) When all viscera is removed, sever the muscle from the remaining shell. Wash the scallop meat in cold water, place in moisture- and vapor-proof wrapping and ice immediately.

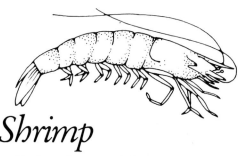

Shrimp

Shrimp is one of the most popular shellfish in the United States. This is not surprising because shrimp have a distinctive flavor, and the pink-white cooked meat is tender, delicate and delicious.

The shrimp is a ten-legged crustacean that wears its skeleton on the outside. Shrimp from the waters of the Gulf and the South Atlantic grow larger than their cold water cousins. The species of warm water shrimp most commonly found in the market are white, brown and pink. They are interchangeable in any shrimp recipe. (Rock shrimp are also a warm water species, but they are different. See page 24 for information on rock shrimp.)

"Green" shrimp is a term used to describe raw shrimp of any species in the shell. Regardless of the color of the green shrimp, when cooked, the shells of all species will turn red, the meat will become white with reddish tinges, and the flavor and nutritional values will be the same.

Shrimp are usually sold according to size or grade, based on the number of headless shrimp per pound. The grades are indicated by the names jumbo, large, medium and small.

Fresh shrimp are firm in texture and have a mild odor. Available in a variety of market forms, shrimp may be purchased raw or cooked, peeled or unpeeled, and fresh or frozen. When purchasing frozen shrimp, make sure the shrimp are solidly frozen, have little or no odor, no brown spots and no signs of freezer burn, indicated by a very white, dry appearance around the edges.

Roughly speaking, two pounds of raw, headless, unpeeled shrimp, properly cooked, will yield one pound of cooked, peeled and deveined shrimp—enough protein for six servings. For maximum quality, cook fresh shrimp within one to two days of purchase. If you plan to use the shrimp more than two days after the purchase, they will be fresher if they are frozen on the day of purchase. Cooked shrimp may be stored in the refrigerator for two to three days. Raw, headless shrimp in the shell maintain quality during freezing longer than frozen cooked shrimp and are best if frozen at the peak of freshness. Fresh shrimp can be frozen in a block of ice or glazed (see page 13). Raw shrimp maintain quality during freezing at a temperature of zero degrees or below for approximately six months. Home-frozen cooked shrimp begin to lose quality after approximately one month.

Thaw frozen shrimp by placing them in the refrigerator, allowing eighteen to twenty-four hours for a one-pound package to thaw. To thaw more quickly, place shrimp under cold running water. *Never* thaw shrimp at room temperature and *never* refreeze.

To clean shrimp:

The method is the same for raw or cooked shrimp, but it is simpler to do when the shrimp are raw.

1) To peel, hold the tail of the shrimp in one hand; slip the thumb of the other hand under the shell between swimmerets and lift off several segments of the shell. Repeat, if necessary, removing all but the tail section.

2) If the tail section is to be removed, hold it and squeeze with the thumb and the forefinger. Pull the shrimp meat with the other hand until it is released from the shell.

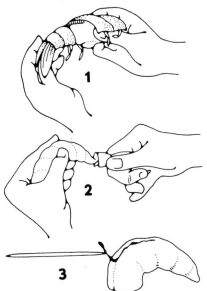

3) The vein (usually black) located near the upper curve is commonly referred to as the "sand vein." Most people prefer to remove it to prevent any sand or grit in the cooked shrimp. It can be removed before or after cooking, but it is much easier to remove before. The vein located on the under curve is part of the circulatory system and need not be removed. To remove the sand vein, make a cut with a sharp knife about one-eighth inch deep along the upper curve of the shrimp. Then rinse away the sand vein under cold running water.

Several varieties of shrimp peeling and deveining tools are available. Some work better than others, but all are designed, when used properly, to remove the shell and vein from the shrimp in one easy motion. All work best when shrimp are peeled and deveined in the raw state.

Shrimp may be prepared in hundreds of ways and served for almost any course in a menu. Shrimp are an excellent source of high-quality protein, vitamins and minerals, and because they are low in calories and easy to digest, they can fit into many special diets.

Even though shrimp cooked by simmering are generally referred to as "boiled" shrimp, shrimp and other seafoods should *not* be boiled. Care should be taken not to overcook shrimp, and the liquid in which the shrimp are cooked should only simmer, never boil, with the shrimp in it. The size of shrimp may vary, so it is best to test for doneness near the end of the recommended cooking time for each size to prevent overcooking. Overcooking toughens the protein, dries out the shrimp and causes the loss of valuable weight. A shrimp is done when it has lost the translucent, watery appearance in its center and has become opaque and white.

Shrimp may be simmered before or after cleaning, depending on personal preference. People tend to eat more shrimp when the shrimp are served peeled and deveined. They do not eat quite as many if they have to work at it. Although raw shrimp are easier to clean, cooking shrimp with the shell on gives them a richer pink color and a more natural curve when they are served. Cooking time varies only slightly between peeled and unpeeled shrimp. The cleaned shrimp require a little closer attention to avoid overcooking. The amount of salt required for shrimp simmered in the shell is one-quarter cup diluted in five cups of water, while peeled and deveined shrimp should be simmered in only two tablespoons of salt diluted in five cups of water.

Rock Shrimp

Rock shrimp, indisputably a member of the shrimp family, could easily be mistaken for miniature lobster tails. Deriving their name from an extremely tough, rigid exoskeleton, rock shrimp were for centuries the prized catch of fishermen but little known to the public. Only in the last few years, with development of machinery to split the shells, have rock shrimp become a popular commercial product. Not only the hard shell but also the texture of the meat is like lobster, while the flavor is between that of lobster and shrimp.

This uniquely delicious creature is far more perishable than either the Florida lobster or its Southern shrimp relatives. Because the flavor and texture can be adversely affected by temperature changes or poor handling practices, rock shrimp are best if the heads are removed immediately after they are caught. It is imperative that the heads be removed and the tails frozen within twenty-four hours. Therefore, most rock shrimp are marketed frozen in the raw state, as either whole or split tails. Rock shrimp are just as good and quite often better when purchased frozen. They are purchased according to size, with the largest size generally available being twenty-one to twenty-five per pound. Whether purchasing rock shrimp tails fresh or frozen, the

quality can be determined by the odor and color of the flesh. Properly handled rock shrimp will have some transparent or clear white flesh. The odor of fresh, high-quality rock shrimp will be mild, with no objectionable off-odor.

When purchasing rock shrimp, it is helpful to know that properly cleaned and cooked they yield about half the weight of the green tails. Therefore, two pounds of green tails will yield one pound of cooked, peeled, deveined rock shrimp.

Split tails are easier to prepare. Cleaning the whole tail is not difficult, but hands combat the hard shell better if armored with rubber gloves. Thaw the rock shrimp under cold running water as they are being cleaned and be ready to cook them immediately. Cooked rock shrimp maintain quality for two to three days in the refrigerator but lose quality rapidly under refrigeration or at room temperature in the green form.

To clean rock shrimp:

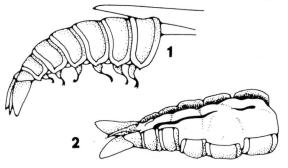

1) Hold the tail section in one hand with the swimmerets down toward the palm of the hand. Using kitchen shears, insert one blade of the scissors in the sand vein opening and cut through the shell along the outer curve to the end of the tail.

2) Pull the sides of the shell apart and remove the meat. Wash thoroughly in cold water to remove all the sand vein. The rock shrimp are then ready for simmering.

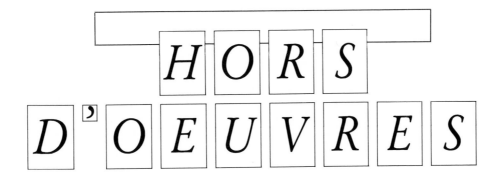

HORS
D'OEUVRES

Smothered Oysters

24 fresh oysters, in the shell
¼ cup minced green pepper
¼ cup minced green onions
¼ cup minced celery
¼ cup chopped chives
2 tablespoons water

1 teaspoon lemon juice
1 teaspoon Worcestershire sauce
¼ teaspoon liquid hot pepper sauce
Rock salt
¼ cup bacon bits
¼ cup grated Cheddar cheese

Preheat oven to 375 degrees. Rinse unopened oysters under cold running water to remove any foreign particles. Shuck oysters, reserving half the shells. Clean shells. In a small saucepan, combine green pepper, green onions, celery, chives and water. Cover and simmer slowly for approximately 7 minutes or until crisp-tender; remove from heat. Add lemon juice, Worcestershire sauce and liquid hot pepper sauce to vegetables; mix well. Pour ½ inch of rock salt in a 13 x 9 x 2-inch baking pan. Arrange oysters in reserved shells; place shells firmly on rock salt. Top each oyster with vegetable mixture. Sprinkle bacon bits and cheese on top of vegetables. Bake at 375 degrees for 10 minutes. Yield: 4 servings or 24 appetizers.

Spectacular Shrimp Spread

½ pound cooked, peeled, deveined rock shrimp
1 can (13 ounces) artichoke hearts, drained
1 cup mayonnaise

½ cup Parmesan cheese
¼ teaspoon lemon-pepper
⅛ teaspoon salt
⅛ teaspoon cayenne
Melba toast or assorted crackers

Preheat oven to 400 degrees. Finely chop rock shrimp and artichoke hearts. Add mayonnaise (½ cup mayonnaise and ½ cup plain yogurt may be substituted), cheese and seasonings; mix well. Place mixture in a 9-inch pie plate or 1-quart shallow baking dish. Bake at 400 degres for 10 minutes or until hot and bubbly. Serve hot with melba toast or crackers. Yield: 4½ cups.

Red Snapper and Pasta Pinwheels

1½ pounds cooked, flaked red snapper or other flaked fish
1 cup mayonnaise
½ cup finely minced celery
½ cup finely minced green onions
½ cup finely minced delicatessen-style dill pickles
¼ cup toasted, slivered almonds

2 teaspoons Dijon mustard
1 teaspoon salt
½ teaspoon white pepper
¼ teaspoon dried dillweed
9 lasagna noodles
2 teaspoons paprika
Bibb lettuce (garnish)

In medium mixing bowl, combine all ingredients except noodles, paprika and lettuce. Mix well. Cook noodles according to package directions. Drain, pat dry; arrange flat on work surface. Spread filling over noodles leaving 1-inch border on one short end. From borderless end, roll noodles up tightly; dip curly edges in paprika. Place noodles seam side down on tray. Cover and chill 1 to 2 hours. To serve, arrange lettuce on individual plates. Cut each roll in half and arrange with cut side down on lettuce. Yield: 6 servings or 18 hors d'oeuvres. **(Photo, page 33)**

Smoked Fish Dip

½ pound smoked Spanish mackerel or other smoked fish, fresh or frozen
1 cup dairy sour cream
2 tablespoons lemon juice
2 teaspoons chopped chives

1 teaspoon instant minced onion
½ teaspoon salt
¼ teaspoon dried rosemary
6 peppercorns, crushed
⅛ teaspoon ground cloves
Assorted chips or raw vegetables

Remove skin and bones from fish. Flake the fish. Combine all ingredients except crackers. Chill at least one hour before serving to blend flavors. Sprinkle with parsley. Serve with chips. Yield: 3½ cups.

Coconut Fried Shrimp

2 pounds peeled, deveined large
   shrimp, fresh or frozen (tail
   section may be left on)
2 cups all-purpose flour
1½ cups milk
1½ teaspoons baking powder

1 teaspoon curry
½ teaspoon salt
2 cups shredded coconut
Vegetable oil for deep-frying
Sweet and Sour Sauce
   (see recipe on page 52)

Thaw shrimp if frozen. Measure ½ cup of flour and set aside. In a 1-quart mixing bowl, combine the remaining 1½ cups flour, milk, baking powder, curry and salt. Place reserved flour and coconut in two separate shallow pans. Dredge shrimp in flour, dip in batter, then roll in coconut. Fry in hot oil at 350 degrees, until coconut is golden brown. Drain on absorbent paper before transferring to warming tray. Serve hot with Sweet and Sour Sauce. Yield: 6 servings. **(Photo, page 35)**

Bacon-Baked Oysters

24 fresh oysters, shucked, half of
   shells reserved
6 slices bacon, cut into 1-inch pieces
½ cup mayonnaise
1 cup butter-flavored cracker
   crumbs, crushed

2 tablespoons dehydrated chives
1 teaspoon hot pepper sauce
½ teaspoon Dijon mustard
1 teaspoon lemon juice
¼ cup grated Parmesan cheese

Preheat oven to 400 degrees. In 10-inch skillet, cook bacon until limp. Set aside. In small bowl, combine remaining ingredients except Parmesan cheese and mix well. Pour ½ inch of coarse salt into baking pan. Arrange oysters, each in half-shell, on salt until they sit firmly. Top each oyster with crumb mixture. Sprinkle with Parmesan cheese and place one piece of bacon on top. Bake at 400 degrees, for 8 to 10 minutes, or until oysters are hot and tender. Yield: 4 to 6 servings.

Rock Shrimp Rémoulade

2 pounds cooked, peeled, deveined
  rock shrimp
½ cup mayonnaise
¼ cup horseradish mustard
¼ cup chopped green onions
2 tablespoons vegetable oil
1 tablespoon chopped parsley

2 teaspoons tarragon vinegar
1 teaspoon prepared horseradish
½ teaspoon paprika
¼ teaspoon salt
¼ teaspoon Worcestershire sauce
¼ teaspoon liquid hot pepper sauce

In a 1-quart bowl, combine all ingredients except rock shrimp; mix well. Stir in rock shrimp. Cover; refrigerate for several hours. Yield: 4 servings or 12 appetizers. **(Photo, page 33)**

Catchy Clams Casino

24 clams (1½- to 2-inch diameter), in
  the shell
4 slices bacon, chopped
⅓ cup chopped onion
¼ cup butter or margarine

1 clove garlic, minced
2 tablespoons chopped pimiento
1½ teaspoons Worcestershire sauce
½ teaspoon white pepper
¼ cup dry white wine

Preheat oven to 425 degrees. Rinse unopened clams under cold running water to remove any foreign particles. Shuck clams, reserving half of the shells. Scrub shells and place in boiling water; boil 2 minutes. Remove shells and drain. Fry bacon until crisp. Add remaining ingredients except clams and white wine. Cook until onion is tender, stirring occasionally. Add wine; remove from heat. Place clams in reserved shells. Arrange shells in a shallow baking pan. Pour wine mixture over clams. Bake at 425 degrees 10 to 15 minutes. Yield: 6 servings. **(Photo, page 35)**

Rock Shrimp Conga

½ pound split and deveined rock
    shrimp tails, fresh or frozen
½ teaspoon salt
¼ teaspoon pepper

2 tablespoons lime juice
4 tablespoons melted butter
1½ ounces cream cheese
½ ounce Roquefort or bleu cheese

Thaw shrimp if frozen. Preheat oven to 400 degrees. Place rock shrimp tails in a single layer in a 1½-quart shallow casserole. Sprinkle shrimp with seasonings and lime juice. In a small bowl, combine cooled melted butter and cream and Roquefort cheeses. Spread over rock shrimp tails. Cover with aluminum foil, crimping it to edges of dish. Bake in a 400-degree oven for 8 to 10 minutes. Yield: 30 hors d'oeuvres.

Oysters with Almond Cream

1 pint oysters, drained, fresh or
    frozen
1 tablespoon minced onion
1½ tablespoons sliced almonds

¼ cup butter or margarine
¼ cup heavy cream
1 tablespoon dry white wine
2 tablespoons minced parsley

Thaw oysters if frozen. Remove any remaining shell particles. In large skillet, sauté the oysters, onion and almonds in butter for 3 minutes. Add cream and wine. Cook, stirring, for 2 minutes more. Sprinkle parsley on top and serve with crackers. Yield: 4 servings.

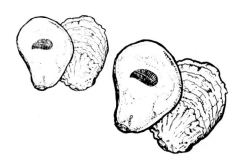

Angels On Horseback

1 pint oysters, fresh or frozen
12 slices bacon, cut in half
½ teaspoon salt
⅛ teaspoon pepper
⅛ teaspoon paprika
2 tablespoons chopped parsley

Thaw oysters if frozen. Preheat oven to 450 degrees. Drain oysters. Remove any shell particles. Place each oyster on half a slice of bacon; sprinkle with seasonings and chopped parsley. Roll bacon around oyster and secure with a wooden toothpick. Place oysters on a rack in shallow baking pan. Bake in hot (450 degrees) oven for about 10 minutes or until bacon is crisp. Remove toothpicks; serve hot. Yield: 24 hors d'oeuvres.

Grouper Teriyaki Kabobs

2 pounds grouper (or other fish) fillets, skinned, fresh or frozen
2 cups cherry tomatoes
1 large green pepper, seeded and cut into 1-inch squares
1 large onion cut into wedges
½ cup lemon juice
¼ cup dry sherry
¼ cup soy sauce
2 tablespoons brown sugar
1 teaspoon ground ginger
1 teaspoon dry mustard
1 teaspoon garlic salt

Thaw fish if frozen. Cut fillets into 1-inch cubes. Place fish and vegetables in a single layer in a shallow dish. Combine lemon juice, sherry, soy sauce, brown sugar, ginger, mustard and garlic salt. Mix well. Pour marinade over fish and vegetables. Cover and marinate in refrigerator for 1 hour. Remove fish and vegetables from marinade, reserving marinade for basting. Alternate fish cubes, cherry tomatoes, green pepper and onions on skewers; place kabobs on broiler pan. Broil about 4 inches from source of heat for 8 minutes. Turn and baste with sauce. Broil 7 to 10 minutes longer or until fish flakes easily when tested with a fork. Yield: 6 servings.

Lobster Pinwheels

¾ pound cooked spiny lobster meat, fresh or frozen
1 package (8 ounces) cream cheese, softened
3 tablespoons half-and-half
3 tablespoons chopped green onions
1 tablespoon Worcestershire sauce
1 tablespoon lemon juice

¼ teaspoon salt
2 teaspoons garlic salt
⅛ teaspoon liquid hot pepper sauce
1 pullman loaf of unsliced white bread
2 tablespoons butter or margarine
20 stuffed pimiento olives
12 midget sweet pickles

Thaw lobster meat if frozen; drain. Shred lobster meat in food processor or blender. Combine cream cheese with half-and-half; beat until smooth. Add other seasonings and lobster. Mix thoroughly.

Cut crusts from bread. Cut bread lengthwise into 8 slices, approximately ¼-inch thick. Flatten bread with rolling pin. Spread bread with butter and then with approximately ⅓ cup lobster mixture. Place a row of 5 olives or 3 pickles across short end of each slice of bread. Start with olive end of the bread and roll jelly-roll style, being careful to keep the olives in place. Wrap each roll in waxed paper or plastic wrap, twisting ends securely. Refrigerate several hours or overnight. To serve, slice each roll crosswise into ¼-inch slices. Yield: 88 pinwheels.

Smoked Fish Spread

1½ pounds smoked, flaked amberjack or other smoked fish, fresh or frozen
2 teaspoons minced onion
2 teaspoons finely chopped celery
2 tablespoons finely chopped sweet pickle

1 clove garlic, minced
1¼ cups mayonnaise
1 tablespoon mustard
⅛ teaspoon Worcestershire sauce
2 tablespoons chopped parsley (garnish)

Mix all ingredients together and chill at least one hour. Yield: 3½ cups.

Red Snapper and Pasta Pinwheels, page 27

Rock Shrimp Rémoulade, page 29

Marinated Oysters, page 37

Coconut Fried Shrimp, page 28

Catchy Clams Casino, page 29

Brewed Oysters

2 pints (15½ ounces) oysters
1 can (12 ounces) beer
¼ cup butter or margarine, melted

2 tablespoons Worcestershire sauce
1 teaspoon seasoned salt

Remove any remaining shell particles. Pour beer in medium-sized skillet. Add oysters to beer and cook over low heat until edges begin to curl. Remove oysters with slotted spoon. Combine remaining ingredients and pour over oysters. Place in chafing dish for serving. Yield: 6 servings.

Marinated Oysters

1 pint oysters, fresh or frozen
2 cups cherry tomatoes
1½ cups fresh whole mushrooms
6 green onions, cut into 2-inch lengths
¼ cup chopped pimiento
1 cup cider vinegar
½ cup salad or olive oil

½ cup water
2 cloves garlic, minced
1 teaspoon sugar
1 teaspoon salt
½ teaspoon dried oregano leaves, crumbled
¼ teaspoon pepper
Salad greens

Thaw oysters if frozen. Drain. Remove any remaining shell particles. Rinse tomatoes in cold water. Clean mushrooms thoroughly with a damp cloth. Cut large mushrooms in half. In a 2-quart bowl, combine oysters, tomatoes, mushrooms, green onions and pimiento. In a 1-quart bowl, combine remaining ingredients except salad greens; stir until sugar is dissolved. Pour marinade over oysters and vegetables. Cover loosely and marinate in the refrigerator at least 12 hours. Drain. Serve on salad greens. Yield: 6 servings, approximately 1½ quarts. **(Photo, page 34)**

Tipsy Pickled Rock Shrimp

1 pound peeled, deveined rock
  shrimp, fresh or frozen
2 cans (12 ounces each) beer
1 medium red onion, cut into slices
½ cup lime juice
2 tablespoons vegetable oil
1 tablespoon capers

½ teaspoon salt
½ teaspoon whole allspice
¼ teaspoon whole black peppercorns
¼ teaspoon liquid hot pepper sauce
2 whole bay leaves
2 cloves garlic, halved

Thaw rock shrimp if frozen. Pour 1 can beer in 2-quart saucepan and bring to a boil. Add rock shrimp and cook 2 to 5 minutes, depending on size, until pink and firm. Drain. Mix remaining ingredients, including second can of beer, in 2-quart mixing bowl. Add rock shrimp to marinade. Cover and marinate in refrigerator at least 6 hours before serving. Serve on wooden toothpicks as hors d'oeuvres. Yield: 6 servings.

Shrimp Ceviche

2 pounds raw peeled, deveined
  shrimp, fresh or frozen
2 cups lemon juice
2 cups sliced onions
3 medium tomatoes, peeled and
  chopped
½ cup tomato paste

½ cup tomato juice
¼ cup sliced green olives with
  pimiento
2 tablespoons instant parsley flakes
2 tablespoons Worcestershire sauce
1 tablespoon salt
½ teaspoon liquid hot pepper sauce

Thaw shrimp if frozen. In a large mixing bowl combine all ingredients and mix well. Pour in a glass bowl and cover tightly. Refrigerate at least 24 hours. Yield: 6 servings.

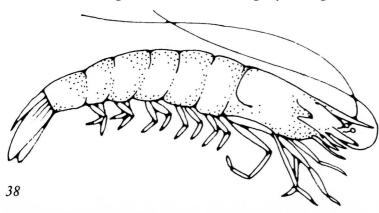

Pickled Stone Crab Claws

2½ pounds stone crab claws,
  fresh or frozen
2 medium onions, sliced
2 cups vegetable oil
2 cups white vinegar

¾ cup sugar
⅓ cup capers with juice
2 teaspoons salt
2 teaspoons celery seed

Thaw stone crab claws if frozen. Crack and remove outer shell leaving meat attached to one side of claw. Make alternate layers of crab claws and onion rings in a sealable container. Mix remaining ingredients and pour over crab claws and onions. Seal and place in refrigerator for 6 hours or more, shaking or inverting occasionally. Remove stone crab claws from marinade and serve. Yield: 6 servings or 15 to 20 hors d'oeuvres.

Rock Shrimp Mini Quiches

½ pound peeled, deveined rock
  shrimp, fresh or frozen
1 package (8 ounces) refrigerated
  butter-flake rolls
1 egg, beaten
½ cup evaporated milk

1 tablespoon cooking sherry
½ teaspoon salt
½ teaspoon white pepper
2 ounces Cheddar cheese or
  ¼ cup Parmesan cheese

Preheat oven to 375 degrees. Thaw rock shrimp if frozen. Finely chop rock shrimp. Grease two miniature muffin tins. Divide rolls into 24 equal pieces and press into muffin tins to form a shell. Place ½ teaspoon of chopped shrimp in each lined muffin well. Combine egg, milk, sherry, salt and pepper. Divide mixture evenly among muffins. Slice cheese into 24 pieces. Place one piece on top of each muffin or top with ½ teaspoon Parmesan cheese. Bake at 375 degrees for 25 minutes. Cool and freeze. Reheat at 375 degrees for 10 to 12 minutes. Yield: 24 hors d'oeuvres.

Fish Rounds

1 cup cooked, flaked fish, fresh or frozen
2 packages (3 ounces each) cream cheese with chives, softened
½ cup finely chopped pecans, divided
1½ teaspoons prepared horseradish
1 teaspoon finely chopped celery
1 teaspoon finely chopped green pepper
1 teaspoon garlic salt
1 teaspoon lemon juice
¼ cup chopped parsley

Thaw fish if frozen. Combine all ingredients, except ¼ cup of pecans and parsley; mix well. Combine remaining ¼ cup pecans and parsley. Set aside. Roll fish mixture into one-inch balls. Coat each ball with pecan-parsley mixture; chill. Serve on wooden toothpicks. Yield: 36 hors d'oeuvres.

Sesame Fish Bites

1 pound tilefish fillets, fresh or frozen
⅓ cup white wine
3 tablespoons mango chutney
3 tablespoons vegetable oil
1 teaspoon curry powder
½ teaspoon salt
¼ cup sesame seeds

Thaw fish if frozen. Cut into 1-inch cubes. Combine wine, chutney, oil, curry powder and salt. Pour over fish and turn several times to coat. Cover and marinate 1 hour in the refrigerator, turning once. Remove fish from marinade and sprinkle on all sides with sesame seeds. Place in a well-greased 15 x 10 x 1-inch baking pan. Broil 5 to 6 inches from source of heat for 5 to 7 minutes or until fish flakes easily when tested with a fork. Serve bites warm. Yield: 32 hors d'oeuvres.

Clam Nachos

24 clams, in the shell
1 jar (8 ounces) process cheese
  spread
¼ cup minced green onions and tops

1 tablespoon chopped hot jalapeño
  pepper
1 box (7 ounces) restaurant-style
  nacho chips
1 jar (8 ounces) taco sauce (optional)

Rinse unopened clams under cold running water to remove any foreign particles. Shuck and mince the clams. Combine clams, cheese, green onions and jalapeño pepper. Place nacho chips on a 15 x 10 x 1-inch baking sheet. Place approximately 1 teaspoon clam mixture on top of each chip. Broil 4 to 5 inches from source of heat or until cheese bubbles, about 2 to 3 minutes. Remove from oven; top each nacho with ½ teaspoon taco sauce, if desired. Yield: 36 appetizers.

Clamdigger Dip

1 can (7½ to 8 ounces) minced clams
1 package (8 ounces) cream cheese,
  softened
1 tablespoon lemon juice
1 tablespoon grated onion
1 teaspoon chopped parsley

1 teaspoon Worcestershire sauce
¼ teaspoon salt
⅛ teaspoon liquid hot pepper sauce
  Assorted chips, crackers or raw
  vegetables

Drain clams and reserve liquor. Combine clams, cream cheese, lemon juice, onion, parsley, Worcestershire sauce, salt and hot pepper sauce. Mix thoroughly. Chill at least 1 hour to blend flavors. Note: If necessary to thin dip, add clam liquor gradually. Serve with chips, crackers or vegetables. Yield: 1½ cups.

Oven-Style Shrimp Barbecue

1½ pounds raw, peeled, deveined
   jumbo shrimp, fresh or frozen
½ cup melted butter or margarine
1½ teaspoons Worcestershire sauce
1¼ teaspoons dry barbecue seasoning

1 teaspoon garlic salt
1 teaspoon paprika
½ teaspoon salt
¼ teaspoon cayenne

Thaw shrimp if frozen. Preheat oven to 400 degrees. Place shrimp in a 1½-quart
rectangular baking dish. Combine melted butter and remaining ingredients. Mix well.
Pour sauce over shrimp. Bake at 400 degrees for 8 to 10 minutes, basting often. Note:
If using smaller shrimp, cooking time will be less. Yield: 4 to 6 servings.

Yellowfin Tuna Buttermilk Bites

2 pounds yellowfin tuna steaks,
   skinned, fresh or frozen
1 cup buttermilk

1 cup biscuit mix
1 teaspoon salt
Oil for deep frying

Thaw fish if frozen. Preheat oven to 350 degrees. Cut steaks into chunks. Place in
single layer in a shallow dish. Pour buttermilk over fish and let stand for 30 minutes,
turning once. Combine biscuit mix and salt. Remove fish from buttermilk and roll in
biscuit mix. Fry in oil, 350 degrees, for 3 to 5 minutes or until brown and fish flakes
easily when tested with a fork. Drain on absorbent paper. Place toothpicks in fish bites
and serve with your favorite seafood sauce. Yield: 12 hors d'oeuvres.

Fresh Tuna Tomato Teasers

½ pound cooked, flaked yellowfin tuna
1 package (3 ounces) cream cheese, softened
1 ripe avocado, mashed
1½ tablespoons lemon juice
½ teaspoon chili powder

2 teaspoons finely chopped green onions
½ teaspoon Worcestershire sauce
½ teaspoon salt
¼ teaspoon liquid hot pepper sauce
2 pints cherry tomatoes

Combine cream cheese and avocado. Add seasonings and tuna. Mix thoroughly and chill. Wash tomatoes and hollow out center. Turn upside down to drain. Fill each tomato with a heaping teaspoonful of tuna mixture. Yield: 40 hors d'oeuvres.

Shrimp Apollo

1 pound raw, peeled, deveined shrimp, fresh or frozen
1 cup Italian dressing (oil base)
¼ cup honey
¼ cup maple syrup

3 tablespoons lemon juice
2 tablespoons soy sauce
1 tablespoon Dijon mustard
2 teaspoons curry powder
1 teaspoon ground ginger

Thaw shrimp if frozen. Drain and pat dry. Place shrimp in shallow baking dish. Combine all remaining ingredients in shaker jar and shake until blended. Pour over shrimp. Marinate approximately one hour. Remove shrimp from marinade, reserving marinade for basting. Place shrimp on broiler pan and broil 5 to 6 inches from source of heat for 3 minutes, basting with marinade. Yield: 4 to 6 servings.

Stone Crab Crystal River

32 stone crab claws, fresh or frozen
1 can (13 ounces) lobster, crab or shrimp bisque
2 tablespoons butter or margarine, melted
1 tablespoon chopped fresh dill (or ½ teaspoon dill weed)

2 cups shredded Swiss cheese
½ teaspoon salt
¼ teaspoon dry mustard
¼ teaspoon white pepper
1 loaf French or Italian bread, cut into 1-inch chunks

Thaw stone crab claws if frozen. In a fondue pot or saucepan, heat bisque, butter and dill weed over medium heat. When this mixture is heated through but not boiling, stir in cheese a little at a time, stirring after each addition, until cheese is melted. Add salt, mustard and pepper. Keep over low heat while serving with stone crab claws and bread. If mixture thickens during serving, blend in a small amount of milk. Yield: Enough fondue for 80 hors d'oeuvres.

Crab Picker's Spread

1 pound blue crab meat, fresh, frozen or pasteurized
1 package (6/10 ounce) Italian salad dressing mix
1 cup dairy sour cream

½ cup mayonnaise or salad dressing
1 tablespoon horseradish mustard
Chopped parsley (garnish)
Assorted chips, crackers or raw vegetables

Thaw crab meat if frozen. Remove any remaining shell or cartilage. Combine crab meat, salad dressing mix, sour cream, mayonnaise and horseradish mustard; chill several hours. Garnish with parsley. Serve with crackers, chips or vegetables. Yield: 3 cups.

Snappy Shrimp

1 pound raw, peeled, deveined
   shrimp, fresh or frozen
½ teaspoon chopped chives
1 clove garlic, minced
¼ cup butter or margarine

1 teaspoon salt
1½ tablespoons sherry
1 tablespoon grated Parmesan
   cheese

Thaw shrimp if frozen. In a 10-inch skillet, sauté chives and garlic in butter until
tender. Add shrimp and salt and simmer 2 to 3 minutes or until the largest shrimp is
opaque in the center when tested by cutting in half. Add sherry and sprinkle cheese
over shrimp. Serve warm. Yield: 80 hors d'oeuvres, using small shrimp.

Coral Shrimp Dip

¾ pound cooked, peeled, deveined
   shrimp, fresh or frozen
1 can (10¾ ounces) condensed cream
   of shrimp soup
1 package (8 ounces) cream cheese,
   softened

1 teaspoon lemon juice
2 tablespoons chopped parsley
¼ teaspoon garlic powder
¼ teaspoon paprika
Parsley sprigs (garnish)
Assorted crackers

Thaw shrimp if frozen. Chop shrimp. Combine all ingredients except parsley sprigs
and crackers. Chill at least one hour to blend flavors. Garnish with parsley sprigs.
Serve with assorted crackers. Yield: 3¾ cups.

Clams on the Half-Shell

36 clams, in the shell
Crushed ice

Lemon wedges (garnish)

Rinse unopened clams under cold running water to remove any foreign particles. Shuck clams, reserving shells. Scrub shells. Place shells in boiling water; boil 2 minutes. Remove shells and drain. Arrange a bed of crushed ice in 6 shallow bowls or plates. Place 6 half-shell clams on each plate of ice with a small container of cocktail sauce in the center. Garnish with lemon wedges. Yield: 6 servings.

Clamlets

30 large clams, in the shell

10 slices bacon

Preheat oven to 375 degrees. Rinse clams under cold running water to remove any foreign particles. Shuck clams, reserving half of the shells. Scrub shells. Place shells in boiling water; boil 2 minutes. Remove shells and drain. Cut bacon slices into thirds. Wrap a piece of bacon around each clam and secure with a wooden toothpick. Place clam wrap-ups in reserved clam shells and arrange on broiler pan. Bake at 375 degrees for 25 minutes or until bacon is done, turning once during cooking. Yield: 6 servings.

Oyster Fritters

1 can (15½ ounces) oysters, fresh or frozen
2 cups sifted all-purpose flour
1 tablespoon baking powder

1½ teaspoons salt
2 eggs, beaten
1 cup milk
1 tablespoon vegetable oil

Thaw oysters if frozen. Remove any remaining shell particles. Drain oysters and chop. Sift dry ingredients together. Combine beaten eggs, milk and oil. Pour into dry ingredients and stir until smooth. Add chopped oysters. Mix well, drop batter by teaspoonful into hot oil, preheated to 350 degrees, and fry about 3 minutes or until golden brown. Drain on absorbent paper. Yield: 6 servings.

Swedish Squid

2 pounds whole squid, fresh or frozen
2 tablespoons vegetable oil
2 cloves garlic, crushed
1 teaspoon dill weed
Salt and pepper to taste

1 cup wine (Chablis)
1 teaspoon lemon juice
½ teaspoon sugar
1 tablespoon flour
½ cup water

Thaw squid if frozen. Clean. Cut mantles into 2-inch pieces. In a large saucepan heat oil; add garlic, dill weed, salt, pepper and squid. Pour wine over mixture and cook 25 to 30 minutes. Add lemon juice and sugar. Blend flour with water until smooth and pour into squid mixture. Heat until sauce thickens. Serve squid hot on toothpicks. Yield: 6 servings.

Tasty Shark Hors D'Oeuvres

1 cup cooked, flaked shark
2 packages (3 ounces each) cream cheese, softened
3 tablespoons mayonnaise or salad dressing
2 tablespoons butter or margarine

1½ tablespoons finely chopped green onions
24 bread rounds (2-inch diameter)
1 tablespoon butter or margarine
1 cup freshly grated Parmesan or Swiss cheese

In a 1-quart bowl, combine first 5 ingredients. Butter bread rounds on one side; place in a single layer on a baking sheet and broil until lightly browned. Turn and brown remaining side. Portion 1 tablespoon of fish mixture over buttered side of rounds; dip top of rounds in cheese and place in a single layer on a baking sheet. Broil approximately 4 inches from source of heat 3 to 5 minutes or until thoroughly heated and cheese is lightly browned. Yield: 24 hors d'oeuvres.

Shrimp St. George Sauté

1 pound medium shrimp, peeled and deveined, fresh or frozen
2 teaspoons paprika
½ teaspoon salt
½ teaspoon white pepper
¼ teaspoon garlic powder
3 tablespoons butter

Thaw shrimp if frozen and pat dry with paper towel. Combine shrimp, paprika, salt, pepper and garlic powder; mix well and set aside. Melt butter in skillet until hot but not smoking. Add shrimp and cook on medium for 30 seconds. Stir shrimp and cook for 45 seconds longer, stirring constantly. Remove from heat; serve immediately. Yield: 6 servings.

Easy Baked Clams

24 clams, in the shell
¼ cup butter or margarine
¼ cup chopped green onions
1 clove garlic, minced
⅓ cup Parmesan cheese
3 tablespoons minced parsley
2 cups coarse bread crumbs
1 tablespoon lemon juice
⅛ teaspoon cayenne (optional)

Preheat oven to 375 degrees. Rinse unopened clams under cold running water to remove any foreign particles. Shuck clams, reserving shells. Scrub shells. Place shells in boiling water; boil 2 minutes. Remove shells and drain. Sauté onions and garlic in butter until onions are tender. Add cheese and parsley. Chop clams coarsely; add to butter-onion-garlic mixture. Stir well. Add bread crumbs and lemon juice to clam mixture, mixing thoroughly. Equally distribute clam mixture among cleaned clam shells. Sprinkle with cayenne. Bake at 375 degrees for 10 to 15 minutes or until heated through and browned slightly. Yield: 8 to 12 hors d'oeuvres.

Shrimp Appetizer

36 large cooked, peeled, deveined shrimp, fresh or frozen, with tail section left intact
1 package (3 ounces) cream cheese, softened
2 teaspoons crumbled bleu cheese
2 teaspoons chopped celery
2 teaspoons chopped green onions and tops
2 teaspoons chopped sweet pickle
½ teaspoon hot dry mustard

Thaw shrimp if frozen. Split shrimp halfway through and spread open. Combine remaining ingredients; mix well. Stuff each shrimp with cheese mixture; chill. Yield: 36 hors d'oeuvres.

Herbed Oyster Wrap-Up

1 pint oysters, fresh or frozen
1 cup herb-seasoned stuffing mix
½ cup chicken broth
¼ cup finely chopped green onions
3 tablespoons finely chopped celery
¼ teaspoon salt
¼ teaspoon Worcestershire sauce
18 slices bacon

Thaw oysters if frozen. Drain oysters. Remove any remaining shell particles. Combine stuffing mix, chicken broth, green onions, celery, salt and Worcestershire sauce; mix well. Cut each piece of bacon in half crosswise. On each piece of bacon, place one oyster and approximately one teaspoon stuffing mixture. Roll bacon around oyster and stuffing mixture and secure with a wooden toothpick. Place on a broiler pan. Broil approximately 4 inches from source of heat for 12 to 15 minutes or until bacon is done, turning once during broiling. Serve warm. Yield: 36 hors d'oeuvres.

Shrimp Mousse

1½ pounds cooked, peeled, deveined
 shrimp, fresh or frozen
1 can (10¾ ounces) condensed
 tomato soup
1 package (8 ounces) cream cheese
2 tablespoons unflavored gelatin
1 cup mayonnaise or salad dressing

¾ cup finely chopped celery
½ cup finely chopped green onions
½ cup finely chopped green pepper
1 teaspoon Worcestershire sauce
1 teaspoon lemon juice
Rich, rectangular butter-flavored
 crackers

Thaw shrimp if frozen. Chop shrimp. Heat tomato soup and cream cheese in top of double boiler until cream cheese melts; cool slightly. Stir in gelatin; mix well. Add shrimp, mayonnaise, celery, green onions, green pepper, Worcestershire sauce and lemon juice; mix well. Pour into a well-greased 1½-quart mold. Cover; refrigerate at least 8 hours. Serve with crackers. Yield: 5½ cups.

Oysters and French Bread

1 pint oysters, fresh or frozen
⅓ cup butter or margarine, melted
⅓ cup reserved oyster liquor
1 tablespoon chopped parsley

1 clove garlic, peeled and minced
1 loaf French bread, sliced and
 toasted

Thaw oysters if frozen. Drain oysters, reserving liquor. Remove any remaining shell particles. Melt butter in medium skillet. Add oyster liquor, parsley and garlic; cook 2 minutes. Add oysters; cook 3 to 5 minutes longer or until edges of oysters begin to curl. Serve in individual dishes with melted butter and French bread. Yield: 4 to 6 hors d'oeuvres.

Crab Pâté

1 pound blue crab meat, fresh,
  frozen or pasteurized
1 cup water
1 teaspoon salt
1 envelope unflavored gelatin

1 cup mayonnaise
¼ cup finely minced green onions
1 teaspoon dry (hot) mustard
Leaf lettuce (garnish)
French bread (optional)

Thaw crab meat if frozen. Remove any remaining shell or cartilage. In small saucepan, combine water and salt. Soften gelatin in cold salted water for 4 minutes. Stir over low heat 1 to 2 minutes to dissolve. Cool slightly. Separate crab meat into two equal portions. In food processor or blender, purée one of the crab portions with mayonnaise, green onions and mustard. Add gelatin mixture. Process 2 seconds more or until combined. Gently fold in remaining crab meat. Pour into well-greased 1-quart mold or terrine. Chill until firm, 3 hours or overnight. Unmold onto lettuce. Serve with warm French bread. Yield: 6 servings.

Sunshine Blue Crab

1½ cups blue crab meat, fresh, frozen
  or pasteurized
2 jars (6 ounces each) marinated
  artichoke hearts

⅓ cup butter or margarine, melted
2 tablespoons lime juice
Salad greens

Thaw blue crab meat if frozen. Remove any remaining shell or cartilage. Drain artichoke hearts. Combine butter and lime juice. Arrange artichoke hearts and crab meat on salad greens. Just before serving, pour lime butter over each appetizer. Yield: 6 servings.

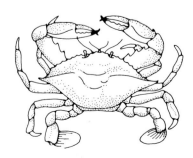

Snapper Nuggets with Sweet-Sour Sauce

2 pounds snapper fillets, fresh or frozen
1 cup all-purpose flour
1½ teaspoons seasoned salt
½ teaspoon paprika
½ teaspoon pepper
Vegetable oil for frying
Sweet-Sour Sauce

Thaw fish if frozen. Cut fillets into 1-inch pieces. Combine flour and seasonings in a bag. Add fish and shake well. In a 10-inch skillet, place fish in a single layer in oil that is hot but not smoking. Fry at moderate heat for 2 to 3 minutes or until brown. Turn carefully. Fry 2 to 3 minutes longer or until fish are brown and flake easily when tested with a fork. Drain on absorbent paper. Serve with Sweet-Sour Sauce. Yield: 6 servings.

Sweet-Sour Sauce

¾ cup finely chopped onions
¾ cup finely chopped green pepper
¼ teaspoon crushed garlic
1 tablespoon vegetable oil
1 cup water
2 tablespoons white vinegar
1 tablespoon sugar
¼ teaspoon powdered ginger
¼ teaspoon salt
¼ cup water
1 teaspoon cornstarch
½ cup catsup

Cook onions, green pepper and garlic in oil in a 2-quart saucepan until tender. Add water, vinegar, sugar, ginger and salt. Bring to a boil; boil 10 minutes, stirring occasionally. Combine water and cornstarch. Add cornstarch mixture and catsup to vegetable mixture. Cook until thick, stirring constantly. Serve hot. Yield: 2 cups.

BRUNCH

Mullet à la Tangerine

2 pounds mullet (or other fish)
fillets, fresh or frozen
½ cup orange juice
½ teaspoon salt
¼ teaspoon ground ginger
⅛ teaspoon white pepper

2 tablespoons vegetable oil
¼ cup butter or margarine, melted
2 tablespoons chopped parsley
2 teaspoons cornstarch or arrowroot
2 medium tangerines, peeled and
separated into sections

Thaw fish if frozen, and place in shallow baking dish. Combine orange juice, salt, ginger and pepper. Pour over fillets and marinate for 10 minutes. Transfer fillets to broiler pan, reserving marinade. Brush fillets with oil; set aside. Pour reserved marinade into small saucepan; cook over low heat until reduced by one half. Add parsley and cornstarch or arrowroot to melted butter. Stir into marinade; cook until thickened. Broil fillets about 3 to 4 inches from source of heat for 4 to 5 minutes or until fish flakes easily when tested with a fork. Add tangerine sections to sauce; heat thoroughly. Place fillets on serving platter and cover with tangerine sauce. Serve immediately. Yield: 6 servings.

Shrimp and Rice Bake

1½ pounds cooked, peeled, deveined
shrimp, fresh or frozen
2 cups sliced fresh mushrooms
1 cup onions, chopped
3 tablespoons butter or margarine

3 cups cooked rice
1 cup dairy sour cream
2 teaspoons mustard
1½ cups Cheddar cheese, shredded

Thaw shrimp if frozen. Preheat oven to 450 degrees. Cut large shrimp in half. Sauté mushrooms and onions in butter until tender. Spread rice in bottom of a well-greased 2-quart shallow baking dish. Top with shrimp. Combine sour cream and mustard. Pour over shrimp. Top with onion-mushroom mixture. Sprinkle with Cheddar cheese. Bake at 450 degrees for 6 to 8 minutes or until cheese melts. Yield: 6 servings.

Rock Shrimp Strata

¾ pound cooked, peeled, deveined
    rock shrimp, fresh or frozen
6 cups soft bread cubes
3 cups grated sharp Cheddar cheese
6 eggs, beaten

1½ cups milk
1 teaspoon salt
1 teaspoon dry mustard
⅛ teaspoon cayenne

Thaw rock shrimp if frozen. Preheat oven to 350 degrees. Layer half the bread cubes in a well-greased 7½ x 12 x 2-inch baking dish. Cover bread cubes with half of the cheese. Place all rock shrimp over bread cubes and cheese layers. Repeat bread cubes and cheese layers. Combine eggs, milk and dry mustard; pour over strata mixture. Let set in refrigerator several hours or overnight. Bake at 350 degrees for 30 to 35 minutes or until egg mixture is set. Yield: 6 servings. **(Photo, page 70)**

Note: 1½ pounds of green rock shrimp tails will yield ¾ pound of cooked, peeled, deveined rock shrimp.

Ginger-Style Mullet

2 pounds mullet (or other fish)
    fillets, fresh or frozen
1 cup firmly packed brown sugar
¼ cup butter or margarine

1 cup crushed gingersnap cookies
1 cup white vinegar
1½ cups chicken broth

Thaw fish if frozen. Divide into 6 portions. Melt butter in a 10-inch skillet over low heat. Stir sugar into melted butter. Continue cooking on medium-high heat, stirring frequently, until sugar is melted. Meanwhile, combine gingersnaps and vinegar. When sugar has melted, remove skillet from heat and gradually add vinegar mixture, stirring constantly. When sugar-vinegar mixture is smooth, stir in chicken broth. Return to heat and bring liquid to a boil, stirring constantly. Add fillets in a single layer, skin side down. Cover. Reduce heat and simmer 10 to 15 minutes or until fish flakes easily when tested with a fork. Carefully remove fillets to a warm serving platter. If desired, accompany with some of the cooking liquid. Yield: 6 servings.

Fisherman's Brunch

1 cup cooked, flaked mullet or other cooked, flaked fish
8 frozen pastry shells (3-inch diameter)
½ cup grated Swiss cheese

1 tablespoon finely chopped onion
4 eggs, slightly beaten
1 teaspoon salt
1 teaspoon pepper
Paprika

Preheat oven to 350 degrees. Bake pastry shells at 350 degrees for 5 minutes or until slightly browned. Remove from oven. Place equal amount of fish, onion and Swiss cheese in each shell. Combine eggs, salt and water in small bowl and mix thoroughly. Pour equal amounts of egg mixture into each shell. Sprinkle with paprika. Bake at 350 degrees for 15 to 20 minutes or until knife inserted in center comes out clean.
Yield: 4 servings.

Note: Leftover baked, broiled or fried fish may be flaked and used. Simmering is the simplest method for preparing cooked, flaked fish. To prepare one cup cooked, flaked fish, place ¾ pound fish fillet in 2 cups boiling, salted water. Cover and reduce heat. Simmer for 8 to 10 minutes or until fish flakes easily. Drain and flake.

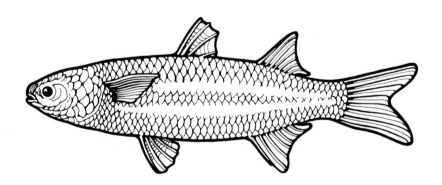

The average sport fisher spends $10.13 for each fish he or she catches.

Saucy Oysters and Eggs

1 pint oysters, fresh or frozen
1 tablespoon butter or margarine, melted
1 tablespoon all-purpose flour
½ teaspoon salt
1 can (10¾ ounces) condensed cream of celery soup
½ cup evaporated milk

2 hard-cooked eggs, sliced
1 can (2 ounces) mushroom stems and pieces, drained
2 tablespoons chopped pimiento
2 tablespoons chopped parsley
4 large baking powder biscuits or patty shells

Thaw oysters if frozen. Drain oysters, reserving liquor. Remove any remaining shell particles. Melt butter in a 2-quart saucepan; add oysters and oyster liquor. Cook slowly until edges of oysters begin to curl, stirring constantly. Stir in flour and salt. Add soup and milk. Cook, stirring constantly, until sauce is smooth and hot. Add eggs, mushrooms, pimiento and parsley; mix well and heat. Spoon over split hot baking powder biscuits or into patty shells. Yield: 4 servings.

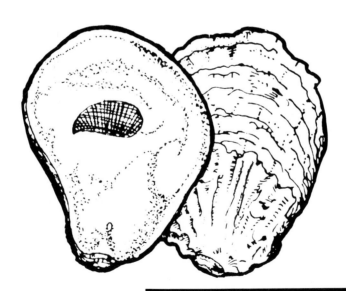

It is a myth that oysters should not be eaten in months without an r (summer months).

Shrimp St. Augustine

1½ pounds peeled, deveined shrimp, fresh or frozen	2 tablespoons chopped pimiento
½ pound fresh sliced mushrooms	1 teaspoon soy sauce
⅓ cup chopped green onions	1 package (10 ounces) frozen chopped spinach, thawed and drained
2 tablespoons chopped green pepper	
3 tablespoons butter or margarine	¼ cup melted butter or margarine
1 tablespoon all-purpose flour	¼ cup grated Swiss cheese
1 cup dairy sour cream	Paprika (garnish)

Thaw shrimp if frozen. Preheat oven to 400 degrees. In a 10-inch skillet, lightly sauté mushrooms, green onions and green pepper for one minute in 3 tablespoons butter. Blend in flour; stir and cook one minute more. Remove from heat. Blend in sour cream, pimiento and soy sauce; mix with sautéed vegetables. Divide spinach among 4 buttered 16-ounce au gratin dishes or individual ramekins. Drizzle each with one tablespoon of melted butter. Spread shrimp on top. Pour sauce over shrimp and sprinkle with cheese and paprika. Bake at 400 degrees for ten minutes. Yield: 4 servings.

Peppered Shrimp and Eggs

½ pound cooked, peeled, deveined shrimp	½ teaspoon salt
3 slices bacon	¼ teaspoon cayenne
¾ cup chopped green peppers	6 eggs, well beaten
½ cup chopped onion	¼ cup half-and-half
	½ teaspoon Worcestershire sauce

Cut large shrimp in half. In a 10-inch skillet, fry bacon until crisp. Remove bacon to absorbent paper, reserving drippings; crumble bacon. Sauté green peppers and onion in bacon drippings until tender. Add salt, cayenne and shrimp; heat. Combine eggs, half-and-half, Worcestershire sauce and crumbled bacon. Pour over shrimp mixture and cook over medium heat until eggs are firm, stirring occasionally. Yield: 6 servings.

Shrimply Delicious Quiche

¾ pound peeled, deveined rock
   shrimp, fresh or frozen
1 tablespoon salt
2 cups water
1½ cups sliced fresh mushrooms
⅔ cup sliced green onions
¼ cup butter or margarine, melted

4 eggs, well beaten
1½ cups half-and-half
1 teaspoon salt
⅛ teaspoon dry mustard
1 cup shredded mozzarella cheese
2 unbaked 9-inch pie shells

Thaw rock shrimp if frozen. Preheat oven to 425 degrees. Add salt to water and bring to a boil. Place shrimp in boiling water; cook 30 seconds. Drain. Rinse under cold running water for 1 to 2 minutes. Remove any remaining particles of sand vein. Chop rock shrimp. Cook mushrooms and green onions in butter until tender but not brown. Combine eggs, half-and-half, salt and dry mustard; beat until smooth. Layer half of the rock shrimp, half of the mushroom mixture and half of the mozzarella cheese in each pie shell. Pour half of the egg mixture into each pie shell. Bake in hot oven, 425 degrees, for 15 minutes; reduce heat to 300 degrees and continue to bake for 30 minutes or until knife, when inserted in the center of quiche, comes out clean. Let stand for 15 minutes before serving. Yield: 6 servings.

Shrimp in Sour Cream

1 pound cooked, peeled, deveined
   shrimp, fresh or frozen
1 cup sliced mushrooms
2 tablespoons chopped green onions
2 tablespoons butter or margarine,
   melted

1 can (10¾ ounces) condensed cream
   of shrimp soup
1 tablespoon all-purpose flour
1 cup dairy sour cream
⅛ teaspoon white pepper
Patty shells, toast points or rice

Thaw shrimp if frozen. In a 10-inch skillet, sauté mushrooms and onions in butter until tender but not brown. Blend in flour. Add soup; cook over medium heat until thickened, stirring constantly. Add shrimp, sour cream and pepper. Heat thoroughly, stirring occasionally. Serve in patty shells, on toast points or over rice. Yield: 6 servings.

Cheesy Fish Rolls

2 cups cooked, flaked croaker or
  other flaked fish*
1 package (10 ounces) frozen
  chopped spinach, thawed and well
  drained
½ cup minced celery
3 tablespoons grated onion
½ teaspoon garlic salt

½ teaspoon salt
1 can (8 ounces) refrigerated
  crescent rolls
1 can (4 ounces) refrigerated
  crescent rolls
1 egg yolk, slightly beaten
Cheese Sauce

Preheat oven to 375 degrees. Combine fish, spinach, celery, onion, garlic salt and salt. Separate packages of crescent rolls into 6 rectangles and pinch dough to remove any perforations. On lightly floured surface, with lightly floured rolling pin, roll out each rectangle to 7 x 6 inches. Spoon equal amounts of fish mixture evenly along the seven-inch side of dough, about ½ inch from the edges. Fold in edges and gently roll up dough. Place seam side down on well-greased 15 x 10-inch cookie sheet. Brush rolls with egg yolk. Bake 20 to 25 minutes at 375 degrees or until golden brown. Serve with Cheese Sauce. Yield: 6 servings.

*For flaked fish: Thaw 1½ pounds croaker fillets. Place in 1-quart boiling water salted with 1 tablespoon salt. Cover and return to the boiling point. Reduce heat and simmer for 10 minutes or until fish flakes easily when tested with a fork. Drain. Remove skin and bones; flake.

Cheese Sauce

1 tablespoon butter or margarine
1 tablespoon all-purpose flour

¾ cup milk
¾ cup grated sharp Cheddar cheese

In a 1-quart saucepan, melt butter and stir in flour. Add milk gradually, stirring constantly until thick and smooth. Stir in cheese and cook over low heat until cheese is melted, stirring constantly. Serve over Fish Rolls. Yield: 1¼ cups.

Shrimp Croquettes with Velvet Sauce

1 pound peeled, deveined shrimp, fresh or frozen
2 cups soft bread crumbs
1 hard-cooked egg, minced
¼ cup minced green onions
2 tablespoons chopped red pepper
¼ cup minced green pepper
2 tablespoons mayonnaise
1 egg, well beaten

1 teaspoon salt
1 teaspoon prepared mustard
¼ teaspoon seasoned salt
⅛ teaspoon cayenne
⅛ teaspoon pepper
½ cup bread crumbs (for coating)
Vegetable oil for pan frying
Velvet Sauce

Thaw shrimp if frozen. Drain and pat dry. Coarsely chop shrimp. Mix all ingredients except ½ cup bread crumbs and Velvet Sauce. Shape into 12 croquettes and coat each thoroughly with remaining bread crumbs. Cover and refrigerate for two hours. In large skillet fry croquettes in vegetable oil over moderate heat. Turn, browning on all sides. Serve with Velvet Sauce. Yield: 6 servings.

Velvet Sauce

1 cup mayonnaise
¾ cup dairy sour cream
1 hard-cooked egg, finely minced
¼ cup minced green onions
1½ tablespoons catsup
2 teaspoons lemon juice

1 teaspoon Dijon mustard
1 teaspoon Worcestershire sauce
⅛ teaspoon cayenne
⅛ teaspoon pepper
⅛ teaspoon salt

Combine all ingredients, mixing well. Refrigerate for two hours. Yield: 2½ cups.

Elegant Shrimp Pie with Rice Crust

1 pound raw shrimp, peeled and
  deveined, fresh or frozen
1 cup thinly sliced green onions
2 tablespoons butter or margarine
3 tablespoons all-purpose flour
½ cup half-and-half
½ cup clam liquor or similar seafood
  broth
½ teaspoon salt

½ teaspoon Worcestershire sauce
¼ teaspoon minced garlic
¼ teaspoon white pepper
1 cup grated Cheddar cheese
1 tablespoon dry vermouth
  (optional)
2 eggs, well beaten
Green olives, sliced (garnish)
Rice Crust

Thaw shrimp if frozen; pat dry with paper towel. Preheat oven to 350 degrees.
Coarsely chop shrimp. Set aside. In a 10-inch skillet, sauté onions in butter until
tender. Stir in flour and cook several minutes longer. Add half-and-half and clam
liquor. Stir until thickened. Add seasonings, cheese and vermouth. Stir a little of the
sauce into eggs; add to remaining sauce, stirring constantly. Add shrimp; mix well.
Pour into baked Rice Crust and bake at 350 degrees for 35 to 45 minutes or until knife
inserted in center comes out clean. Let stand 10 to 15 minutes before serving. Garnish
with sliced olives and cut into pie wedges to serve. Yield: 6 servings.

Rice Crust

3 cups cooked rice
2 eggs, well beaten

¼ cup chopped green olives with
  pimientos

Preheat oven to 450 degrees. Combine rice, eggs and olives. Press firmly into a greased
10-inch pie plate. Bake at 450 degrees for 10 minutes.

Rock Shrimp Asparagus Casserole

2 pounds raw, peeled, deveined split rock shrimp tails, fresh or frozen
2 tablespoons salt
1 quart water
2 cans (15 ounces each) extra long green asparagus spears, drained
4 hard-cooked eggs, sliced
2 envelopes (1¼ ounces each) hollandaise sauce mix

1½ cups milk
2 tablespoons cooking oil
½ cup sour cream
1 tablespoon butter or margarine, melted
¾ cup dry bread crumbs
1 tablespoon grated Parmesan cheese

Thaw rock shrimp if frozen. Preheat oven to 350 degrees. Add salt to water and bring to a boil. Place shrimp in boiling water; cook 30 seconds. Drain. Rinse under cold running water for 1 to 2 minutes. Remove any remaining particles of sand vein. Arrange asparagus spears in bottom of a well-greased 12 x 8 x 2-inch baking dish or divide equally among 6 individual baking dishes. Place rock shrimp evenly over asparagus. Arrange egg slices on top of shrimp. Combine the hollandaise sauce mix, milk and cooking oil and cook over low heat, stirring constantly until mixture thickens. Remove from heat and stir in the sour cream. Spoon hollandaise mixture evenly over shrimp and eggs. Combine melted butter, bread crumbs and Parmesan cheese. Sprinkle over top. Bake in moderate oven, 350 degrees, for 10 to 15 minutes or until thoroughly heated. Yield: 6 servings. (**Photo, page 36**)

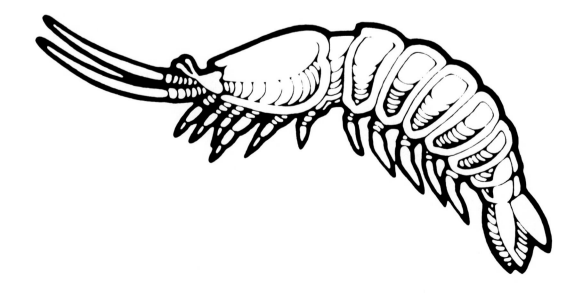

Brunch–Sebastian Style

1 pound cooked, peeled, deveined rock shrimp
½ cup chopped green onions
1 can (4 ounces) sliced mushrooms, drained
2 tablespoons butter or margarine
1 tablespoon all-purpose flour
½ teaspoon salt

⅛ teaspoon cayenne
1 cup light cream
3 tablespoons pitted ripe olives, chopped
6 eggs, poached
6 slices firm white bread, toasted and buttered
Paprika (garnish)

In a medium skillet, sauté onions and mushrooms in butter until onions are soft. Stir in flour, salt and cayenne. Slowly add cream, stirring constantly until thickened. Add ripe olives and rock shrimp. Heat thoroughly. Serve over poached eggs on toast. Garnish with paprika. Yield: 6 servings; 2½ cups sauce.

Cedar Key Crab Tart

1 pound blue crab meat, fresh, frozen or pasteurized
1 package (1¼ ounces) onion soup mix
1 cup milk
1 egg, slightly beaten
½ teaspoon rosemary leaves

⅛ teaspoon white pepper
1 package (8 ounces) shredded mozzarella cheese
¼ cup sliced ripe olives
1 package (15 ounces) refrigerated pie crust for 2 (9-inch) crusts
Aluminum foil (for baking sheet)

Thaw crab meat if frozen. Preheat oven to 375 degrees. Remove any remaining shell or cartilage from crab meat. In small bowl thoroughly blend soup mix, milk, egg, rosemary and pepper. Stir in cheese and olives. Freeze one hour or refrigerate 2 hours or until mixture is slightly thickened and not runny. On aluminum foil-lined baking sheets, unfold pie crusts. Fill center of each prepared crust with ½ soup mixture; spread evenly to edge. Fold crust edges over 1 inch to form rim. Brush rim if desired with 1 egg yolk beaten with 2 tablespoons of water. Bake 25 minutes at 375 degrees or until crusts are golden brown. Yield: 6 servings.

Crab Quiche

1 pound crab meat, fresh, frozen or pasteurized
1 unbaked (deep-dish style) frozen pie shell
1 teaspoon Worcestershire sauce
1 cup grated Swiss cheese
¾ cup sliced pitted ripe olives

3 eggs, slightly beaten
1 cup half-and-half
¼ cup chopped green onions
½ teaspoon salt
5-6 drops liquid hot pepper sauce
Paprika

Thaw crab meat if frozen. Remove any remaining pieces of shell or cartilage. Bring frozen pie shell to room temperature and transfer to ceramic quiche dish or glass pie plate, pressing pastry firmly against sides to prevent shrinkage during cooking. Sprinkle Worcestershire sauce over crust; spread evenly with pastry brush. Prick pie crust with fork several times. Cook in microwave oven for 3 minutes or until done. Let cool. Sprinkle cheese over bottom of pie shell. Add crab and olives. Mix eggs, half-and-half, onion, salt and liquid hot pepper sauce together and pour over crab and olives. Sprinkle with paprika. Cook 15 to 18 minutes in microwave oven, rotating the dish a quarter turn every 2 to 3 minutes. To test quiche for doneness, insert knife in center. Quiche is done if knife comes out clean. Let stand 2 minutes to finish cooking. May be served hot or at room temperature. Yield: 6 servings.

Crab Pineapple Imperial

1 pound blue crab meat, fresh, frozen or pasteurized
¼ cup mayonnaise or salad dressing
1 teaspoon chopped pimiento
½ teaspoon salt
½ teaspoon Worcestershire sauce

3 drops liquid hot pepper sauce
6 large pineapple slices, drained
⅔ cup fine cornflake crumbs
1 tablespoon melted butter or margarine
¼ cup fine cornflake crumbs

Thaw crab meat if frozen. Preheat oven to 350 degrees. Remove any remaining pieces of shell or cartilage. Combine mayonnaise, pimiento, salt, Worcestershire sauce and liquid hot pepper sauce. Add to crab meat and mix lightly. Dip both sides of pineapple slices in ⅔ cup of crumbs. Place in a well-greased 12 x 8 x 2-inch dish. Place ⅓ cup crab mixture on top of each pineapple slice. Combine butter and ¼ cup crumbs; sprinkle over top of crab mixture. Bake in a moderate oven, 350 degrees, for 20 to 25 minutes or until crumbs are lightly browned. Yield: 6 servings. (Photo, page 69)

Curried Shrimp Crepes

1 pound cooked, peeled, deveined shrimp, fresh or frozen	¼ cup seedless raisins
½ cup finely chopped celery	½ teaspoon curry powder
¼ cup finely chopped onion	1 can (10¾ ounces) condensed cream of shrimp soup
¼ cup butter, margarine or cooking oil	¼ cup heavy cream
1½ cups finely chopped, peeled raw apple	1 teaspoon lemon juice
	12 thin crepes

Thaw shrimp if frozen. Preheat oven to 350 degrees. Chop half of shrimp. Cut remaining shrimp in half, lengthwise. In a 10-inch skillet, sauté celery and onion in butter until tender but not brown. Stir in chopped shrimp, apple, raisins, curry powder and ½ cup undiluted soup; heat thoroughly, mixing well. Spoon equal amounts of filling (about 3 tablespoons) on each crepe and roll up. Arrange filled crepes on an ovenproof platter. Cover with aluminum foil. Heat at 350 degrees about 10 minutes or to serving temperature. In a 1-quart saucepan, combine cream and remaining shrimp and soup; heat. Stir in lemon juice. Spoon sauce over hot crepes. Yield: 12 crepes. **(Photo, page 70)**

Crepes

1 cup pancake mix	¾ cup milk
2 eggs	2 tablespoons cooking oil

Combine all ingredients; beat until smooth. Bake on lightly greased hot griddle, using about 3 tablespoons of batter for each. Turn pancake when edges are dry and top is bubbly. Brown on underside. Yield: 12 crepes.

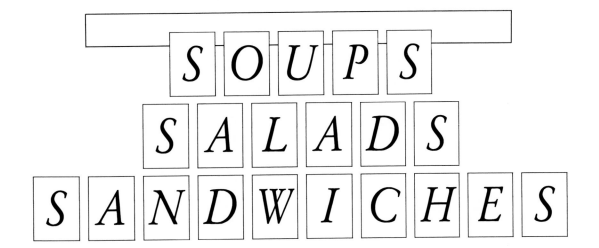

SOUPS
SALADS
SANDWICHES

Fernandina Fish Chowder

½ pint oysters, fresh or frozen
½ pound flounder (or other fish) fillets, fresh or frozen
¼ pound calico or bay scallops, fresh or frozen
¼ pound peeled, deveined shrimp, fresh or frozen
1 tablespoon vegetable oil
1 cup diced potatoes
1 cup diced onions

¾ cup diced celery
¾ cup diced carrots
¼ cup sliced scallions
2 teaspoons fresh lime juice
1 teaspoon dry dill weed
¼ teaspoon salt
⅛ teaspoon cayenne
1 quart half-and-half
½ cup heavy cream
2 egg yolks, well beaten

Thaw seafood if frozen. Cut fillets into ½-inch chunks. Drain oysters, reserving liquor. Remove any remaining shell particles. In a large preheated saucepot, sauté vegetables in oil until tender but not brown. Add reserved oyster liquor, lime juice, dill weed, salt, cayenne and half-and-half; simmer 10 minutes. In a small mixing bowl, combine cream and egg yolks, blending well. Add seafood and cream-egg mixture to vegetables in saucepot, stirring constantly. Do not let chowder boil. Simmer for 10 minutes or until seafood is done. Yield: 6 servings.

Gulf Gazpacho

½ pound cooked, peeled, deveined, shrimp
¾ cup chopped celery
¾ cup seeded and chopped cucumber
½ cup chopped green onions
¼ cup chopped green pepper

2 cloves garlic, minced
1 cup tomato-based vegetable juice
1 can (10¾ ounces) beef bouillon
3 tablespoons lemon juice
1 teaspoon sugar
⅛ teaspoon cayenne

Combine all ingredients except shrimp in blender (or food processor fitted with steel blade). Blend (or pulse) for 2 seconds. Add shrimp. Refrigerate several hours. Serve cold. Yield: 6 servings.

Crab Pineapple Imperial, page 65 ▶

Curried Shrimp Crepes, page 66

Rock Shrimp Strata, page 55

Bouillabaisse Salad, page 95

Golden Oyster Stew, page 74

Delightful Rock Shrimp Salad, page 107

Rock Shrimp and Oyster Manquechou

½ pound rock shrimp, peeled and
  deveined, fresh or frozen
½ pint oysters, drained,
  reserving liquor
4 slices bacon, chopped
1 large onion, finely chopped
½ cup green pepper, finely chopped
1 teaspoon finely chopped garlic

2½ cups peeled tomatoes, chopped
  and drained, reserving liquid
2 cups fresh corn or frozen corn,
  thawed
Reserved oyster liquor and water to
  make 1 cup liquid
1½ teaspoons salt
½ teaspoon cayenne

Thaw rock shrimp if frozen. In a heavy 4-quart casserole, fry bacon until limp. Add
onion, garlic and green pepper; cook until onion is translucent but not brown. Stir in
corn and tomatoes. Add tomato liquid, reserved oyster liquor, salt and cayenne;
simmer mixture 10 minutes or until corn is tender. Add rock shrimp and oysters.
Cook 2 minutes more or until edges of oysters begin to curl. Serve at once with hot
bread and cole slaw. Yield: 4 to 6 servings. **(Photo, page 89)**

Dinner Bell Fish Soup

1 pound fish fillets, fresh or frozen
2 cups water
1½ cups chopped onion
1 cup sliced carrots
1 cup elbow macaroni
1 teaspoon salt

⅛ teaspoon cloves
⅛ teaspoon pepper
1 can (11½ ounces) condensed split
  pea with ham soup
2 cups milk
Chopped parsley (garnish)

Thaw fish if frozen. Skin fillets; cut into 1-inch pieces. In a 5-quart Dutch oven,
combine water, onion, carrots, macaroni, salt, cloves and pepper; bring to a boil.
Reduce heat; cover and simmer for 4 to 6 minutes or until carrots are almost tender.
Add soup and milk, stirring until well mixed. Add fish; cover and simmer for 8 to 10
minutes longer or until fish flakes easily when tested with a fork. Garnish with
chopped parsley. Yield: 6 servings.

Golden Oyster Stew

1 can (pint) oysters, undrained
½ cup chopped onion
½ cup sliced celery
¼ cup butter or margarine
2 cups sliced fresh mushrooms
¼ cup all-purpose flour
1 teaspoon salt

¼ teaspoon pepper
2 cups milk
1½ cups grated sharp Cheddar cheese
1 can (10½ ounces) cream of potato soup
1 jar (2 ounces) diced pimiento
¼ teaspoon liquid hot pepper sauce

Remove any remaining shell particles from oysters. Cook onions and celery in butter until tender. Add mushrooms and cook one minute. Over low heat, stir flour, salt and pepper into vegetable mixture. Add milk gradually and stir until thickened. Add cheese; stir until melted. Add oysters, soup, pimiento and liquid hot pepper sauce. Heat for 5 to 10 minutes or until oysters begin to curl. Yield: 6 servings.
(Photo, page 72)

Landlubber's Fish Stew

1 pound shark steaks, fresh or frozen
1 cup chopped onion
3 strips bacon
2 cans (10¾ ounce) condensed cream of potato soup
2 cups diluted evaporated or whole milk

1 can (1 pound) stewed tomatoes
1 package (10 ounces) frozen mixed vegetables, thawed
1 can (8 ounces) whole kernel corn, drained
1 teaspoon salt
⅛ teaspoon pepper
1 small bay leaf

Thaw fish if frozen. Cut into chunks. Fry bacon in Dutch oven until crisp. Remove bacon to absorbent paper; crumble. Cook onion in bacon drippings until tender. Add soup, milk, tomatoes, vegetables, corn, salt, pepper and bay leaf; heat, stirring occasionally, until simmering. Add fish and bacon; simmer until fish flakes easily when tested with a fork, about 10 minutes. Yield: 9 cups. **(Photo, page 91)**

Rock Shrimp Asparagus Soup

1 pound peeled, deveined rock shrimp, fresh or frozen
¼ cup butter or margarine, melted
¼ cup all-purpose flour
1 tablespoon salt
⅛ teaspoon ground nutmeg
⅛ teaspoon pepper

1½ quarts milk
2 packages (10 ounces each) frozen chopped asparagus, cooked and drained
3 cups shredded sharp Cheddar cheese
Paprika (garnish)

Thaw rock shrimp if frozen. Cut shrimp in half. Melt butter in a 4-quart saucepan; blend in flour, salt, nutmeg and pepper. Gradually add milk; cook until thickened and smooth, stirring constantly. Add rock shrimp, asparagus and cheese; continue cooking over low heat, 3 to 4 minutes, stirring occasionally, until cheese melts. Garnish with paprika. Serve hot. Yield: 6 servings.

Clam-Corn Chowder

30 clams, in the shell
1 cup clam liquor and water
3 slices bacon, chopped
1 cup chopped onions
2 cups diced potatoes
1½ cups drained whole-kernel corn
3 cups milk
2 tablespoons all-purpose flour

1 tablespoon melted butter or margarine
1 teaspoon celery salt
1 teaspoon salt
⅛ teaspoon pepper
½ cup coarse cracker crumbs (optional)

Rinse unopened clams under cold running water to remove any foreign particles. Shuck clams, reserving liquor. Chop clams. Add enough water to reserved clam liquor to make one cup of liquid. In a 4-quart saucepan, fry bacon until crisp; add onions and cook until tender. Add potatoes, clam liquor and water. Cover; simmer until potatoes are tender. Add corn and milk. Blend flour and butter together; stir into soup. Cook slowly until mixture thickens slightly, stirring constantly. Add seasonings and clams; simmer 5 minutes. Top with cracker crumbs. Serve hot. Yield: 6 servings.

Creole Bouillabaisse

1 pound mullet (or other fish) fillets, fresh or frozen
1 pound croaker (or other fish) fillets, fresh or frozen
½ pound peeled, deveined rock shrimp, fresh or frozen
2 tablespoons butter or margarine
2 tablespoons olive oil
¼ cup all-purpose flour
1 cup chopped onions
½ cup chopped celery

1 clove garlic, minced
5 cups water
1 can (16 ounces) tomatoes, chopped, reserving liquid
½ cup dry white wine
2 tablespoons chopped parsley
1 tablespoon lemon juice
1 bay leaf
½ teaspoon salt
¼ teaspoon cayenne

Thaw fish and shrimp if frozen. Remove skin and bones from fish. Cut each fish into 2-inch chunks. In a 4- to 5-quart Dutch oven, melt butter. Add olive oil and blend in flour. Cook, stirring constantly, until light brown in color. Add onion, celery and garlic. Cook, stirring constantly, until vegetables begin to brown. Gradually stir in water. Add tomatoes, tomato liquid, wine, parsley, lemon juice, bay leaf, salt, cayenne and the fish. Bring to a boil and simmer for 10 minutes. Add rock shrimp and cook another 1½ minutes. Yield: 8 servings.

Mullet Chowder

1 pound skinless mullet (or other skinless fish) fillets, fresh or frozen
2 tablespoons chopped bacon
½ cup chopped onions
2 cups hot water

1 cup diced potatoes
¾ teaspoon salt
⅛ teaspoon pepper
2 cups milk
Chopped parsley (garnish)

Thaw fish if frozen. Cut fish into 1-inch pieces. In a 5-quart Dutch oven, fry bacon until browned. Add onions; cook until tender. Add water, potatoes and seasonings. Cover; simmer about 10 minutes. Add fish and simmer 5 to 10 minutes longer or until fish flakes easily when tested with a fork and potatoes are tender. Gradually add milk; heat through but do not boil. Garnish with parsley. Yield: 6 servings.

Seafood Gumbo

½ pound skinless fish fillets, fresh or frozen

½ pound peeled, deveined shrimp, fresh or frozen

½ pound blue crab meat, fresh, frozen, pasteurized or canned

¼ cup butter or margarine, melted

1 cup chopped onions

1 cup thinly sliced celery

¾ cup chopped green peppers

1 tablespoon finely chopped parsley

1 clove garlic, peeled and minced

1 tablespoon all-purpose flour

1½ teaspoons chili powder

1½ teaspoons salt

1 teaspoon paprika

⅛ teaspoon cayenne

1 can (1 pound) tomato wedges or whole tomatoes, drained

1 can (8 ounces) tomato sauce

½ cup water

1 package (10 ounces) frozen whole okra, thawed

2 cups cooked rice

Chopped parsley (garnish)

Thaw fish, shrimp and crab meat if frozen. Cut fish into 1½-inch pieces. Remove any remaining shell particles from crab meat. In a 5-quart Dutch oven sauté onions, celery, green peppers, parsley and garlic in butter until tender but not brown, stirring occasionally. Combine flour, chili powder, salt, paprika and cayenne. Stir into vegetables. Add tomato wedges, tomato sauce and water; simmer 4 to 6 minutes. Add fish and okra; reduce heat, cover and simmer for 5 to 7 minutes. Add shrimp and crab meat and simmer for 5 minutes longer. Serve over cooked rice. Garnish with chopped parsley. Yield: 6 servings.

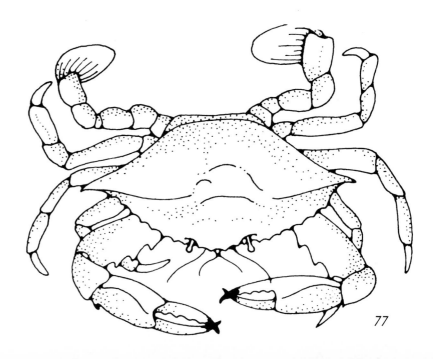

Oyster Chowder

1 pint oysters, fresh or frozen
¼ cup butter or margarine, melted
½ cup chopped onions
½ cup sliced celery
3 cups oyster liquor and enough
  milk to make volume
1 cup half-and-half

1 cup cooked diced potatoes
1 can (8 ounces) whole kernel corn,
  undrained
1½ teaspoons salt
¼ teaspoon pepper
Chopped parsley (garnish)

Thaw oysters if frozen. Drain oysters, reserving liquor. Remove any remaining shell particles. Sauté onions and celery in butter until tender. Add oyster liquor, half-and-half, potatoes, corn, salt and pepper; heat, stirring occasionally. Add oysters and heat for 3 to 5 minutes longer or until edges of oysters begin to curl. Do not let chowder boil. Garnish with chopped parsley. Yield: 6 servings. **(Photo, page 92)**

Everybody's Favorite Fish Soup

2 pounds mullet (or other fish)
  fillets, fresh or frozen
1 cup chopped onion
1 cup chopped celery
1 cup chopped green pepper
1 clove garlic, minced
2 tablespoons vegetable oil
1 cup chicken broth

1 can (28 ounces) tomatoes,
  undrained
¼ cup white wine
¼ cup chopped parsley
1 teaspoon salt
½ teaspoon sugar
¼ teaspoon basil

Thaw fish if frozen. Skin fillets and cut them into 1-inch cubes. In a 5-quart soup pot, cook onion, celery, green pepper and garlic in oil over medium heat until tender but not brown. Add tomatoes, chicken broth, wine, parsley, salt, sugar and basil; heat to boiling. Reduce heat; cover and simmer for 10 minutes. Add fish and cook over low heat for 10 minutes or until fish flakes easily when tested with a fork, stirring occasionally. Yield: 6 servings.

Clam Chowder

Brown Roux*
3 cups roasted tomatoes*
3 tablespoons peanut oil
3 cups sliced mushrooms
1 cup diced leek (white part only)
1 cup diced carrots
1 cup diced turnips
1 cup diced celery
1 cup diced red pepper
1 cup diced bliss potatoes
3 cloves garlic, minced
1½ teaspoons dried thyme

1 teaspoon dried tarragon
2 bay leaves, crumbled
1 tablespoon minced lemon zest
1 teaspoon curry powder
½ teaspoon crushed red pepper (optional)
1½ tablespoons chopped parsley
1 cup diced clams
5½ cups clam juice
1 cup tomato juice
Salt to taste
Croutons (optional)

*Make brown roux by combining ¼ cup peanut oil and ¾ cup all-purpose flour in a heavy-bottomed skillet. Cook over medium-high heat until a deep rich brown color is achieved. The color of almond skins is ideal. Remove from heat, cool, retain.

*To roast tomatoes cut tomatoes in half, remove core and seeds, discard. Slice and place on greased oven pan. Brown on both sides under broiler. Retain.

In a 4-quart heavy-bottomed saucepan, add 3 tablespoons oil over high heat until oil begins to smoke. Add mushrooms. When mushrooms are a deep dark brown color, add leek, carrots, celery, turnips and garlic. Continue cooking until vegetables are slightly brown, about 2 minutes. Add all remaining ingredients including roasted tomatoes but not roux. Bring soup to a boil, reduce heat and simmer about 5 minutes or until vegetables are tender. Add brown roux, stirring constantly. Continue simmering another 2 minutes. Serve right away or store tightly covered in refrigerator for up to 5 days. Garnish with fresh croutons. Yield: 8 to 10 cups.

Easy-Do Fish Stew

2 pounds flounder (or other fish) fillets, fresh or frozen
6 slices bacon, diced
1 cup sliced celery
½ cup chopped onion
½ cup chopped green pepper
2 cans (10½ ounces each) condensed cream of potato soup

2 cans (10½ ounces each) chicken broth
1 can (16 ounces) green peas and sliced carrots, drained
1 can (8 ounces) whole kernel corn, drained
⅛ teaspoon pepper
1 medium bay leaf

Thaw fish if frozen. Skin fillets and cut into 1½-inch pieces. In a 5-quart soup pot, brown bacon. Remove bacon and cook celery, onion and green pepper in bacon drippings over medium heat until tender but not brown, stirring occasionally. Add bacon and cream of potato soup, chicken broth, vegetables, pepper and bay leaf; heat to boiling. Reduce heat; add fish, cover and simmer for 12 to 15 minutes or until fish flakes easily when tested with a fork, stirring occasionally. Remove bay leaf and serve. Yield: 6 servings.

Country-Flavored Fish Soup

1 pound skinless fish fillets, fresh or frozen
2 teaspoons butter, margarine or vegetable oil
2 teaspoons all-purpose flour
1½ teaspoons instant minced onion
¾ teaspoon salt

¼ teaspoon white pepper
¼ teaspoon ground nutmeg
1 cup half-and-half
1 can (8½ ounces) whole kernel corn, undrained
Chopped parsley (garnish)

Thaw fish if frozen. Cut fish into 1-inch pieces. In a 3-quart saucepan, melt butter; blend in flour and seasonings. Gradually add half-and-half, stirring constantly. Add fish and corn. Cook over medium heat, stirring occasionally, 8 to 10 minutes or until fish flakes easily when tested with a fork. Garnish with chopped parsley. Yield: 3 servings.

Crab Bisque

1 pound blue crab meat, fresh, frozen or pasteurized
2 tablespoons finely chopped onion
2 tablespoons finely chopped celery
¼ cup melted butter or margarine
3 tablespoons all-purpose flour

1 teaspoon salt
¼ teaspoon paprika
⅛ teaspoon white pepper
1 quart milk
¼ cup chopped parsley (garnish)

Thaw crab meat if frozen. Remove any pieces of shell or cartilage from meat. Cook onion and celery in butter until tender but not brown. Blend in flour and seasonings. Add milk gradually, stirring constantly; cook until thick. Add crab meat and heat. Just before serving, sprinkle with parsley. Yield: 6 servings.

Scallop Chowder

2 pounds calico or bay scallops, fresh or frozen
4 slices bacon, cut into ½-inch pieces
1 tablespoon butter or margarine
1 cup sliced celery
1 cup sliced carrots
½ cup chopped onion
½ cup chopped green pepper
2 cloves garlic, crushed
2 cups water

2 cups diced potatoes
3 chicken bouillon cubes
1½ teaspoons salt
½ teaspoon white pepper
2 cups milk
1 cup half-and-half
¼ cup all-purpose flour
2 tablespoons cornstarch
¼ cup butter or margarine, melted
Parsley (garnish)

Thaw scallops if frozen. Rinse under cold running water to remove any remaining shell particles. In large saucepan or Dutch oven, fry bacon until crisp. Stir in 1 tablespoon butter. Add celery, carrots, onion, green pepper and garlic; cook until tender. Add water, potatoes, bouillon, salt and white pepper. Cover and bring to boiling point. Simmer 15 minutes or until potatoes are tender. Add milk and half-and-half. Mix flour and cornstarch in melted butter; add to chowder. Blend well. Add scallops. Cook over medium-high heat until chowder starts to bubble and thicken. Reduce heat; simmer 8 to 10 minutes or until scallops are opaque. Garnish with parsley. Yield: 6 to 8 servings.

Seafood Stew with Cornbread Dumplings

2 pounds fish fillets, fresh or frozen
1 large onion, sliced
¼ cup butter, margarine or
  cooking oil
1 package (10 ounces) frozen mixed
  vegetables, thawed
1 can (4 ounces) sliced mushrooms,
  drained
1 cup milk

2 cans (10½ ounces each) condensed
  cream of celery soup
1 teaspoon salt
½ teaspoon thyme
4 slices bacon, chopped
½ package (18 ounces) corn
  muffin mix
Milk

Thaw fish if frozen. Preheat oven to 400 degrees. Skin fillets; cut into 1-inch pieces. In a 6-quart Dutch oven, cook onion in butter until tender, not brown. Add mixed vegetables, mushrooms, soup, 1 cup milk, salt and thyme. Heat and stir until hot. Add fish; cover and bake in a hot oven, 400 degrees, for 12 to 15 minutes. Fry bacon until crisp; drain on absorbent paper. Prepare muffin mix as directed on package label, reducing milk by half. Fold in bacon; drop 6 to 8 mounds of batter onto hot fish mixture. Return to oven and bake uncovered for 20 minutes or until dumplings are done and fish flakes easily when tested with a fork. Yield: 6 servings.

Oyster-Mushroom Stew

2 cans (15½ ounces each) oysters,
  fresh or frozen
1 can (10¾ ounces) condensed cream
  of mushroom soup
2 cups oyster liquor and milk

¼ cup butter or margarine
½ teaspoon salt
1 tablespoon sherry
Paprika (garnish)

Thaw oysters if frozen. Drain oysters, reserving liquor. Remove any remaining shell particles. Add enough milk to reserved oyster liquor to equal 2 cups liquid. In a 3-quart saucepan, combine all ingredients, except oysters and sherry; heat, stirring occasionally. Add oysters; simmer 3 to 5 minutes longer or until edges of oysters begin to curl. Add sherry. Sprinkle with paprika. Yield: 6 servings.

Trout and Cabbage Stew

1 pound trout (or other fish) fillets, fresh or frozen
4 slices bacon, chopped
1 cup chopped onion
1 clove garlic, minced
1 can (14½ ounces) beef broth, divided
1 beef bouillon cube
¾ teaspoon salt
¼ teaspoon soy sauce
⅛ teaspoon pepper
1 cup thinly sliced carrots
2 cups shredded cabbage
2¼ tablespoons all-purpose flour
Chopped parsley (garnish)

Thaw fish if frozen. Skin fillets; cut into 1-inch pieces. In a 3-quart saucepan, cook bacon until brown. Add onion and garlic and cook until tender. Add 1½ cups beef broth, bouillon cube, salt, soy sauce and pepper; bring to a boil. Add carrots; cover and simmer for 4 to 6 minutes or until carrots are almost tender. Add fish and cabbage; cover and simmer for 4 to 6 minutes longer or until cabbage is almost tender. Combine flour with remaining beef broth and add to soup mixture; stir. Cover; simmer for 4 to 6 minutes or until fish flakes easily when tested with a fork. Garnish with chopped parsley. Yield: 3 servings.

Southern-Style Fish Chili

2 pounds fish fillets, fresh or frozen
1 large onion, sliced
1 cup chopped green pepper
1 clove garlic, minced
2 tablespoons butter, margarine or cooking oil
2 teaspoons salt
1½ teaspoons chili powder
½ teaspoon oregano
¼ teaspoon pepper
1 can (1 pound) red kidney beans, undrained
1 can (1 pound) whole tomatoes, undrained
1 can (6 ounces) tomato paste
Chopped parsley (garnish)

Thaw fish if frozen. Skin fillets; cut into 1-inch pieces. In a 5-quart Dutch oven, cook onion, green pepper and garlic in butter until onion is tender, not brown. Stir in salt, chili powder, oregano and pepper. Add beans, tomatoes, and tomato paste. Heat almost to boiling point, stirring occasionally. Add fish. Reduce heat; cover and simmer 8 to 10 minutes or until fish flakes easily when tested with a fork. Garnish with chopped parsley. Yield: 6 servings.

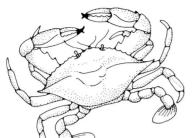

Crab-Carrot Salad

1 pound blue crab meat, fresh, frozen or pasteurized
1 cup grated carrots
2 hard-cooked eggs, chopped
1 tablespoon chopped onion
1 cup mayonnaise or salad dressing
¼ cup lemon juice
1 teaspoon prepared mustard

1 teaspoon salt
¼ teaspoon pepper
18 tomato slices
6 lettuce leaves
Salt (optional)
1 can (14½ ounces) asparagus spears, drained
Paprika (garnish)

Thaw crab meat if frozen. Remove any remaining shell or cartilage. Combine carrots, eggs, onion and crab meat. In separate bowl, combine mayonnaise, lemon juice, mustard, salt and pepper. Add mayonnaise mixture to crab mixture and toss lightly. Chill. Arrange 3 tomato slices on each lettuce leaf and sprinkle with salt. Place asparagus spears on tomatoes. Top each serving with crab salad. Sprinkle with paprika. Yield: 6 servings.

Blue Crab Trio

1 pound blue crab meat, fresh, frozen or pasteurized
3 cups cooked twisted trio macaroni
1 cup sliced fresh mushrooms
½ medium green pepper, seeded and sliced
½ red pepper, seeded and sliced
¼ cup sliced green onions

¼ cup grated Parmesan cheese
2 tablespoons chopped parsley
1 tablespoon chopped pimiento
¼ teaspoon pepper
¾ cup herb and spice dressing (from packaged mix)
Salad greens

Thaw crab meat if frozen. Remove any remaining shell or cartilage. Combine all ingredients; mix well. Cover and chill. Serve on salad greens. Yield: 6 servings.

Oyster Salad

1 pint oysters
¼ teaspoon celery salt
1 tablespoon butter
½ cup lettuce, chopped
2 hard-cooked eggs, diced
½ cup celery, diced
1 pimiento, chopped

1 teaspoon onion, grated
1 teaspoon lemon juice
½ cup mayonnaise or salad dressing
½ teaspoon salt
⅛ teaspoon pepper
Lettuce

Drain oysters. Add celery salt and cook in butter until edges begin to curl. Chill and dice oysters. Combine all ingredients and serve on lettuce cups. Garnish with paprika. Yield: 6 servings.

Sea Slaw

1½ pounds fish fillets, fresh or frozen
1 quart boiling water
1 tablespoon salt
¼ cup mayonnaise or salad dressing
2 tablespoons chopped onion
2 tablespoons sweet pickle relish

1 tablespoon lemon juice
1 teaspoon salt
1 cup shredded green cabbage
1 cup thinly sliced celery
6 lettuce cups
Lemon wedges

Thaw frozen fillets. Place fillets in boiling salted water. Cover and simmer about 10 minutes or until fish flakes easily when tested with a fork. Drain. Remove skin and bones; flake. Combine mayonnaise, onion, relish, lemon juice, salt and fish. Chill at least 1 hour to blend flavors. Add cabbage and celery; toss lightly. Serve in lettuce cups with lemon wedges. Yield: 6 servings.

South-of-the-Border Salad

2 pounds smoked mullet or other smoked fish, fresh or frozen
½ cup cooked, drained garbanzo beans
½ medium head lettuce, torn into 2-inch pieces
1 large peeled avocado, cut into 1-inch pieces

1 medium tomato, chopped
1 cup diagonally sliced celery
½ cup chopped green onions
½ cup grated carrot
1 cup shredded mild Cheddar cheese
½ cup buttermilk-style salad dressing
1 package (4 ounces) tortilla chips, lightly crushed

Thaw fish if frozen. Remove skin and bones. Break fish into bite-sized pieces. Combine all ingredients except salad dressing and tortilla chips. Toss well. Add dressing and tortilla chips and serve immediately. Yield: 6 large servings.
(Photo, page 90)

Yellowfin Tuna Louis

1 pound cooked yellowfin tuna steaks
1 head of lettuce, shredded
⅔ cup mayonnaise
⅓ cup chili sauce
¼ cup chopped green olives

2 tablespoons minced onion
1 tablespoon vegetable oil
1 tablespoon capers (optional)
1 teaspoon dry mustard
½ teaspoon salt
½ teaspoon pepper

Break tuna into bite-sized pieces. Toss shredded lettuce and tuna chunks; set aside. Combine remaining ingredients and chill for one hour. Spoon dressing over tuna mixture, toss lightly and serve. Yield: 6 servings.

Smoked Fish Potato Salad

1 pound smoked mullet or other smoked fish, fresh or frozen	½ cup mayonnaise
2 cups diced cooked potatoes	1 tablespoon prepared mustard
1 cup chopped celery	1 teaspoon lemon juice
½ cup chopped, peeled cucumber	1 teaspoon vinegar
½ cup sliced pitted ripe olives	½ teaspoon salt
¼ cup grated carrot	¼ teaspoon celery seed
¼ cup chopped onion	⅛ teaspoon pepper
2 tablespoons chopped parsley	Salad greens
	Tomato wedges (garnish)

Remove skin and bones from fish. Flake the fish. Combine mayonnaise, mustard, lemon juice, vinegar and seasonings; blend well. Add mayonnaise mixture to fish mixture; toss lightly. Chill. Serve on salad greens. Garnish with tomato wedges. Yield: 6 servings.

Pinellas Hickory Salad

2 cups flaked smoked shark or other smoked fish, fresh or frozen	⅔ cup mayonnaise or salad dressing
4 crisp red apples	½ cup chopped celery
4 tablespoons lemon juice	¼ cup coarsely chopped walnuts or slivered almonds
3 pink grapefruit, peeled and sectioned	2 tablespoons lemon juice
1 head lettuce, shredded	

Core but do not peel three of the apples; cut into 12 slices each, sprinkle with lemon juice to keep from browning. On a bed of shredded lettuce, alternate apple slices and grapefruit sections, flower-fashion. Combine smoked fish, remaining ingredients and the fourth apple, cored, peeled and diced. Mound fish mixture in center of the apple-grapefruit flower. Yield: 4 to 6 servings.

Tangy Squid Salad

2 pounds whole squid, fresh or frozen
Boiling water
1 cup sliced celery
1 cup sliced onion, red or white
1 cup coarsely shredded carrot
½ cup vegetable or olive oil

⅓ cup lemon juice
1 tablespoon chopped parsley
1 teaspoon oregano
½ teaspoon salt
1 clove garlic, sliced
4 to 6 tomatoes or avocado halves

Thaw squid if frozen. To clean squid, grasp head and mantle (body) firmly in hands; pull off head, tentacles and ink sack. Pull transparent backbone or quill from the mantle. Squeeze any remaining entrails from inside mantle. Under cold running water, peel off speckled membrane covering mantle. Wash mantle thoroughly, inside and out. Slice mantle crosswise into ½-inch rings. Drop sliced squid into boiling water, cover and simmer for 20 minutes or until cooked. Drain. Place celery, onion, carrot and drained squid in bowl. Combine oil, lemon juice, parsley, oregano, salt and garlic; mix. Pour oil mixture over ingredients in bowl; mix well. Cover, chill several hours or overnight. Remove garlic. Serve on tomatoes, cut top to bottom into eighths, not quite through, or on avocado halves, as desired. Yield: 4 cups of salad mixture, 4 to 6 servings.

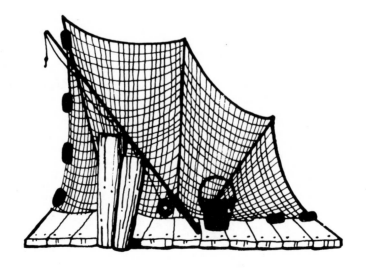

Cold Rock Shrimp and Pasta Salad, page 94

Rock Shrimp and Oyster Manquechou, page 73

Landlubber's Fish Stew, page 74

Squid Salad, page 107

◀ *South-of-the-Border Salad, page 86*

Smoked Fish Salad Parmesan

2 cups flaked, smoked red snapper
   or other smoked fish, fresh or
   frozen
1 cup cauliflower flowerets,
   broken into pieces

6 cups shredded lettuce
½ cup sliced ripe olives
⅓ cup sliced green onions
Parmesan Dressing
Salad greens

Thaw fish if frozen. In large bowl, combine fish, lettuce, cauliflower, olives and green onions. Toss lightly with Parmesan Dressing. Serve on salad greens. Yield: 6 servings.

Parmesan Dressing

½ cup dairy sour cream
⅓ cup mayonnaise

¼ cup grated Parmesan cheese

Combine all ingredients; chill. Yield: 1 cup.

Midsummer Salad

2 cups cooked, flaked fish
1 cup red grapes, halved and seeded
1 cup chopped celery
½ cup mayonnaise or salad dressing

¼ cup sliced almonds
¼ teaspoon salt
¼ teaspoon curry powder
Lettuce

Combine all ingredients except lettuce, being careful not to break fish into too-small pieces. Chill. Serve in lettuce cups. Yield: 6 servings.

Cold Rock Shrimp and Pasta Salad

1 pound cooked, peeled, deveined
   rock shrimp
3 cups cooked, drained noodles
   (include colorful noodles such as
   spinach or tomato)

1 cup diagonally sliced celery
Summer Dressing
Bibb lettuce
Tomatoes and avocado (garnish)

In medium-sized bowl, combine shrimp, celery and noodles. Toss with ¼ cup of dressing. Serve on a bed of bibb lettuce. Garnish with tomato and avocado slices. Serve with remaining dressing. Yield: 6 servings. **(Photo, page 89)**

Summer Dressing

1 cup salad oil
½ cup half-and-half
3 tablespoons white vinegar
2 teaspoons sugar
2 hard-cooked egg yolks, sieved
1 tablespoon chopped capers
1 teaspoon salt

½ teaspoon onion salt
½ teaspoon pepper
½ teaspoon dry mustard
½ teaspoon lemon juice
⅛ teaspoon Worcestershire sauce
2 small cloves of garlic, crushed

Combine all ingredients in a container with a tight-fitting lid. Shake thoroughly before using. Yield: 1½ cups.

Bouillabaisse Salad

¼ pound cooked lump crab or
   lobster meat
½ pound cooked, peeled, deveined
   medium-sized shrimp
¼ pound cooked scallops (cut large
   scallops into ½-inch cubes)
½ pound delicately flavored, skinned
   and boned cooked fish, cut into
   bite-sized pieces

1 small head lettuce or mixed salad
   greens, torn into pieces
Melon balls or other fruit
Strawberries or other fruit
Louis Dressing
Wafers or crackers

Combine fish and shellfish. Arrange over salad greens in a shallow serving bowl or on
a small platter. Garnish with melon balls, strawberries or other fruit and serve with
wafers or crackers. Serve with Louis Dressing. Yield: 4 servings. **(Photo, page 71)**

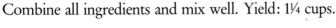

Louis Dressing

¾ cup mayonnaise
4 tablespoons chili sauce
1 hard-cooked egg, chopped
   (optional)
1 teaspoon prepared horseradish

2 teaspoons finely chopped green
   pepper
¼ teaspoon Worcestershire sauce
1 teaspoon lemon juice
2 tablespoons chopped scallions

Combine all ingredients and mix well. Yield: 1¼ cups.

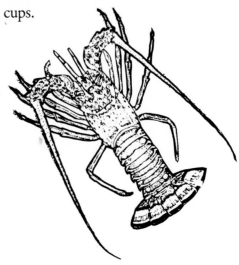

Mullet Salad

2 cups flaked mullet
1 cup creamed cottage cheese
½ cup chopped apple
⅓ cup chopped celery
2 tablespoons chopped green onion
2 tablespoons mayonnaise or salad dressing

2 tablespoons chopped pecans
1 tablespoon lemon juice
½ teaspoon salt
Dash pepper
6 lettuce cups
12 thin apple slices
Celery Seed Dressing

Combine all ingredients except lettuce, apple slices, and Celery Seed Dressing. Toss lightly. Chill. Serve in lettuce cups. Garnish with apple slices. Serve with Celery Seed Dressing. Yield: 6 servings.

Celery Seed Dressing

¾ cup mayonnaise or salad dressing
2 tablespoons lemon juice

1 tablespoon celery seeds

Combine all ingredients and mix well. Yield: ¾ cup.

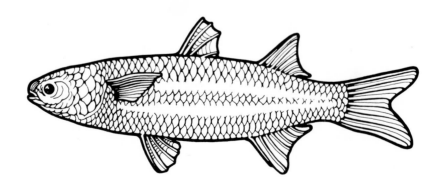

Mullet-Cantaloupe Mousse

1 cup flaked mullet
1 cup coarsely shredded cantaloupe
¼ cup mayonnaise or salad dressing
3 tablespoons lemon juice
2 tablespoons chopped pimiento
1 tablespoon white vinegar
Dash white pepper
Dash liquid hot pepper sauce
1 package (3 ounces) lime gelatin

½ teaspoon salt
1 cup boiling water
¼ cup whipping cream
2 tablespoons chopped parsley
Salad greens
Cantaloupe balls
Honeydew melon balls
Mayonnaise or salad dressing

Combine fish, cantaloupe, ½ cup mayonnaise, lemon juice, pimiento, vinegar, pepper and hot pepper sauce. Dissolve gelatin and salt in boiling water. Cool until slightly thickened. Add fish mixture. Chill until partially set. Whip cream. Fold cream and parsley into fish-gelatin mixture. Pour into a 1-quart ring mold. Chill until firm. Unmold on salad greens. Fill center with cantaloupe and honeydew melon balls. Serve with mayonnaise or salad dressing. Yield: 6 servings.

Rock Shrimp Luncheon Salad

1 pound cooked, peeled, deveined rock shrimp, fresh or frozen
3 cups cooked rice
1 can (16 ounces) chunky cut fruit in heavy syrup, drained (reserving ⅓ cup liquid)

1 banana, peeled and sliced
½ red apple, unpared, diced
½ orange, peeled, seeded, cut in small pieces
2 tablespoons shredded coconut
Broccoli flowerets (garnish)

Thaw rock shrimp if frozen. Mix rock shrimp together with rice and spread evenly on platter. Gently toss all fruit ingredients together. Spoon fruit attractively over shrimp and rice. Garnish with broccoli. Yield: 6 servings.

Springtime Crab Salad

1 pound blue crab meat, fresh, frozen or pasteurized
3 hard-cooked eggs, chopped
½ cup mayonnaise
¼ cup sliced celery
¼ cup chopped green pepper
¼ cup chopped green onions

¼ cup pitted ripe olives, chopped
1 teaspoon lemon juice
½ teaspoon salt
¼ teaspoon pepper
¼ teaspoon dry mustard
Lettuce cups

Thaw crab meat if frozen. Remove any pieces of shell or cartilage from meat. Combine crab meat with remaining ingredients, except lettuce, mixing well. Chill several hours. Serve in lettuce cups. Yield: 6 servings.

Crab Meat Three-Bean Salad

1 pound blue crab meat, fresh, frozen or pasteurized
2 jars (14 ounces each) three-bean salad, drained*
½ cup creamy Italian salad dressing

2 tablespoons chopped green pepper (optional)
Lettuce cups
Tomato wedges (garnish)

Thaw crab meat if frozen. Remove any shell or cartilage from meat. Combine crab meat, three-bean salad, salad dressing and green pepper; mix well. Chill for at least 30 minutes. Serve in lettuce cups. Garnish with tomato wedges. Yield: 6 servings.

*Note: If unavailable, use any equivalent marinated bean salad, including homemade.

Spicy Rock Shrimp Salad

1 pound cooked, peeled, deveined rock shrimp, fresh or frozen
1 large ripe avocado, cut into bite-sized pieces
¾ cup finely chopped onions
2 large tomatoes, coarsely chopped
4 hard-cooked eggs, coarsely chopped
Spicy Dressing
6 cups finely shredded lettuce
Green and black olives (garnish)

Thaw rock shrimp if frozen. Gently toss all ingredients except lettuce. Cover with dressing and toss gently again, until all ingredients are well coated. Refrigerate for 2 to 3 hours (tossing once or twice while refrigerated.) Serve on bed of finely shredded lettuce; garnish with green and black olives. Yield: 6 servings.

Spicy Dressing

1 cup dairy sour cream
½ cup mayonnaise
¼ cup peanut oil
¼ cup lemon juice
2 tablespoons garlic powder
1 tablespoon chili powder
1 tablespoon cumin
½ teaspoon salt
¼ teaspoon liquid hot pepper sauce

Place all ingredients in a blender; blend on high speed for 1 to 2 minutes. Yield: 2 cups.

Scallop Vegetable Salad

1½ pounds calico or bay scallops, fresh
    or frozen
1 quart boiling water
2 tablespoons salt
1 can (1 pound) cut green beans,
    drained

1 cup sliced celery
¼ cup chopped onion
¼ cup chopped green pepper
1 tablespoon chopped pimiento
Marinade
6 lettuce cups

Thaw scallops if frozen; rinse under cold running water to remove any remaining shell particles. Place scallops in boiling, salted water. Cover; return to boiling point. Reduce heat; simmer for 3 to 4 minutes, depending on size. Drain and cool. Combine all ingredients except lettuce. Cover and let stand in refrigerator for at least 1 hour. Drain; serve in lettuce cups. Yield: 6 servings.

Marinade

½ cup cider vinegar
1 tablespoon sugar
¼ teaspoon salt

⅛ teaspoon pepper
¼ cup olive oil or salad oil

Combine vinegar, sugar, salt and pepper. Add oil gradually, blending thoroughly.

Refreshing Fish and Apple Salad

2 cups cooked, flaked fish
1 apple, cored and chopped
1 medium banana, sliced
1 can (8 ounces) pineapple chunks, drained
½ cup raisins
½ cup chopped pecans
½ cup mayonnaise or salad dressing
1 tablespoon lemon juice
Salad greens
1 apple, wedged (garnish)

In a 2-quart bowl, combine first 8 ingredients; toss lightly. Serve on crisp salad greens. Garnish with apple wedges. Yield: 4 servings.

Rock Shrimp Orange Salad Olé

1 pound cooked, peeled, deveined rock shrimp, fresh or frozen
⅓ cup vegetable oil
⅓ cup red wine vinegar
¼ cup chopped green onions
2 tablespoons lemon juice
1 teaspoon sugar
½ teaspoon salt
½ teaspoon chili powder
4 large navel oranges
1 ripe avocado (garnish)
6 to 8 large pitted ripe olives (garnish)
Salad greens

In large mixing bowl, combine shrimp, oil, vinegar, green onions, lemon juice, sugar, salt and chili powder. Cut oranges in half and carefully remove sections; add to shrimp mixture and toss to coat. Refrigerate for several hours. Serve on salad greens and garnish with thin slices of avocado and ripe olives. Yield: 6 servings.

Fruity Shrimp Salad

1 pound cooked, peeled, deveined shrimp, fresh or frozen
2 cups diced, unpared fresh pears
2 cups diced, unpared fresh red apples
1 cup thinly sliced celery
½ cup mayonnaise or salad dressing

2 tablespoons milk
1 tablespoon cider vinegar
2 teaspoons grated onion
1 teaspoon salt
Salad greens
Paprika (garnish)

Thaw shrimp if frozen. Cut large shrimp in half. Combine shrimp, pears, apples and celery. Combine mayonnaise, milk, vinegar, onion and salt; mix well. Pour over shrimp mixture; toss lightly. Chill for at least 30 minutes. Serve on salad greens. Garnish with paprika. Yield: 6 servings.

Gulf Fish Salad

¾ pound cooked, flaked fish
2 cups cooked rice
1 cup sliced celery
½ cup chopped parsley
¼ cup sliced ripe olives

½ cup mayonnaise or salad dressing
2 tablespoons lemon juice
1 teaspoon curry powder
2 tablespoons French dressing
Salad greens

Combine rice, celery, parsley, olives and flaked fish. Combine mayonnaise, French dressing, lemon juice and curry powder; mix thoroughly. Add mayonnaise mixture to fish mixture; toss lightly. Chill. Serve on salad greens. Yield: 6 servings.

Tossed Fish Salad

2 cups flaked sea trout*
1 clove garlic
2 cups chopped raw spinach
1 cup thinly sliced celery
1 cup drained bean sprouts

½ cup chopped cucumber
¼ cup chopped green onions
½ cup French dressing
Tomato wedges (garnish)

*1½ pounds of fish fillets, fresh or frozen, may be poached in the microwave oven to yield approximately 2 cups cooked, flaked fish. To poach fish, place thawed fish in a single layer in a baking dish. Cover with plastic wrap. Cook 5 to 7 minutes or until fish flakes easily when tested with a fork. Drain. Remove skin and bones; flake fish.

Drain fish. Break into large pieces. Rub the inside of a salad bowl with the cut surface of a clove of garlic. Combine fish, spinach, celery, bean sprouts, cucumber, green onion and dressing; toss lightly. Garnish with tomato wedges. Yield: 6 servings.

Shrimp Seashell Salad

1 pound cooked, peeled, deveined shrimp, fresh or frozen
1½ cups cooked seashell macaroni
1 cup finely chopped celery
2 hard-cooked eggs, peeled and chopped
⅓ cup finely chopped green pepper
¼ cup mayonnaise or salad dressing

3 tablespoons chopped sweet pickle or sweet pickle relish
1 tablespoon grated onion
1 teaspoon lemon juice
1 teaspoon salt
⅛ teaspoon pepper
Salad greens

Thaw shrimp if frozen. Cut large shrimp in half. Combine all ingredients, except salad greens; chill. Serve on salad greens. Yield: 6 servings.

Curried Fish-Filled Avocado

1½ cups cooked fish fillets, cut into
    1-inch cubes
½ cup diced celery
¼ cup cooked tiny green peas
¼ cup slivered almonds, toasted
¼ cup mayonnaise or salad dressing
2 tablespoons sugar
2 teaspoons lemon juice

½ teaspoon curry powder
½ teaspoon salt
¼ teaspoon pepper
2 ripe avocados
Lemon juice
Lettuce leaves
Pimiento strips (garnish)

Combine fish, celery, peas and almonds in medium mixing bowl. Blend mayonnaise, sugar, lemon juice, curry powder, salt and pepper in small bowl. Pour over fish mixture; toss lightly. Halve and pit avocados; rub cut sides with lemon juice to prevent darkening. Arrange on lettuce-lined plates. Fill avocado centers with fish mixture. Garnish with pimiento strips, if desired. Yield: 4 servings.

Shrimp Salad Veronique

¾ pound cooked, peeled, deveined
    shrimp, fresh or frozen
1 cup pineapple chunks, fresh or
    canned in natural juice, drained
    (reserving ¼ cup juice)
1 cup fresh orange segments,
    drained (reserving ¼ cup juice),
    seeded and membrane removed

1 cup seedless grapes
1 small red apple, unpared, cored
    and cut into 1-inch chunks
1 teaspoon lemon juice
½ teaspoon arrowroot or cornstarch
¼ cup raisins
Lettuce leaves

In a 2-quart mixing bowl, combine shrimp, pineapple, orange segments, grapes and apple. Cover; chill. Place reserved pineapple, orange and lemon juices in a 1-quart saucepan. Bring to a gentle boil; stir in arrowroot. Cook until thickened, stirring constantly. Remove from heat. Stir in ¼ cup raisins; cool. Serve salad on lettuce-lined salad plates. Spoon 1 tablespoon raisin dressing over each serving. Yield: 4 servings.

Shrimp Waldorf Salad

1 pound cooked, peeled, deveined
   shrimp, fresh or frozen
4 cups lettuce (broken into small
   pieces)
2 cups diced, unpared red apples
1 cup minced celery
⅓ cup chopped pecans
¼ cup minced green onions
½ teaspoon salt
⅛ teaspoon pepper
4½ tablespoons mayonnaise
1½ tablespoons vinegar
1½ tablespoons sugar

Thaw shrimp if frozen. Cut large shrimp in half. Combine shrimp, lettuce, apples, celery, pecans, green onions, salt and pepper. In separate bowl, combine mayonnaise, vinegar and sugar; mix well. Pour over shrimp mixture; toss lightly. Yield: 4 to 6 servings.

Curried Shrimp Salad

1 pound cooked, peeled, deveined
   shrimp, fresh or frozen
1 cup chopped celery
⅓ cup dairy sour cream
¼ cup mayonnaise
2 hard-cooked eggs, chopped
3 tablespoons chopped green pepper
2 tablespoons lemon juice
1½ tablespoons grated onion
1½ tablespoons curry powder
1 tablespoon chili sauce
1 tablespoon chopped pimiento
1 teaspoon salt
¾ cup toasted sliced almonds
Salad greens

Thaw shrimp if frozen. Cut shrimp into halves or thirds if large. Combine all ingredients except almonds. Chill in refrigerator for several hours. Add almonds before serving. Serve on salad greens. Yield: 6 servings.

Crab Salad in Lime Mold

1 pound crab meat, fresh, frozen or
   pasteurized, or 2 cans (6½ ounces
   each) crab meat, drained
1 can (20½ ounces) pineapple tidbits
½ cup chopped pecans

½ cup mayonnaise or salad dressing
1 teaspoon lemon juice
¼ teaspoon salt
Lime Mold
Salad greens

Thaw frozen crab meat; remove any remaining shell or cartilage from meat. Drain pineapple, reserving juice. Combine pineapple, pecans, mayonnaise, lemon juice, salt and crab meat. Toss lightly. Chill. Unmold gelatin on salad greens; fill center with crab salad. Yield: 6 servings.

Lime Mold

2 packages (3 ounces each) lime-
   flavored gelatin
1 teaspoon salt
1½ cups boiling water

2 cups pineapple juice and water to
   make volume
¼ cup lemon juice

Dissolve gelatin and salt in boiling water. Add pineapple juice and lemon juice; mix well. Pour into a lightly greased 1-quart ring mold. Chill until firm.

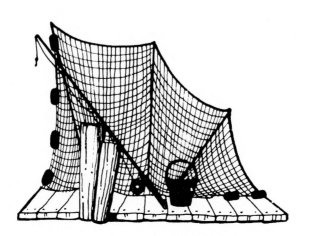

Squid Salad

2 pounds whole squid, fresh or frozen
2 quarts boiling water
2 teaspoons salt
4 cups cooked seashell macaroni
1 cup sliced celery
½ cup chopped red onions
½ cup shredded carrot (optional)

½ cup shredded purple cabbage (optional)
½ cup vegetable oil
¼ cup lemon juice
1 clove garlic, crushed
1 tablespoon chopped parsley
1 teaspoon salt
¼ teaspoon pepper

Thaw squid if frozen. From opening in mantle, cut mantle lengthwise with a sharp knife. Spread inside of mantle open flat. Pressing mantle with one hand, grasp head and arms and pull off with intestines. Remove pen. With knife, scrape away any visceral remains adhering to inside of mantle wall. Turn mantle to other side. Starting at tail end, pinch fins, pulling fins and outer membrane from mantle. Remove any remaining membrane with knife. Rinse under cold running water. Place squid in boiling, salted water. Cover and simmer 3 to 5 minutes or until tender. Rinse under cold running water; drain. Cut squid into strips or pieces. Combine all ingredients in large bowl; mix well. Cover; refrigerate several hours. Yield: 6 servings.
(Photo, page 91)

Delightful Rock Shrimp Salad

1 pound cooked, peeled, deveined rock shrimp, fresh or frozen
1 ripe avocado, peeled and sliced
1 can (11 ounces) mandarin oranges, drained
1 pound fresh spinach, washed and torn into 1-inch pieces

4 strips bacon, cooked, drained and crumbled
Russian salad dressing
1 package (2¾ ounces) sliced almonds (garnish)

Thaw rock shrimp if frozen. Cut large shrimp in half. In large mixing bowl, combine shrimp, avocado, orange slices, spinach and bacon. Toss lightly. Garnish with sliced almonds. Serve immediately with salad dressing on the side. **(Photo, page 72)**

Shrimp Cheese Dreams

½ pound cooked, peeled, deveined
  shrimp, fresh or frozen
2 packages (3 ounces each) cream
  cheese, softened
½ cup toasted slivered almonds
½ cup crushed pineapple

¼ cup chopped pitted ripe olives
1 tablespoon lemon juice
6 slices buttered white bread
6 slices buttered whole wheat bread

Thaw shrimp if frozen. Chop shrimp. Combine all ingredients except bread. Spread 6 slices of white bread with approximately ½ cup shrimp mixture; cover with 6 slices whole wheat bread. Cut each sandwich diagonally into 4 triangles. Yield: 6 servings.

Fish Sandwich Surprise

1 pound mullet (or other fish) fillets,
  fresh or frozen
1 quart boiling water
1 tablespoon salt
3 hard-cooked eggs, chopped
¾ cup chopped pimiento-stuffed
  olives

⅓ cup mayonnaise or salad dressing
1 tablespoon horseradish
½ teaspoon salt
⅛ teaspoon pepper
12 large slices buttered rye bread
6 lettuce leaves

Thaw fillets, if frozen. Place fillets in boiling salted water. Cover and return to the boiling point. Reduce heat and simmer for ten minutes or until fish flakes easily when tested with a fork. Drain. Remove skin and bones; flake. Combine egg, olives, mayonnaise or salad dressing, horseradish, salt, pepper and fish; mix thoroughly. Chill. Spread six slices bread with approximately one-half cup mullet mixture. Cut in half. Yield: 6 servings.

Sauerkraut Seafest Sandwich

1 cup cooked, flaked fish
½ cup drained sauerkraut
¼ cup dill pickle cubes
¼ cup mayonnaise
1 tablespoon horseradish mustard

8 slices rye bread
4 slices processed Swiss cheese (4 ounces)
2 tablespoons butter or margarine

Combine fish, sauerkraut, pickles, mayonnaise and mustard in 2-quart mixing bowl. Mix well. Spread ¼ of mixture on each of four slices of bread; cover each with cheese slice and top with remaining bread. Melt butter in heated skillet. Place sandwiches in skillet and grill on each side until golden brown. Yield: 4 servings.

Crab Sandwich Caladesi

1 pound blue crab meat
¾ cup diced American cheese
½ cup buttermilk dressing
1½ teaspoon prepared mustard

2 tablespoons finely chopped, pimiento-stuffed olives
6 junior pita bread
6 lettuce leaves

Remove any remaining shell or cartilage from crab meat. Combine all ingredients except bread and lettuce; mix well. Chill for 1 hour. Place 1 lettuce leaf in bread and stuff with crab mixture. Yield: 6 servings.

Smoked Amberjack Sandwich

2 cups cooked, flaked amberjack	½ teaspoon garlic powder
⅓ cup mayonnaise	16 dill pickle slices
1 tablespoon prepared mustard	4 slices white bread, toasted
1 teaspoon liquid smoke	4 slices mozzarella cheese

Combine fish, mayonnaise, mustard, liquid smoke and garlic powder. Place 4 pickles on each piece of toast; top with equal amounts of fish mixture. Cover each with cheese. Broil until cheese is bubbly. Yield: 4 open-faced sandwiches.

Note: 2 cups of smoked, flaked amberjack can be substituted in this recipe, omitting liquid smoke.

Davy Jones's Submarine Sandwich

2 cups cooked, flaked fish	1 onion
1 cup chopped celery	6 lettuce leaves
½ cup mayonnaise or salad dressing	3 submarine rolls, 12 inches each
2 tablespoons chopped sweet pickle or drained pickle relish	6 slices (1 ounce each) provolone cheese
3 tomatoes	¼ cup mayonnaise or salad dressing

Combine celery, mayonnaise, pickle and fish; chill. Wash and slice tomatoes, crosswise, into 18 slices. Peel onion and slice, crosswise, into thin slices. Separate into rings. Wash lettuce and drain. Cut rolls in half lengthwise. Spread bottom half with approximately ¾ cup fish mixture. Top with tomato slices, onion rings, cheese and lettuce. Spread top half of rolls with mayonnaise. Cover sandwiches and secure with toothpicks. Cut in half crosswise. Yield: 6 servings.

Sea Trout Burgers

1½ pounds sea trout fillets, skinned,
   fresh or frozen
1 quart boiling water
1 tablespoon salt
3 eggs, beaten
⅓ cup grated Parmesan cheese
1 tablespoon chopped parsley

1 clove garlic, finely chopped
½ teaspoon salt
⅛ teaspoon pepper
½ cup dry bread crumbs
Vegetable oil for frying
6 toasted sesame hamburger buns
Tartar sauce

Thaw fish if frozen. Add 1 tablespoon salt to boiling water. Place fillets in boiling
water. Cover and return to boiling point. Reduce heat and simmer for 7 to 10 minutes
or until fish flakes easily when tested with a fork. Drain. Flake. In medium-sized bowl
combine eggs, cheese, parsley, garlic, salt, pepper and fish. Chill for two hours. Shape
into 6 burgers and roll in crumbs. Fry in hot oil at moderate heat until brown on one
side. Turn carefully and brown the other side. Cooking time will be approximately 6
to 8 minutes. Drain on absorbent paper. Place burger on bottom half of bun. Spread
with tartar sauce and cover with top half of bun. Yield: 6 servings.

Croque-Monsieur

(Pronounced Croak-Messuer)

½ pound blue crab meat, fresh,
   frozen or pasteurized
3 tablespoons butter or margarine
6 slices Swiss cheese

6 slices firm white bread,
   thickly sliced
Delicatessen-style dill pickles (garnish)

Thaw crab if frozen. Remove any remaining cartilage. Melt butter in a large skillet.
Add bread and fry on one side until golden. Place crab on bread; top with cheese.
Cook, covered, over reduced heat for approximately 4 minutes or until cheese melts
and crab is well heated. Garnish with delicatessen-style dill pickle slices. Yield: 6
servings.

ENTRÉES

Rolled Amberjack with Asparagus

1½ pounds amberjack (or other fish) fillets, fresh or frozen
1 package (6 ounces) cream cheese with herbs and spices
⅓ cup butter or margarine
⅓ cup lemon juice
1 teaspoon seasoned salt
¼ teaspoon lemon-pepper seasoning
¼ teaspoon arrowroot
1 (10 ounces) package frozen chopped asparagus spears, thawed
1½ cups cooked rice
1 cup shredded sharp Cheddar cheese
Paprika

Thaw fish if frozen. Preheat oven to 375 degrees. (Split horizontally to make two fillets.) Spread cream cheese equally on each fillet. Set aside. In small saucepan, melt margarine; add lemon juice, salt, lemon-pepper and arrowroot stirring until thickened. Remove from heat, reserving ¼ cup lemon mixture. Set aside. In medium bowl, combine asparagus, rice, cheese and ¼ cup lemon mixture. Mix well. Divide among fillets and roll turban style. Place seam side down in 13 x 9 x 2-inch baking dish. Pour remaining sauce over rolled fillets and top with paprika. Bake at 375 degrees for 25 minutes or until fish flakes easily when tested with a fork. Yield: 4 servings.

Parmesan Amberjack

1½ pounds amberjack (or other fish) fillets, fresh or frozen
¼ cup soft bread crumbs
¼ cup grated Parmesan cheese
½ teaspoon paprika
½ teaspoon basil
½ teaspoon salt
¼ teaspoon curry powder
¼ teaspoon lemon-pepper seasoning
4 tablespoons butter or margarine, melted

Thaw fish if frozen. Preheat oven to 400 degrees. Combine bread crumbs, cheese and seasonings. Place fillets in a well-greased baking pan. Spread mixture evenly over each fillet. Drizzle melted butter over fillets. Bake at 400 degrees for 15 minutes or until fish flakes easily when tested with a fork. Yield: 4 servings.

Amberjack with Pea Pods

1½ pounds amberjack (or other fish) fillets, fresh or frozen
½ teaspoon paprika
½ teaspoon salt
½ teaspoon seasoned pepper
½ cup butter, divided
1 package (6 ounces) frozen pea pods, cooked according to package directions
2 cups sliced fresh mushrooms
¼ teaspoon herb seasoning
3 tablespoons all-purpose flour
1½ cups chicken bouillon
2 tablespoons dry sherry (optional)

Thaw fish if frozen. Preheat oven to 375 degrees. Cut into serving-sized portions; sprinkle with paprika, salt and pepper. In skillet, sauté fish in ¼ cup of butter for 5 minutes, turning once. Place fish in large baking dish and spread pea pods among portions. In same skillet over low heat, combine mushrooms, herb seasoning and remaining butter; stir flour in gently. Add bouillon and sherry, stir. Simmer for 5 minutes. Pour sauce over fish and bake at 375 degrees for 20 minutes. Yield: 4 servings.

Broiled Marinated Amberjack

1½ pounds amberjack (or other fish) fillets, fresh or frozen
½ cup olive or vegetable oil
3 tablespoons lemon juice
2 teaspoons Dijon mustard with white wine
2 cloves garlic, finely chopped
½ teaspoon white pepper

Thaw fish if frozen. Place fish in rectangular dish. Combine other ingredients in a shaker jar; shake well. Pour mixture over fillets; cover and marinate in refrigerator for one hour, turning once. Remove fillets from marinade and broil 5 to 6 inches from heat for 10 minutes, basting occasionally. Yield: 4 servings.

Amberjack Pizzaiola

2 pounds amberjack (or other fish) fillets, fresh or frozen
1 can (14½ ounces) Italian tomatoes, drained, reserving liquid
1 can (6 ounces) tomato paste
¼ cup olive oil

2 tablespoons chopped chives
2 cloves garlic, finely chopped
1 teaspoon fine herb blend
½ teaspoon salt
¼ teaspoon creole seasoning
¼ cup grated Parmesan cheese
Hot cooked linguine

Thaw fillets if frozen. Preheat oven to 375 degrees. Cut into ½-inch pieces. Place fish in 13 x 9 x 2-inch baking dish, set aside. Chop tomatoes. Combine tomatoes, tomato liquid, tomato paste, olive oil, chives, garlic and seasonings; stir well. Pour tomato mixture over fish and bake at 375 degrees for 20 minutes. Sprinkle with cheese and bake an additional 5 minutes. Serve over linguine. Yield: 6 servings.

Sour Cream-Baked Amberjack

1½ pounds amberjack (or other fish) fillets, fresh or frozen
½ cup plain yogurt
1½ tablespoons all-purpose flour
1 cup dairy sour cream
3 tablespoons chopped pimiento

½ teaspoon salt
½ teaspoon celery seed
½ teaspoon white pepper
½ teaspoon thyme
1 tablespoon chopped fresh dill weed

Thaw fish if frozen. Preheat oven to 350 degrees. Place fillets in well-greased baking dish. In small bowl combine yogurt and flour. Add sour cream, pimiento, salt, celery seed, white pepper and thyme. Mix well. Spread sauce over fish. Sprinkle with dill weed. Bake at 350 degrees for 25 minutes or until fish flakes easily when tested with a fork. Yield: 4 servings.

Ale-Poached Fish with Pimiento Sauce

1½ pounds black sea bass (or other fish) fillets, fresh or frozen
1 cup water
1 cup beer
1 small onion, sliced
1 teaspoon salt
1 teaspoon Worcestershire sauce
3 peppercorns
1 clove garlic, peeled
Pimiento Sauce

Thaw fish if frozen. Remove skin and bones from fish. In a 10-inch skillet, combine water, beer, onion, salt, Worcestershire sauce, peppercorns and garlic; bring ingredients to a gentle boil. Place fillets in poaching liquid; cover and simmer 5 to 10 minutes or until fish flakes easily when tested with a fork. Carefully remove fish to warm platter. Pour Pimiento Sauce over fish. Yield: 4 servings. **(Photo, page 147)**

Pimiento Sauce

2 tablespoons butter or margarine
2 tablespoons flour
1 can (10¾ ounces) chicken broth
3 tablespoons chopped pimiento
1 teaspoon curry
1 teaspoon lemon juice
¾ teaspoon sugar

In a medium saucepan, melt butter. Stir in flour; add chicken broth gradually and cook until thick and smooth, stirring constantly. Add remaining ingredients and heat. Yield: 1½ cups.

Blackened Fish Fillets

1½ pounds black drum (or other fish)
   fillets, fresh or frozen
 2 teaspoons ground thyme
 2 teaspoons ground marjoram
 2 teaspoons garlic powder
 1 teaspoon ground oregano

 1 teaspoon cayenne
 1 teaspoon paprika
 1 teaspoon salt
 1 teaspoon white pepper
 ½ cup melted butter or margarine

Thaw fish if frozen. Mix all ingredients except butter. Heat large, lightly oiled cast-iron skillet over high heat until a drop of water sizzles in pan (about 10 minutes). Coat both sides of fish with butter. Sprinkle fish with spices, shaking off excess. Place fillets in hot skillet and cook 2 to 3 minutes per side or until fish flakes easily when tested with a fork. Yield: 4 servings.

Fish Crunch

 2 pounds bluefish (or other fish)
   fillets, fresh or frozen
 3 cups water
 ¾ cup lemon juice
1½ cups cornflake crumbs
 1 tablespoon paprika

1¾ teaspoon seasoned salt
 ⅓ cup mayonnaise
 4 teaspoons prepared mustard
 1 tablespoon lemon juice
 1 teaspoon seasoned salt

Thaw fish if frozen. Preheat oven to 400 degrees. Place in shallow baking dish. Combine water and ¾ cup lemon juice; pour over fillets. Marinate in refrigerator for 30 minutes. Combine cornflake crumbs, paprika and 1¾ teaspoon seasoned salt. Combine mayonnaise, mustard, 1 tablespoon lemon juice and 1 teaspoon seasoned salt; mix thoroughly. Remove fillets from marinade and pat dry with paper towels. Dip in mustard mixture, then roll in crumb mixture. Place on a well-greased bake-and-serve platter, approximately 15 x 10 x ½-inches. Bake at 400 degrees for 12 to 15 minutes or until fish flakes easily when tested with a fork. Yield: 6 servings.

Indian River Clambake

6 dozen clams
12 small Vidalia onions
6 medium baking potatoes
6 ears of corn in the husks

6 live spiny lobsters (1 pound each)
Seaweed (optional)
Lemon wedges
Melted butter or margarine

Wash clam shells thoroughly. Peel onions and wash potatoes. Parboil onions and potatoes for 15 minutes; drain. Remove silk from corn and replace husks. Cut 12 pieces of cheesecloth and 12 pieces of heavy-duty aluminum foil, 18 x 36 inches each. Place 2 pieces of cheesecloth on top of 2 pieces of foil. Place 2 onions, 1 potato, 1 ear of corn, 1 lobster, 1 dozen clams and seaweed on cheesecloth. Tie opposite corners of cheesecloth together. Pour 1 cup of water over the package. Bring foil up and close all edges with tight double folds. Make 6 packages. Place packages on a grill about 4 inches from hot coals. Cover with hood or aluminum foil. Cook for 45 to 60 minutes or until onions and potatoes are cooked. Serve with lemon wedges and melted butter. Yield: 6 servings.

Stuffed Clams

24 clams, in the shell
½ cup dry bread crumbs
½ cup finely chopped mushrooms
2 slices bacon, finely chopped

½ teaspoon minced parsley
⅛ teaspoon pepper
Butter or margarine

Preheat oven to 350 degrees. Rinse unopened clams under cold running water to remove any foreign particles. Shuck clams, reserving shells. Scrub shells and place in boiling water; boil 2 minutes. Remove shells and drain. Chop the clams. Combine clams with bread crumbs, mushrooms, bacon and parsley. Season with pepper. Fill reserved clam shells with clam mixture; dot with butter. Bake at 350 degrees 15 minutes or until top is brown. Yield: 6 servings.

Clam Fritters

18-24 clams, shucked and drained
2½ cups self-rising flour
1 teaspoon baking powder
⅛ teaspoon salt
⅛ teaspoon pepper
⅛ teaspoon ground thyme
½ cup milk
1 egg, slightly beaten

1 tablespoon lime juice
⅛ teaspoon liquid hot pepper sauce (optional)
½ cup minced green pepper
⅓ cup minced onion
1 clove garlic, minced
Vegetable oil for deep-frying
Tangy Sauce

Preheat oven to 375 degrees. Chop clams; set aside. Combine flour, baking powder, salt, pepper and thyme. Add milk, egg, lime juice and liquid hot pepper sauce; mix until batter is smooth. Stir in clams, celery, green pepper, onion and garlic. Drop clam batter by teaspoons into hot oil, 375 degrees, and fry until lightly browned. Serve with Tangy Sauce. Yield: 6 servings.

Tangy Sauce

½ cup seafood cocktail sauce or catsup
¼ cup mayonnaise

3 tablespoons lime juice
⅛ teaspoon liquid hot pepper sauce (optional)

Combine all ingredients; chill. Yield: ¾ cup.

Company Crab

1 pound blue crab meat, fresh, frozen or pasteurized
1 can (15 ounces) artichoke hearts, drained
1 can (4 ounces) sliced mushrooms, drained
2 tablespoons butter or margarine
2½ tablespoons flour

½ teaspoon salt
⅛ teaspoon cayenne
1 cup half-and-half cream
2 tablespoons sherry
2 tablespoons cereal crumbs
1 tablespoon grated Parmesan cheese
Paprika

Thaw crab meat if frozen. Preheat oven to 450 degrees. Remove any remaining pieces of shell or cartilage. Cut artichoke hearts in half. Place artichokes in a well-greased shallow 1½-quart casserole. Cover with mushrooms and crab meat. Melt butter in a 1-quart saucepan. Blend in flour and seasonings. Add cream gradually and cook until thick, stirring constantly. Stir in sherry. Pour sauce over crab meat. Combine crumbs and cheese. Sprinkle over sauce. Sprinkle with paprika. Bake in a hot oven, 450 degrees, for 12 to 15 minutes or until bubbly. Yield: 6 servings. (**Photo, page 207**)

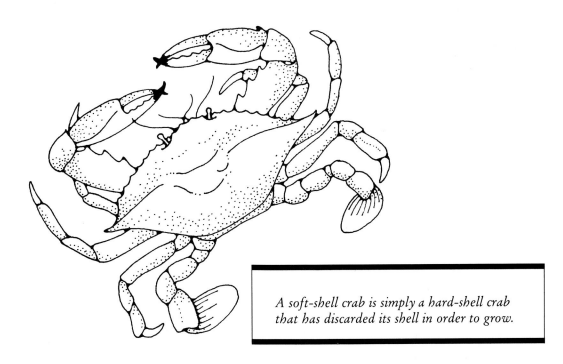

A soft-shell crab is simply a hard-shell crab that has discarded its shell in order to grow.

Crab Delight

1 pound blue crab meat, fresh, frozen or pasteurized
3 medium acorn squash
1 cup diced cooked ham
1 cup finely chopped onions
2 cloves garlic, finely chopped
⅓ cup butter or margarine

2 cups fresh bread crumbs
¼ cup chopped parsley
1 teaspoon salt
¾ teaspoon powdered thyme
¾ teaspoon liquid hot pepper sauce
Parsley sprigs (garnish)

Thaw crab meat if frozen. Preheat oven to 375 degrees. Remove any remaining shell or cartilage. Scrub acorn squash. Halve lengthwise; discard seeds and pulp. Place cut side down in a 17¼ x 11⅜ x 2¼-inch baking pan. Add ¼ inch water. Bake at 375 degrees for 40 minutes. Cook onions and garlic in butter until tender; add crab meat and ham; cook 3 minutes. Stir in bread crumbs, chopped parsley, salt, thyme and liquid hot pepper sauce. Remove squash from oven, drain water, and turn cut side of squash up in pan. Fill each half with the crab meat stuffing. Return to oven and bake 15 minutes longer or until stuffing is heated throughout. Yield: 6 servings.

Crab Oscar

1 pound blue crab meat, fresh, frozen or pasteurized
1 package (12 ounces) frozen asparagus spears, cooked according to package directions
1 cup dairy sour cream

¼ cup mayonnaise
1 tablespoon lemon juice
¼ teaspoon salt
¼ teaspoon cayenne
¼ cup Parmesan cheese
Paprika (garnish)

Thaw crab meat if frozen. Preheat oven to 350 degrees. Remove any remaining shell or cartilage. In a 1-quart saucepan, combine sour cream, mayonnaise, lemon juice, salt and cayenne. Cook over low heat for 4 minutes. Arrange cooked asparagus in 12 x 8 x 2-inch baking dish. Place crab over asparagus. Pour sauce over all. Sprinkle with Parmesan cheese. Bake at 350 degrees for 20 minutes. Sprinkle with paprika. Yield: 4 servings.

Crab Spaghetti

1 pound blue crab meat, fresh, frozen or pasteurized
½ cup chopped onion
½ cup chopped celery
2 cloves garlic, finely chopped
2 tablespoons chopped parsley
¼ cup butter or margarine, melted

1 cup canned tomatoes
1 can (8 ounces) tomato sauce
½ teaspoon paprika
¼ teaspoon salt
⅛ teaspoon pepper
3 cups cooked spaghetti
Grated Parmesan cheese (optional)

Thaw crab meat if frozen. Remove any remaining shell or cartilage. In large saucepan cook onion, celery, garlic and parsley in butter until tender. Add tomatoes, tomato sauce and seasonings. Simmer for 20 minutes, stirring occasionally. Add crab meat; heat. Serve over spaghetti. Sprinkle with Parmesan cheese. Yield: 6 servings.

Crab Meat Florida

1 pound blue crab meat, fresh, frozen or pasteurized
3 tablespoons vegetable oil
2 tablespoons minced onion
3 tablespoons all-purpose flour
2 cups skim milk
½ teaspoon dehydrated celery flakes
⅛ teaspoon grated orange peel
1 tablespoon snipped parsley

1 tablespoon minced green pepper
1 pimiento, minced
⅛ teaspoon liquid hot pepper sauce
2 tablespoons dry sherry
1 egg, beaten
⅛ teaspoon pepper
½ cup toasted dry bread crumbs
1 tablespoon vegetable oil

Thaw crab meat if frozen. Preheat oven to 350 degrees. Remove any remaining shell or cartilage from meat. Sauté onion in oil until transparent. Add flour and cook, stirring, 1 minute. Add milk and simmer until sauce is thick, stirring constantly. Add celery flakes, orange peel, parsley, pepper, pimiento and pepper sauce. Remove from heat and add sherry. Stir some of the sauce into the beaten egg; pour egg mixture slowly into the sauce, stirring constantly. Add pepper and crab meat. Turn into 8 greased individual casserole dishes or shells. Mix bread crumbs with oil. Sprinkle on top of each casserole. Bake at 350 degrees, uncovered, 15 to 20 minutes or until lightly brown. Yield: 8 servings.

Crab Meat Chantilly

1 pound lump crab meat, fresh, frozen or pasteurized	⅛ teaspoon salt
2 tablespoons butter	⅛ teaspoon pepper
½ cup sherry	2 packages (10 ounces each) frozen asparagus
2 tablespoons all-purpose flour	1 cup whipped cream
2 cups light cream	4 tablespoons Parmesan cheese

Thaw crab meat if frozen. Remove any remaining shell or particles. Add sherry and simmer until reduced by half. Add flour, cream and seasonings; cook until thickened. While heating, fork stir to keep the crab meat in lumps. Cook asparagus according to package directions; drain. Place asparagus in the bottom of a well-greased casserole dish. Pour crab meat mixture over the asparagus. Spread the whipped cream on top. Sprinkle with the cheese. Brown lightly under the broiler. Yield: 4 servings.

Crab Cakes

1 pound blue crab claw meat, fresh, frozen or pasteurized	1 tablespoon chopped parsley
½ cup chopped onion	1 teaspoon prepared horseradish
⅓ cup chopped celery	1 teaspoon salt
⅓ cup chopped green pepper	1 teaspoon Worcestershire sauce
2 cloves garlic, finely chopped	½ teaspoon pepper
⅓ cup melted butter or margarine	¼ teaspoon dry mustard
2 cups soft bread crumbs	1 cup soft bread crumbs
3 eggs, beaten	Vegetable oil for frying

Thaw crab meat if frozen. Remove any remaining shell or cartilage. Cook onion, celery, green pepper and garlic in butter until tender. Combine 2 cups bread crumbs, eggs, parsley, horseradish, salt, Worcestershire sauce, pepper, mustard, cooked vegetables and crab meat. Mix well. Form into 6 large or 12 small patties. Roll patties in remaining 1 cup soft bread crumbs and fry in ⅛ inch of vegetable oil, hot but not smoking, until brown. Yield: 6 servings.

Stir-Fry Fish Hash, page 162 ▶

King Mackerel Rice Casserole, page 156

Croaker and Walnut Specialty, page 133

Deviled Crab, page 130 ▶

Crabber's Creation, page 131

Sea Trout with Pecan Rice, page 224

Crab Meat Supreme

1 pound blue crab meat, fresh, frozen or pasteurized
1 package (1 ounce) white wine sauce mix
1 cup soft bread crumbs
⅓ cup sliced green onions
¼ cup grated mozzarella cheese
2 tablespoons lemon or lime juice
1 tablespoon chopped pimiento
1 teaspoon Worcestershire sauce
¼ teaspoon tarragon
¼ teaspoon salt
½ cup dry bread crumbs
1 tablespoon melted butter or margarine
Paprika

Thaw crab meat if frozen. Preheat oven to 400 degrees. Remove any remaining shell or cartilage. Prepare white wine sauce mix according to package directions. Combine all the ingredients, except ½ cup bread crumbs and butter. Place equal portions in 6 well-greased individual shells or casseroles. Combine ½ cup bread crumbs and butter and sprinkle over crab mixture. Sprinkle with paprika. Bake at 400 degrees for 15 to 20 minutes or until lightly brown and heated throughout. Yield: 6 servings.

Crabber's Casserole

1 pound crab meat, fresh, frozen or pasteurized
¼ cup butter or margarine, melted
½ cup chopped celery
2 tablespoons chopped green pepper
2 tablespoons all-purpose flour
1 cup milk
1 egg yolk, beaten
2 tablespoons lemon juice
½ teaspoon salt
⅛ teaspoon pepper
1 tablespoon melted butter or margarine
¼ cup bread crumbs

Thaw crab meat if frozen. Preheat oven to 350 degrees. Remove any remaining shell or cartilage. Sauté celery and green pepper in ¼ cup butter until tender. Blend in flour. Gradually add milk; cook until thickened, stirring constantly. Stir a little of the hot sauce into the egg yolk; add to remaining sauce, stirring constantly. Add lemon juice, seasonings and crab meat. Place crab meat mixture in a well-greased 1-quart casserole. Combine 1 tablespoon melted butter with bread crumbs; sprinkle over casserole. Bake at 350 degrees for 20 to 25 minutes or until lightly browned. Yield: 6 servings.

Tangy Creamed Crab

1 pound blue crab meat, fresh, frozen or pasteurized
1 package (10 ounces) frozen green peas
½ cup chopped onion
¼ cup chopped green pepper
1 can (6 ounces) sliced mushrooms, drained

4 tablespoons butter or margarine, melted
1 cup mayonnaise
1 cup plain yogurt
1 teaspoon salt
⅛ teaspoon pepper
1 tablespoon chopped pimiento
3 cups cooked rice

Thaw crab meat if frozen. Remove any remaining shell or cartilage. Cook peas according to package directions. Drain. In large skillet, cook onion, green pepper and mushrooms in butter until tender. Combine crab meat, mayonnaise, yogurt, salt, pepper and pimiento, and simmer until thoroughly heated, stirring occasionally. Serve with rice. Yield: 6 servings.

Deviled Crab

1 pound blue crab meat, fresh, frozen or pasteurized
6 tablespoons butter or margarine, melted
3 tablespoons all-purpose flour
1 cup milk
¼ cup mayonnaise or salad dressing
2 tablespoons lemon juice
1 tablespoon chopped parsley
2 teaspoons Worcestershire sauce
2 teaspoons grated onion

2 teaspoons cream-style prepared horseradish
½ teaspoon liquid hot pepper sauce
½ teaspoon salt
⅛ teaspoon pepper
⅛ teaspoon nutmeg
1 tablespoon melted butter or margarine
¼ cup dry bread crumbs
Paprika

Thaw crab meat if frozen. Preheat oven to 350 degrees. Remove any remaining shell or cartilage. Melt 6 tablespoons butter in a 1-quart saucepan; blend in flour. Gradually add milk and cook, stirring constantly, until thickened. Add mayonnaise, lemon juice, parsley, Worcestershire sauce, onion, horseradish, liquid hot pepper sauce, salt, pepper and nutmeg; blend well. Combine sauce and crab meat. Spoon mixture in 6 well-greased ramekins or shells. Combine 1 tablespoon butter and bread crumbs; sprinkle over top of crab meat. Sprinkle with paprika. Bake at 350 degrees for 20 to 25 minutes or until golden brown. Yield: 6 servings. **(Photo, page 127)**

Crabber's Creation

1 pound blue crab meat, fresh, frozen or pasteurized
1 package (7 ounces) long grain and wild rice
2 cups sliced fresh mushrooms (optional)

⅓ cup olive vegetable oil
1 teaspoon salt
½ teaspoon white pepper
2 tablespoons extra dry vermouth
2 tablespoons lemon juice

Thaw crab meat if frozen. Preheat electric skillet to 325 degrees. Remove any shell or cartilage from crab meat. Prepare rice according to package directions; add fresh mushrooms 5 minutes before end of cooking time. Add oil, salt and pepper to preheated skillet. Stir in crab meat, vermouth and lemon juice. Cook 2 to 3 minutes, stirring frequently until crab meat is heated thoroughly. Serve immediately over wild rice mixture. Yield: 6 servings. **(Photo, page 128)**

Devilishly Stuffed Soft-Shell Crab

8 soft-shell crabs, cleaned, fresh or frozen
¼ cup chopped onion
¼ cup chopped celery
2 tablespoons chopped green pepper
1 clove garlic, minced
¼ cup butter or margarine, melted
1 cup finely crushed butter-flavored crackers

2 tablespoons milk
1 egg, beaten
1 tablespoon chopped parsley
½ teaspoon dry mustard
½ teaspoon Worcestershire sauce
¼ teaspoon salt
⅛ teaspoon cayenne
¼ cup butter or margarine, melted

Thaw crabs if frozen. Preheat oven to 400 degrees. Wash crabs thoroughly; drain well. Cook onion, celery, green pepper and garlic in butter until tender. In a medium bowl, combine mixture with the next 8 ingredients. Place crabs in a shallow, well-greased baking pan. Remove top shell from crabs and fill each cavity with 1 tablespoon stuffing mixture. Replace top shell. Brush crabs with melted butter. Bake at 400 degrees for 15 minutes or until shells turn red and crabs brown slightly. Yield: 4 servings. **(Photo, page 168)**

Crawfish Étouffée

2 pounds cooked, peeled crawfish, fresh or frozen
¼ cup butter or margarine, melted
3 tablespoons all-purpose flour
1 cup chopped onions
½ cup chopped celery
¼ cup chopped green pepper

2 tablespoons chopped parsley
1 clove garlic, minced
½ cup water
1 tablespoon lemon juice
¼ teaspoon salt
¼ teaspoon cayenne
3 cups cooked rice

Thaw fish if frozen. In a 10-inch skillet, combine butter and flour. Add onions, celery, green pepper, parsley and garlic. Sauté vegetables over medium heat, stirring constantly, for 5 minutes or until tender. Add water gradually and continue to stir; cook until thick. Stir in crawfish, lemon juice, salt and pepper; heat thoroughly. Serve over rice. Yield: 6 servings. **(Photo, page 186)**

Crawfish Linguine

1 pound peeled crawfish tails, fresh or frozen
½ cup butter or margarine
¼ cup olive oil
1 clove garlic, minced
1 cup fresh sliced mushrooms

½ cup chopped green onions and tops
¼ cup chopped parsley
1 package (8 ounces) linguine, cooked
Parmesan cheese (optional)

Thaw fish if frozen. Melt butter with olive oil in large skillet. Sauté garlic and mushrooms until mushrooms are tender. Add crawfish tails and green onions. Cook 5 minutes over low heat. Stir in chopped parsley. Serve over hot cooked linguine; sprinkle with Parmesan cheese. Note: The crawfish mixture also makes an excellent filling for omelets. If using in omelets, omit the olive oil. Yield: 4 servings. **(Photo, page 148)**

Croaker and Walnut Specialty

1½ pounds croaker (or other fish) fillets, fresh or frozen
1 can (3 ounces) sliced mushrooms, drained
⅓ cup chopped green onion
2 tablespoons butter or margarine, melted
1 cup uncooked long grain white rice

½ cup pimiento-stuffed olives, sliced
½ cup chopped walnuts
⅓ cup grated sharp Cheddar cheese
2 tablespoons chopped parsley
2 cans (10¾ ounces each) condensed golden mushroom soup
1½ teaspoon salt
¼ teaspoon pepper
⅓ cup grated sharp Cheddar cheese

Thaw fish if frozen. Preheat oven to 350 degrees. Skin fillets and cut into 1-inch chunks. Cook onions and mushrooms in butter until onions are tender. Add fish, rice, olives, walnuts, ⅓ cup cheese and parsley. Blend soup and seasonings until smooth; add to fish mixture. Pour fish mixture into well-greased 13 x 9 x 2-inch casserole dish. Sprinkle with ⅓ cup cheese over top of casserole. Bake in a moderate oven, 350 degrees, for 20 to 25 minutes or until rice is tender. Yield: 6 servings. (**Photo, page 126**)

Floridian Croaker

2 pounds croaker (or other fish) fillets, skinned, fresh or frozen
1½ teaspoons salt
¼ teaspoon pepper
1 cup sliced fresh mushrooms
½ cup sliced onion

¼ cup chopped green pepper
1 cup orange juice
3 tablespoons dry sherry
1 tablespoon grated orange rind
1 tablespoon all-purpose flour
Orange and/or lime slices (garnish)

Thaw fish if frozen. Preheat oven to 375 degrees. Cut fish into serving-sized portions. Sprinkle with salt and pepper. Place fish in a single layer in a 13 x 9 x 2-inch baking dish. Combine mushrooms, onions and green pepper; spread mushroom mixture over top of fish. Combine remaining ingredients, except orange or lime slices, in a saucepan. Cook over moderate heat, stirring frequently, until mixture thickens and bubbles. Pour sauce over fish and vegetables. Bake at 375 degrees for 20 to 25 minutes or until fish flakes easily when tested with a fork. Garnish with orange and/or lime slices. Yield: 6 servings. (**Photo, page 168**)

133

Parmesan-Stuffed Croaker

4 pan-dressed croakers, ½ to ¾
   pound each, or other pan-dressed
   fish, fresh or frozen
1 cup milk
1 cup crushed rich crackers
½ cup grated Parmesan cheese

½ teaspoon paprika
Parmesan Stuffing
2 tablespoons butter or margarine,
   melted
Lime wedges

Thaw fish if frozen. Preheat oven to 350 degrees. Rinse and thoroughly dry fish. Pour milk into a shallow dish or pie plate. In another pie plate, combine crushed crackers, cheese and paprika. Dip fish in milk and then in cracker mixture. Place on a well-greased 10 x 16-inch baking pan. Stuff fish with approximately ⅓ cup of Parmesan Stuffing. Close opening with small skewers or wooden toothpicks. Drizzle melted butter over fish. Bake in moderate oven, 350 degrees, for 30 minutes or until fish flakes easily when tested with a fork. Remove skewers. Garnish with lime wedges. Yield: 4 servings. **(Photo, page 206)**

Parmesan Stuffing

1 cup crushed rich crackers
½ cup dry curd cottage cheese
½ cup grated Parmesan cheese
1 egg, well beaten
1 tablespoon chopped parsley

¼ teaspoon oregano leaves
¼ teaspoon basil leaves
¼ teaspoon salt
⅛ teaspoon white pepper

Combine all ingredients and mix thoroughly. Yield: 1½ cups.

Triple Treat

1½ pounds croaker (or other fish) fillets, fresh or frozen
6 medium tomatoes
3 tablespoons butter or margarine, softened
1 tablespoon chopped parsley
1 tablespoon lemon juice
½ teaspoon Worcestershire sauce
½ teaspoon grated onion
½ teaspoon salt
⅛ teaspoon liquid hot pepper sauce
3 cups seasoned mashed potatoes
Chopped parsley (garnish)

Thaw fish if frozen. Preheat oven to 350 degrees. Skin fillets. Divide fish into six equal portions. Cut a slice off the top of each tomato and scoop out center. Set aside. Combine butter, parsley, lemon juice, Worcestershire sauce, onion, salt and liquid hot pepper sauce. Roll fillets turban style and secure with a wooden toothpick. Stand turbans on end in a well-greased 8 x 8 x 2-inch baking dish. Bake in moderate oven, 350 degrees, for 10 to 12 minutes. Remove toothpicks and place a fish turban in each tomato cup. Place stuffed tomatoes in the center of a well-greased 12 x 8 x 2-inch baking dish. Spoon approximately 2 teaspoons butter mixture into each tomato cup. Pipe seasoned mashed potatoes into the dish around the base of the tomatoes. Bake in moderate oven, 350 degrees, for 12 to 15 minutes or until fish flakes easily when tested with a fork and tomatoes are done. Garnish with chopped parsley. Yield: 6 servings.

Croaker Country Style

4 pan-dressed croaker, ½ to ¾ pound each, or 1½ pounds croaker fillets, fresh or frozen
1 teaspoon salt
¼ teaspoon pepper
¼ teaspoon paprika
1½ cups chopped tomatoes
⅔ cup chopped parsley
½ cup sliced pimiento-stuffed olives
⅓ cup diced, peeled lemon

Thaw fish if frozen. Preheat oven to 400 degrees. Sprinkle with salt, pepper and paprika. Place fish in a shallow 12 x 8 x 2-inch baking dish. Combine remaining ingredients and spread over top of fish. Cover. Bake at 400 degrees for 10 minutes. Uncover and continue baking 18 to 20 minutes longer or until fish flakes easily when tested with a fork. Yield: 4 servings. (Photo, page 187)

Fish and Chips

2 pounds croaker (or other fish)
   fillets, fresh or frozen
¼ cup lemon juice
2 tablespoons Italian salad dressing
   (oil base)
2 cups crushed potato chips

½ cup grated Parmesan cheese
¼ cup chopped parsley
1½ teaspoons paprika
½ teaspoon thyme
2 tablespoons vegetable oil

Thaw fish if frozen. Preheat oven to 500 degrees. Cut fish into serving-sized portions. Combine lemon juice and salad dressing. Combine potato chips, Parmesan cheese, parsley, paprika and thyme. Dip fish in lemon juice mixture; coat with potato chip mixture. Place fish, skin side down, on a well-greased 15 x 10 x 1-inch baking pan. Drizzle oil over fish. Bake at 500 degrees for 10 to 12 minutes or until fish flakes easily when tested with a fork. Yield: 6 servings.

Escabeche

3 pounds pan-dressed croaker,
   fresh or frozen
¼ cup all-purpose flour
4 teaspoons salt
4 teaspoons pepper
½ cup vegetable oil
1 clove garlic, minced
2 bay leaves

2 cups sliced onions
1½ cups sliced jalapeño peppers
½ cup sliced carrots
1 teaspoon whole allspice
¾ teaspoon liquid hot pepper sauce
½ teaspoon whole peppercorns
2 cups white vinegar

Thaw fish if frozen; rinse and pat dry. Combine flour, salt and pepper; coat both sides of fish with flour mixture. Add garlic and bay leaves to hot oil. Fry fish for 5 minutes. Turn carefully and fry 4 to 6 minutes longer or until fish is brown and flakes easily when tested with a fork. Remove fish from oil and place in a 1½-quart shallow glass baking dish. Add onions, peppers, carrots and seasonings to remaining oil; sauté until onions are tender. Add vinegar; heat to boiling point. Pour hot vegetable mixture over fish. Cover and refrigerate 4 hours or overnight. Yield: 6 servings.

The South's Best

1½ pounds fish fillets,
fresh or frozen

Oil for frying
Batter and Breading

Thaw fish if frozen. Dip fillets into batter, then roll in breading mixture, making sure that a thin coat covers the entire fish. Deep fry in oil at 350 degrees until light brown. Serve immediately. Yields: 4 servings.

BATTER

¾ cup all-purpose flour
3 tablespoons cornstarch
2 tablespoons onion powder

2 tablespoons garlic powder
1 teaspoon salt
1¼ cups cold water

Combine all dry ingredients in a bowl; slowly add water, mixing well to avoid lumps. Batter will be thin.

BREADING

⅔ cup cornmeal
2 scallions, finely chopped
1 tablespoon finely chopped parsley

2 tablespoons coarse-ground black pepper

Mix all ingredients.

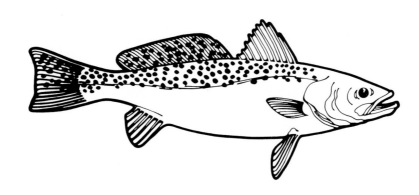

Microwave Fish Cordon Bleu

1½ pounds thin fish fillets, fresh or frozen
4 slices ham
2 slices Swiss cheese
¼ cup chopped tomato
4 teaspoons chopped green onions
½ teaspoon salt
½ teaspoon thyme

¼ teaspoon white pepper
¼ cup butter or margarine, melted
½ cup dry bread crumbs
¼ cup Parmesan cheese
2 tablespoons chopped parsley
Tomato roses (optional garnish)
Parsley (garnish)

Thaw fish if frozen. Cut fillets into 4 serving-sized portions; cover each with plastic wrap. With a meat mallet, gently pound fillet portions until thin and approximately 6½ x 4 inches. Top each fillet portion with 1 slice ham and ½ slice cheese. Add 1 tablespoon chopped tomato and 1 teaspoon green onion to each portion. Sprinkle with salt, thyme and pepper. Roll up each fillet portion jelly-roll style. In a shallow container, combine bread crumbs, Parmesan cheese and parsley. Dip fillet in butter; coat with crumb mixture. Place fillet rolls seam side down in a shallow 1½-quart baking dish. Cook in microwave oven, uncovered, on high for 7 to 9 minutes, rotating dish ½ turn after 5 minutes. Garnish with tomato roses and parsley. Yield: 4 servings.

Sole and turbot have eyes on the left side; flounder on the right.

Grilled Fish with Orange Barbecue Sauce

1½ pounds fish fillets, skinned, fresh
   or frozen
¾ teaspoon salt

¼ teaspoon pepper
Orange Barbecue Sauce
Orange slices (garnish)

Thaw fish if frozen. Cut into serving-sized portions; sprinkle with salt and pepper. Brush both sides of fillets with Orange Barbecue Sauce. Place fillets in well-greased hinged wire grills about 4 inches from moderately hot coals. Cook 5 to 8 minutes and baste with sauce. Turn and cook 5 to 8 minutes longer or until fish flakes easily when tested with a fork. Garnish with orange slices. Yield: 4 servings.

Orange Barbecue Sauce

½ cup orange juice
⅓ cup catsup
3 tablespoons brown sugar
2 tablespoons lemon juice

1 tablespoon instant minced onion
1 tablespoon soy sauce
¼ teaspoon salt

In a ½-quart saucepan, combine all ingredients and heat. Yield: 1 cup.

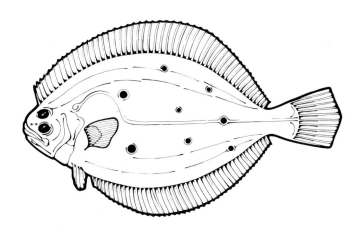

Flounder with Crab Meat Stuffing

6 pan-dressed flounder (approximately ¾ pound each), fresh or frozen
Crab Stuffing
½ cup melted butter or margarine
¼ cup lemon juice
2 tablespoons water
2 teaspoon salt
Paprika

Thaw fish if frozen. Preheat oven to 350 degrees. Clean, wash and dry fish. To make a pocket for the stuffing, lay the fish flat on a cutting board, light side down. With a sharp knife cut down the center of the fish to the backbone from the tail to about one inch from the other end. Turn the knife flat and cut the flesh along both sides of the backbone allowing the knife to run over the rib bones, thereby forming a pocket. Prepare Crab Meat Stuffing. Stuff each fish loosely with approximately ⅔ cup stuffing. Combine butter, lemon juice, water and salt. Place fish in a well-greased baking pan. Pour butter-lemon mixture over fish. Sprinkle with paprika. Bake at 350 degrees for 30 to 40 minutes or until fish flakes easily when tested with a fork. Yield: 6 servings.

Crab Meat Stuffing

1 pound crab meat, fresh, frozen or pasteurized
½ cup chopped onion
⅓ cup celery
⅓ cup chopped green pepper
2 cloves garlic, peeled and finely chopped
⅓ cup melted butter or margarine
2 cups soft bread crumbs
3 eggs, beaten
1 tablespoon chopped parsley
2 teaspoons salt
½ teaspoon pepper

Thaw crab meat if frozen. Remove any remaining shell or cartilage. Sauté onions, celery, green pepper and garlic in butter until tender but not brown. Combine bread crumbs, eggs, parsley, salt, pepper, cooked vegetables and crab meat; mix well. Yield: 4 cups.

Easy Flounder Fillets

2 pounds flounder (or other fish) fillets, skinned, fresh or frozen	2 large tomatoes, cut into small pieces
2 tablespoons grated onion	¼ cup melted butter or margarine
1½ teaspoons salt	1 cup shredded Swiss cheese
⅛ teaspoon pepper	

Thaw fillets if frozen. Place fillets in a single layer on a well-greased 6 x 10-inch bake-and-serve platter. Sprinkle fish with onion, salt and pepper. Cover fillets with tomatoes. Pour butter over tomatoes. Broil about 4 inches from source of heat for 10 to 12 minutes or until fish flakes easily when tested with a fork. Remove from heat; sprinkle with cheese. Broil 2 to 3 minutes longer or until cheese melts. Yield: 6 servings.

Baked Fish Cordon Bleu

2 pounds flounder (or other fish) fillets, fresh or frozen	1 egg, beaten
6 slices (6 ounces) cooked ham	1 cup bread crumbs
6 slices (6 ounces) Swiss cheese	1 tablespoon butter or margarine
1 teaspoon grated orange rind	1 tablespoon all-purpose flour
¼ teaspoon white pepper	1 cup light cream or half-and-half
	¼ cup Parmesan cheese

Thaw fillets if frozen. Place 1 slice each of ham and cheese in the center of each fillet. Cut to fit. Sprinkle with grated orange rind and white pepper. Roll into pinwheels and secure with wooden toothpicks. Gently dip roll in beaten egg; coat with bread crumbs. Place in a greased 12 x 8 x 2-inch baking dish. In saucepan, over medium heat, combine butter and flour. Slowly stir in cream; heat until sauce begins to thicken. Pour sauce over fish roll-ups. Sprinkle with Parmesan cheese. Bake at 350 degrees for 20 to 25 minutes or until fish flakes easily when tested with a fork. Yield: 6 servings. **(Photo, page 146)**

Flounder Kiev

2 pounds flounder (or other thin fish) fillets, skinned, fresh or frozen
½ cup soft butter or margarine
2 tablespoons chopped parsley
1 tablespoon lemon juice
¾ teaspoon Worcestershire sauce
¼ teaspoon liquid hot pepper sauce
1 clove garlic, finely chopped
½ teaspoon salt
⅛ teaspoon pepper
2 tablespoon water
2 eggs, beaten
½ cup all-purpose flour
3 cups soft bread crumbs
Vegetable oil for deep frying

Thaw fish if frozen. Combine butter, parsley, lemon juice, Worcestershire sauce, pepper sauce and garlic. Place butter mixture on waxed paper and form into a roll. Chill until hard. Divide fillets into 12 strips about 6 x 2 inches. Sprinkle fish with salt and pepper. Cut butter roll into 12 pieces. Place a piece at one end of each strip of fish. Roll fish around and secure with a wooden toothpick. Add water to egg and mix thoroughly. Roll fish in flour; dip in egg and roll in crumbs. Chill for 1 hour. Fry in oil, 375 degrees, for 2 to 3 minutes or until golden brown and fish flakes easily when tested with a fork. Drain on absorbent paper. Remove toothpicks. Yield: 6 servings.

Glorified Flounder with Chives

2 pounds flounder (or other fish) fillets, fresh or frozen
2 cups dairy sour cream
¾ cup frozen chopped chives or 6 tablespoons dehydrated chopped chives
1 tablespoon salt
¼ teaspoon pepper
2 cups biscuit mix
Vegetable oil for frying
Paprika (garnish)

Thaw fish if frozen. Cut fish into serving-sized portions. Combine sour cream, chives, salt and pepper, reserving ⅓ cup sour cream mixture for garnish. Dip fish into sour cream mixture, then coat with biscuit mix; repeat. Fry in oil approximately ⅛ inch deep at 360 degrees until both sides are brown and crisp. Garnish servings with equal amounts of sour cream mixture and paprika. Yield: 6 servings.

Southern Stuffed Fish

2 pounds flounder (or other fish) fillets, fresh or frozen
2 tablespoons butter or margarine
1 tablespoon lemon juice

½ teaspoon salt
¼ teaspoon paprika
⅛ teaspoon pepper
Cornbread Stuffing

Thaw fish if frozen. Combine butter, lemon juice, salt, paprika and pepper. Brush both sides of fillets with mixture. Place half of the fillets skin side down on a well-greased shallow baking dish. Place stuffing on fish and cover with remaining fillets, skin side up. Bake in microwave oven on high for 8 minutes. Turn dish and continue baking 4 to 5 minutes or until fish flakes easily when tested with a fork. Let stand 5 minutes. Yield: 6 servings.

Cornbread Stuffing

½ pound mild pork sausage meat
½ cup chopped celery
½ cup chopped onion
½ cup chopped green pepper
2 cups toasted cornbread cubes

⅓ cup tomatoes
¼ cup chicken broth
1 teaspoon browning and gravy sauce
½ teaspoon poultry seasoning
½ teaspoon sage

Crumble sausage in 1-quart round casserole bowl. Add celery, onion and green pepper. Cover and cook in microwave oven on high for 2 minutes. Stir. Cover again and cook 2 more minutes. Add remaining ingredients and mix well. Yield: 3 cups.

At birth, flounder (and other flat fish) have bodies shaped like other fish, with eyes on opposite sides of the head. As they mature, the spine and the head twist and both eyes end up on one side.

Baked Grouper Surprise

2 pounds grouper (or other fish)
   steaks, fresh or frozen
½ cup French dressing
2 tablespoons lemon juice

¼ teaspoon salt
1 can (3½ ounces) French-fried
   onions
¼ cup grated Parmesan cheese

Thaw fish if frozen. Preheat oven to 350 degrees. Place in a shallow dish. Combine dressing, lemon juice and salt. Pour sauce over steaks and let stand for 30 minutes, turning once. Remove from sauce and place in a well-greased 12 x 8 x 2-inch baking dish. Crush onions. Add cheese and mix thoroughly. Sprinkle onion mixture over fish. Bake in a moderate oven, 350 degrees, for 25 to 30 minutes or until fish flakes easily when tested with a fork. Yield: 6 servings.

Grouper Parmesan

2 pounds grouper (or other fish)
   fillets, skinned, fresh or frozen
1 cup dairy sour cream
¼ cup grated Parmesan cheese
1 tablespoon lemon juice

1 tablespoon grated onion
½ teaspoon salt
⅛ teaspoon liquid hot pepper sauce
Paprika
Chopped parsley (garnish)

Thaw fish if frozen. Preheat oven to 350 degrees. Cut fish into serving-sized portions. Place in single layer in a well-greased 12 x 8 x 2-inch baking dish. Combine remaining ingredients except paprika and parsley. Spread sour cream mixture over fish. Sprinkle with paprika. Bake at 350 degrees for 25 to 30 minutes or until fish flakes easily when tested with a fork. Garnish with parsley. Yield: 6 servings.

> *Groupers all start life as females and later become males.*

Baked Fish Cordon Bleu, page 141

Broiled Rock Shrimp, page 181

Ale-Poached Fish with Pimiento Sauce, page 117 ▶

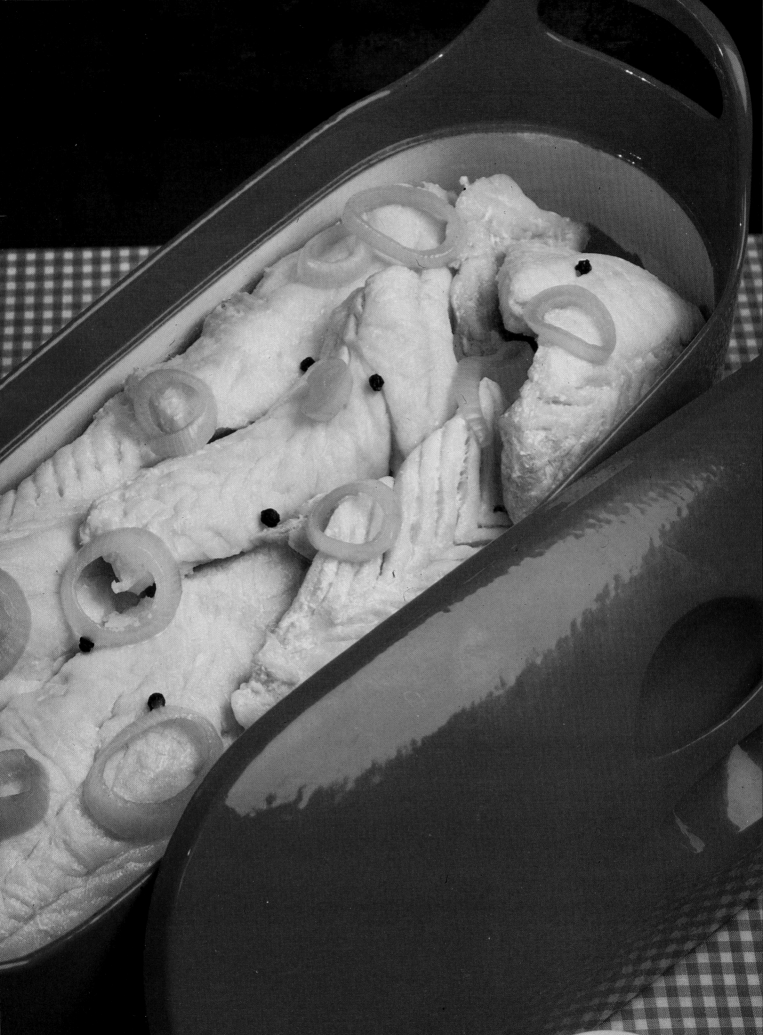

Crawfish Linguine, page 132

Fish Fingers with Creamy Vegetable Sauce, page 218

Stir-Fry Fish and Vegetables

1½ pounds grouper (or other fish) fillets, fresh or frozen
¼ cup soy sauce
2 tablespoons cider vinegar
2½ teaspoons cornstarch
1 teaspoon sugar
2 chicken bouillon cubes
⅓ cup boiling water
¼ cup vegetable oil, divided

2 cloves garlic, halved
½ pound fresh snow peas
1 cup sliced fresh mushrooms
1 cup broccoli flowerets
1 large onion, sliced and separated into rings
1 medium green pepper, seeded and cut into strips
3 cups cooked rice

Thaw fish if frozen. Cut into 1½-inch cubes. In a small bowl combine soy sauce, vinegar, cornstarch and sugar; stir until cornstarch dissolves. Dissolve bouillon cubes in boiling water, and add to cornstarch mixture. Pour 2 tablespoons oil around top of preheated wok, coating sides. Allow to heat at medium high (325 degrees) for 1 minute. Add garlic; stir fry 1 minute; discard garlic. Add fish to wok; stir fry 2 minutes. Remove fish from wok. Pour remaining 2 tablespoons oil around top of wok, coating sides; allow to heat at medium high 1 minute. Add snow peas, mushrooms, broccoli, onion and green pepper. Stir fry 2 minutes. Stir cornstarch mixture and pour over vegetables. Cook, stirring constantly, until slightly thickened. Return fish to wok; stir well. Serve over rice. Yield: 4 to 6 servings.

Broiled Grouper with Sauce Dijon

2 pounds grouper (or other fish) fillets, fresh or frozen
¼ cup vegetable oil
¼ cup tarragon vinegar
1 teaspoon salt
¼ teaspoon paprika

1 clove garlic, sliced
⅛ teaspoon cayenne
Paprika (garnish)
Chopped parsley (garnish)
Sauce Dijon

Thaw fish if frozen. Place in shallow dish. Combine oil, vinegar, salt, paprika, garlic and pepper in a shaker or jar with a tight-fitting lid; shake well. Pour marinade over fillets. Cover and marinate in refrigerator for at least 2 hours, turning several times. Reserving marinade, remove fillets and place on a well-greased broiler pan. Broil about 4 inches from source of heat for 6 to 8 minutes, basting with marinade. Turn carefully; baste. Broil an additional 6 to 8 minutes or until fish flakes easily when tested with a fork, basting with marinade several times. Garnish with paprika and chopped parsley. Serve with Sauce Dijon. Yield: 6 servings.

Sauce Dijon

2 egg yolks, slightly beaten
¼ cup water
2 tablespoons tarragon vinegar
1 tablespoon Dijon or other prepared mustard

1 tablespoon sugar
¼ teaspoon salt
½ cup sour cream

In saucepan, combine egg yolks, water, vinegar, mustard, sugar and salt; mix well. Cook over low heat until thick, stirring constantly. Stir in sour cream. Serve warm. Yield: 1 cup.

Super Grouper

2 pounds grouper (or other fish)
fillets, fresh or frozen
¼ cup chopped onion
1 package (⅝ to ⅞ ounce) brown
gravy mix
1 tablespoon olive oil

1 teaspoon lemon juice
1 teaspoon salt
⅛ teaspoon pepper
¼ cup sliced almonds (garnish)
¼ cup chopped green pepper
(garnish)

Thaw fish if frozen. Preheat oven to 350 degrees. Cut fish into serving-sized portions. Sprinkle onion in a well-greased 13 x 9 x 2-inch baking dish. Place fillets in a single layer on onion. Prepare brown gravy mix according to package directions. To gravy mix, add oil, lemon juice, salt and pepper. Pour gravy mixture over fish. Baked at 350 degrees for 20 to 25 minutes or until fish flakes easily when tested with a fork. Garnish with almonds and green pepper. Yield: 6 servings.

Grouper Italiano

2 pounds grouper (or other fish)
fillets, skinned, fresh or frozen
½ cup butter or margarine, melted

1 clove garlic, peeled and crushed
2 cups Italian-style bread crumbs

Thaw fish if frozen. Preheat oven to 450 degrees. Cut into serving-sized portions. If very thick fillets, carefully slice in half horizontally. Combine melted butter and garlic. Place bread crumbs in shallow dish. Dip fish into garlic butter, then coat with bread crumbs. Place fish on a well-greased baking pan. Drizzle any remaining butter over fish. Bake at 450 degrees for 10 minutes per inch of thickness or until fish flakes easily when tested with a fork. Yield: 4 to 6 servings.

Grouper and Noodles Béarnaise

2 pounds grouper (or other fish) fillets, skinned, fresh or frozen
2 cups finely crushed butter-flavored crackers
½ teaspoon lemon-pepper seasoning

3 egg whites, beaten
Vegetable oil
Béarnaise Sauce
Hot cooked noodles

Thaw fish if frozen. Dry with paper towels. Cut into 1 x 4-inch strips. Combine cracker crumbs and seasoning; mix well. Dip each fish strip into beaten egg whites and coat with cracker crumbs. Fry fish in hot oil until brown or until fish flakes easily when tested with a fork. Drain on absorbent paper. Prepare Béarnaise Sauce. Toss hot noodles with half of the sauce. Arrange grouper over noodles. Top with remaining Béarnaise Sauce. Yield: 4 servings.

Béarnaise Sauce

½ cup butter
2½ tablespoons Chablis or other dry white wine
2½ tablespoons red wine vinegar
1 tablespoon minced green onions or shallots
½ teaspoon tarragon leaves

½ teaspoon chervil (optional)
¼ teaspoon white pepper
3 egg yolks
2 tablespoons water
¼ cup finely chopped parsley
Salt and pepper to taste

Melt butter in small saucepan and keep warm. In the top of a double-boiler combine wine, vinegar, onions, tarragon, chervil and pepper. Cook over hot water until almost all the liquid has evaporated. Cool to lukewarm. In small mixing bowl, beat the egg yolks and water; blend in the wine mixture. Return to top of double-boiler. Place over hot water and cook, beating constantly with a whisk, until thick. Remove from heat. Add a tablespoon of butter at a time, whisking vigorously until all butter is absorbed. (The sauce will separate if the butter is added too fast or if it is heated too quickly.) Add the parsley and stir in until well blended. Stir in the lemon juice, salt and pepper. Serve warm. Yield: 1 cup.

Florida Dilly Lobster

¾ pound cooked spiny lobster meat, fresh or frozen
⅓ cup butter or margarine, melted
⅓ cup all-purpose flour
1 teaspoon salt
⅛ teaspoon white pepper
2½ cups milk
1 tablespoon dry white wine
2 teaspoons lemon juice
¾ teaspoon dill weed
1 can (4½ ounces) sliced mushrooms, drained
1 package (10 ounces) frozen mixed vegetables
6 buttered, toasted English muffins
Parsley sprigs (garnish)

Thaw lobster meat if frozen. Cut into slices ¼ inch thick. Cook frozen vegetables according to package directions; drain. Melt butter in a medium-sized saucepan; blend in flour, salt and pepper. Gradually add milk; cook until thickened, stirring constantly. Stir in wine, lemon juice and dill weed. Add mushrooms, vegetables and lobster; heat. Serve on English muffins. Garnish each serving with a parsley sprig. Yield: 6 servings.

Lobster Thermidor

1 pound cooked lobster meat, fresh or frozen
2 tablespoons butter or margarine
2 tablespoons all-purpose flour
1½ teaspoons dry mustard
½ teaspoon salt
⅛ teaspoon cayenne
1½ cups half-and-half
1 can (4 ounces) mushroom stems and pieces, drained
2 tablespoons grated Parmesan cheese
Paprika

Thaw lobster if frozen. Preheat oven to 400 degrees. Cut lobster meat into ½-inch pieces. Melt butter in a 10-inch skillet; blend in flour and seasonings. Add half-and-half gradually and cook, stirring constantly, until thick and smooth. Add mushrooms and lobster meat. Place in cleaned and rinsed lobster shells or into 6 well-greased 6-ounce baking shells. Sprinkle with cheese and paprika. Bake at 400 degrees for 10 minutes or until top is lightly browned. Yield: 6 servings.

Lettuce-Baked Lobster Tails

6 green lobster tails (½ pound each), fresh or frozen
1 cup melted butter or margarine, divided in half
½ teaspoon garlic powder

½ teaspoon salt
Paprika
10 to 12 lettuce leaves, rinsed and drained

Thaw lobster if frozen. Preheat oven to 400 degrees. Pan-cut lobster tails by cutting off the under shell, leaving the tail fan and upper shell in place. Place lobster, shell side down, on baking sheet; add garlic powder and salt to ½ cup butter and brush onto lobster meat; sprinkle with paprika. Cover tails completely with damp lettuce leaves and bake at 400 degrees for 15 to 20 minutes or until lobster meat is opaque and tender. Discard lettuce leaves. Serve with remaining melted butter. Yield: 6 servings. **(Photo, page 166)**

Baked Stuffed Spiny Lobster

2 live spiny lobsters or 2 frozen whole green lobsters (1 pound each)
1¼ cups soft bread crumbs
½ cup grated Cheddar cheese
¼ cup chopped parsley

2 tablespoons melted butter or margarine
2 tablespoons chopped green onions
¼ cup toasted sliced almonds
Paprika

Thaw lobster if frozen. Preheat oven to 400 degrees. Cut lobster in half lengthwise. (It is difficult to split a live lobster. Place it in the freezer for 20 to 30 minutes to make it easier to handle and clean without harming the quality of the meat.) Remove stomach and intestinal vein. Rinse and clean body cavity thoroughly. Combine bread crumbs, cheese, parsley, butter and onions in a small mixing bowl; mix well. Place stuffing in body cavity and spread over surface of the tail meat. Sprinkle with almonds and paprika. Place on 15 x 10 x 1-inch baking pan. Bake in hot oven, 400 degrees, for 15 to 20 minutes or until lightly browned. Yield: 2 servings. **(Photo, page 186)**

Grilled Spiny Lobster Tails

6 spiny lobster tails (8 ounces each), fresh or frozen
¼ cup butter or margarine, melted

2 tablespoons lemon juice
½ teaspoon salt
Melted butter or margarine

Thaw frozen lobster tails. Cut in half lengthwise. Remove swimmerets and sharp edges. Cut 6 pieces of heavy-duty aluminum foil, 12 x 12-inches each. Place each lobster tail on foil. Combine butter, lemon juice and salt. Baste lobster meat with sauce. Bring the foil up over the lobster and close all edges with tight double folds. Make 6 packages. Place packages on grill, shell side down, about 5 inches from hot coals; cook for 20 minutes. Remove lobster tails from the foil. Place them on grill, flesh side down, and cook for 2 to 3 minutes longer or until lightly browned. Serve with melted butter. Yield: 6 servings.

Onion-Baked Mackerel

2 pounds Spanish mackerel (or other fish) fillets, fresh or frozen
1 teaspoon salt
1 cup sour cream
1 cup mayonnaise

1 package (4/10 ounce) original ranch salad dressing mix
2 cans (3 ounces each) French-fried onions, crushed

Thaw fish if frozen. Preheat oven to 350 degrees. Skin fillets. Cut fillets into serving-sized portions. Sprinkle with salt. Combine sour cream, mayonnaise and salad dressing mix. Dip fillets into 1 cup salad dressing and roll in onions. Place fish on a well-greased 15 x 10 x ½-inch baking pan. Bake in moderate oven, 350 degrees, for 20 to 25 minutes or until fish flakes easily when tested with a fork. Serve with remaining dressing if desired. Yield: 6 servings. **(Photo, page 166)**

Tomally, the lobster's liver, turns green when cooked. Many consider it a delicacy.

If the tail of a cooked lobster is curled, it was alive when cooked.

King Mackerel Rice Casserole

2 pounds king mackerel steaks, fresh or frozen
⅓ cup lemon juice
1 can (1 pound) whole tomatoes, undrained
2 cups sliced onion rings

¼ cup olive liquid
1 can (10½ ounces) beef consommé
1 cup uncooked rice
½ cup sliced pimiento-stuffed olives
1 teaspoon seasoned salt

Thaw fish if frozen. Preheat oven to 350 degrees. Marinate steaks in lemon juice for 30 minutes, turning once. Combine tomatoes, onion, soup, rice, olives and olive liquid. Pour into a well-greased 12 x 8 x 2-inch baking dish. Cover and bake in moderate oven, 350 degrees, for 30 minutes. Remove steaks from lemon juice. Sprinkle steaks with seasoned salt and arrange over rice. Cover and return to oven. Continue cooking 20 to 25 minutes or until fish flakes easily when tested with a fork. Yield: 6 servings.
(Photo, page 126)

Tangy Seafood

2 pounds skinless Spanish mackerel (or other fish) fillets, fresh or frozen
⅔ cup tomato juice
½ cup French dressing

3 tablespoons vinegar
2 tablespoons vegetable oil
2 cloves garlic, minced
½ teaspoon pepper

Thaw fish if frozen. Cut into serving-sized portions. Place fish in a single layer in a shallow baking dish. Combine remaining ingredients and mix thoroughly. Pour sauce over fish and let stand for 1 hour in refrigerator, turning once. Remove fish, reserving sauce for basting. Place fish on a well-greased broiler pan. Broil about 4 inches from source of heat for 4 to 5 minutes. Turn carefully and brush with sauce. Broil 4 to 5 minutes longer or until fish flakes easily when tested with a fork. Yield: 6 servings.

Golden Spanish Mackerel Casserole

2 cups cooked, flaked Spanish mackerel or other cooked, flaked fish, fresh or frozen
1 box (6 ounces) hash brown potatoes with onion
1 package (10 ounces) frozen peas, slightly separated
2 cups sliced celery
1½ cups water
2 tablespoons butter or margarine
¾ teaspoon salt
⅛ teaspoon pepper
1 can (10¾ ounces) cream of shrimp soup
⅔ cup milk
1 cup grated sharp Cheddar cheese

Thaw fish if frozen. Preheat oven to 350 degrees. In saucepan, combine hash brown potatoes, peas, celery, water, butter, salt and pepper. Bring to a boil; reduce heat and simmer uncovered about 5 minutes or until liquid is absorbed. Combine soup and milk. Stir soup mixture, fish and ½ cup cheese carefully into potato mixture. Pour into a well-greased 1½-quart casserole. Bake, uncovered, at 350 degrees for 25 to 30 minutes or until thoroughly heated. Top casserole with remaining ½ cup cheese; continue cooking, uncovered, 2 to 3 minutes or until cheese melts. Yield: 6 servings.

Fish in Foil

2 pounds Spanish mackerel (or other fish) fillets, fresh or frozen
2 green peppers, seeded and sliced
2 onions, sliced
¼ cup butter or margarine, melted
2 tablespoons lemon juice
2 teaspoons salt
1 teaspoon paprika
⅛ teaspoon pepper

Thaw fish if frozen. Cut into serving-sized portions. Cut six pieces of heavy-duty aluminum foil, 12 x 12 inches each. Grease lightly. Place a portion of fillets, skin side down, on foil. Top with green pepper and onion. Combine remaining ingredients. Pour sauce over fillets. Bring the foil up and close all edges with tight double folds. Make six packages. Place packages on a grill about five inches from moderately hot coals. Cook for 45 to 60 minutes or until fish flakes easily when tested with a fork. Yield: 6 servings.

Marinated Spanish Mackerel Fillets

2 pounds Spanish mackerel (or other fish) fillets, fresh or frozen
½ cup vinegar
¼ cup vegetable oil
¼ cup lemon juice
2 tablespoons grated lemon rind
1 tablespoon liquid smoke

1 tablespoon brown sugar
2 teaspoons salt
½ teaspoon Worcestershire sauce
2 bay leaves
⅛ teaspoon white pepper
⅛ teaspoon liquid hot pepper sauce

Thaw fish if frozen. In a saucepan, combine all ingredients, except fish. Heat until mixture comes to the boiling point; cool. Cut fillets into serving-sized portions; place in a single layer in a shallow baking dish. Pour sauce over fillets; marinate in refrigerator for 30 minutes, turning once. Remove fillets, reserving marinade for basting. Place fish in well-greased hinged wire grills; baste fillets with reserved marinade. Cook about 4 inches from moderately hot coals for 8 minutes. Turn fillets; baste with remaining marinade. Cook 7 to 10 minutes longer or until fish flakes easily when tested with a fork. Yield: 6 servings.

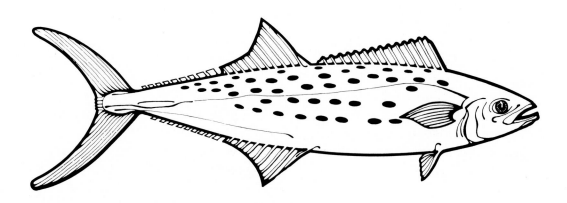

Experts estimate that over twenty thousand species of fish exist.

Mullet Olé

2 pounds mullet (or other fish) fillets, skinned, fresh or frozen
2 teaspoons garlic salt
¾ cup chili sauce
½ cup sliced green onions
½ cup sliced green pepper
½ cup sliced celery
1 can (3 ounces) sliced mushrooms, drained
½ teaspoon dried crushed thyme

Thaw fish if frozen. Preheat oven to 350 degrees. Cut into serving-sized portions. Sprinkle fillets with garlic salt. Place fillets in a single layer in a well-greased 12 x 8 x 2-inch baking dish. Combine remaining ingredients and spread over fillets. Bake at 350 degrees for 20 to 25 minutes or until fish flakes easily when tested with a fork. Yield: 6 servings.

Mullet Casserole Panacea

2 cups cooked, flaked mullet or other flaked fish, fresh or frozen
2 tablespoons butter or margarine
½ cup chopped green pepper
2 tablespoons all-purpose flour
½ teaspoon salt
¼ teaspoon oregano
⅛ teaspoon pepper
1 cup half-and-half
⅔ cup grated Cheddar cheese (divided)
½ cup bread crumbs

Thaw fish if frozen. Preheat oven to 450 degrees. In a large saucepan melt butter. Cook green pepper until tender. Reduce heat, stir in flour, salt, oregano and pepper. Gradually add half-and-half, cook until thickened; add ⅓ cup cheese stirring constantly until cheese melts. Fold in fish, mixing well. Spoon into four individual ramekins. Combine remaining ⅓ cup cheese and bread crumbs; sprinkle over top of casseroles. Bake at 450 degrees for 5 minutes or until bubbly. Yield: 4 servings.

Fisherman's Tartar-Baked Mullet

3 pounds pan-dressed mullet or other pan-dressed fish, fresh or frozen
1½ teaspoons salt
¼ teaspoon pepper

1¾ cups Fisherman's Tartar Sauce
1½ cups dry bread crumbs
¼ cup butter or margarine, melted
Parsley (garnish)

Thaw fish if frozen. Preheat oven to 450 degrees. Sprinkle fish with salt and pepper. Prepare Fisherman's Tartar Sauce. Coat all surfaces of fish with ¾ cup tartar sauce. Coat fish with bread crumbs. Place fish on a well-greased 16 x 10 x 1-inch baking tray. Drizzle butter over fish. Bake at 450 degrees for 15 to 20 minutes or until fish flakes easily when tested with a fork. Serve with remaining 1 cup Fisherman's Tartar Sauce. Garnish with parsley. Yield: 6 servings.

Fisherman's Tartar Sauce

1 cup mayonnaise or salad dressing
¼ cup dairy sour cream
2 tablespoons finely chopped kosher dill pickle
2 tablespoons finely chopped onion

2 tablespoons finely chopped pimiento-stuffed olives
1 teaspoon lemon juice
⅛ teaspoon pepper

Combine all ingredients; chill. Yield: 1¾ cups.

Mullet-Squash Casserole

2 cups cooked, flaked mullet or
  other flaked fish, fresh or frozen
1 medium acorn squash, peeled, cut
  into ½-inch cubes
½ cup chopped onion
1 tablespoon butter or margarine
1 cup dairy sour cream
½ cup shredded sharp Cheddar
  cheese

½ cup shredded Swiss cheese
½ teaspoon garlic salt
⅛ teaspoon paprika
1 egg yolk, beaten
1 tablespoon chopped chives
1 cup soft bread crumbs
1 tablespoon butter or margarine,
  melted

Thaw fish if frozen. Preheat oven to 350 degrees. Cook squash in small amount of boiling, salted water 5 minutes or until tender; drain well. Place in a lightly greased 2-quart shallow baking dish; set aside. In large saucepan, sauté onions in butter until tender. Reduce heat to low. Add sour cream, cheeses, garlic salt and paprika stirring constantly until cheese melts. Remove from heat; stir about ¼ of hot mixture into egg yolk; add to remaining hot mixture, stirring constantly. Stir in mullet and chives. Pour over squash. Combine bread crumbs and 1 tablespoon melted margarine; mix well and sprinkle over top of casserole. Bake at 350 degrees for 20 minutes. Yield: 4 to 6 servings.

Simply Elegant Mullet

2 pounds mullet fillets, fresh or
  frozen
1 can crushed pineapple (8 ounces)
  in natural juice
⅓ cup low-calorie Russian dressing

¾ teaspoon salt
⅛ teaspoon pepper
⅛ teaspoon cloves
½ cup grated mild Cheddar cheese
  Paprika

Thaw fish if frozen. Place fish in single layer in a shallow baking dish. Drain pineapple, reserving juice. Combine dressing, reserved pineapple juice and seasonings. Pour sauce over fish and let stand for 30 minutes, turning once. Remove fish, reserving sauce for basting. Place fish skin side up on a well-greased broiler pan. Broil about 4 inches from source of heat for 3 to 4 minutes. Turn carefully and brush with remaining sauce. Broil 3 to 4 minutes longer or until fish flakes easily when tested with a fork. Combine pineapple and cheese. Spread pineapple mixture over fish and sprinkle with paprika. Broil 2 to 3 minutes longer or until lightly browned. Yield: 6 servings. **(Photo, page 145)**

Stir-Fry Fish Hash

2 pounds mullet (or other fish) fillets, fresh or frozen
2 tablespoons soy sauce
2 tablespoons dry sherry
¼ teaspoon sugar
¼ teaspoon cayenne
⅛ teaspoon ground ginger
½ cup cooking oil

1 cup cashews
4 cups sliced, unpeeled zucchini
4 cups sliced fresh mushrooms
4 cups diagonally sliced Chinese cabbage
2 cups green onions, cut into 3-inch pieces
½ teaspoon salt

Thaw fish if frozen. Skin fillets. Cut fillets into 2-inch cubes. Combine soy sauce, sherry, sugar, cayenne and ground ginger in 1½-quart bowl. Mix well; add fish and stir. Marinate fish in refrigerator for 15 minutes. In a 12-inch skillet or wok, heat oil over medium-high heat. Add cashews, and cook about 3 minutes or until lightly browned, stirring constantly. Remove cashews with slotted spoon onto absorbent paper. Add zucchini, mushrooms, cabbage, green onions and salt to remaining oil and cook until tender-crisp, about 5 minutes. Remove vegetables from pan with slotted spoon; place in 1½-quart bowl; set aside. Add fish to pan, reduce heat and cover. Cook over low heat for 8 to 10 minutes or until fish flakes easily when tested with a fork. Add cashews and cooked vegetables to fish in skillet or wok. Stir carefully. Heat 1 to 2 minutes before serving. Serve immediately. Yield: 6 servings. **(Photo, page 125)**

Heavenly Broiled Mullet

2 pounds skinned mullet (or other fish) fillets, fresh or frozen
2 tablespoons lemon juice
½ cup grated Parmesan cheese
¼ cup butter or margarine, softened

3 tablespoons mayonnaise or salad dressing
3 tablespoons chopped green onions
¼ teaspoon salt
⅛ teaspoon liquid hot pepper sauce

Thaw fish if frozen. Place fillets in a single layer on a well-greased 15 x 10-inch bake-and-serve platter. Brush fillets with lemon juice and let stand for 10 minutes. Combine remaining ingredients. Broil fillets about 4 inches from source of heat for 6 to 8 minutes or until fish flakes easily when tested with a fork. Remove from heat and spread with cheese mixture. Broil 2 to 3 minutes longer or until lightly browned. Yield: 6 servings. **(Photo, page 208)**

Plain Delicious Smoked Fish

4 pounds mullet butterfly fillets or
other butterfly fish fillets, fresh or
frozen
1 gallon water
1 cup salt

1 box (3 ounces) crab boil (in bag)
1 pound hickory chips
2 quarts water
Vegetable oil (for basting)

To prepare hickory chips: Cover hickory chips with water and soak in a cool place for
several hours or overnight.

To prepare for smoking: To smoke fish use a hooded or covered charcoal, electric or
gas grill. The heat must be kept low. If using charcoal, fewer briquets are necessary
than for regular grilling. Cover charcoal or ceramic briquets with approximately ⅓ of
the wet chips to lower the temperature and create smoke, which flavors the fish.
Remaining chips are added as needed throughout the cooking process.

Thaw fish if frozen. Clean and rinse in cold water. In a 2-gallon bowl, combine salt
and 1 gallon water; add bag of crab boil. Add fish and marinate in refrigerator for 30
minutes, stirring occasionally. Remove fish from brine; rinse thoroughly and pat dry.
Place the fish fillets, skin side down, on a well-greased grill approximately 4 to 6
inches from smoking chips. Close hood on grill and open vent slightly to keep smoke
and air circulating. Smoke fish approximately 1 hour at 150 to 175 degrees or for 30 to
45 minutes at 200 degrees. Baste fish with oil near the end of cooking time. The fish is
done when the cut surface is golden brown and the flesh flakes easily when tested with
a fork. Yield: 6 servings.

*Many consider the gizzard of mullet a
delicacy.*

Crunchy Baked Fish Fillets

2 pounds mullet (or other fish) fillets, fresh or frozen
⅓ cup butter or margarine, melted
1 clove garlic, minced
½ teaspoon *fines herbes* blend

1½ cups potato chip crumbs
3 tablespoons grated Parmesan cheese
Paprika

Thaw fish if frozen. Combine margarine, garlic and *fines herbes* blend. Arrange fillets in shallow baking dish. Brush fillets with seasoned butter. Sprinkle ½ of the crumbs over fillets. Turn fillets and repeat process using remaining seasoned butter and crumbs. Sprinkle with Parmesan cheese and paprika. Bake in microwave oven on high for 8 to 10 minutes or until fish flakes easily when tested with a fork. Yield: 6 servings.

Smoked Fish Romanoff

1 pound smoked mullet or other smoked fish
1 package (8 ounces) egg noodles
2 cups large curd, cream-style cottage cheese
2 cloves garlic, minced
2 teaspoons Worcestershire sauce

1¼ cups dairy sour cream
⅔ cup sliced green onions and tops
½ teaspoon liquid hot pepper sauce
¼ teaspoon pepper
½ cup grated Parmesan cheese

Remove skin and bones from fish. Flake the fish. Cook noodles according to package directions; drain well. Combine fish, cooked noodles, cottage cheese, garlic, Worcestershire sauce, sour cream, onions, liquid hot pepper sauce and pepper. Pour into a well-greased 2-quart shallow casserole. Sprinkle Parmesan cheese over top. Bake in a moderate oven, 350 degrees, for 20-25 minutes or until heated throughout. Yield: 6 servings.

Tipsy Shark Steaks, page 195

Onion-Baked Mackerel, page 155

Lettuce-Baked Lobster, page 154

Shrimp Jambalaya, page 203

Floridian Croaker, page 133

Devilishly Stuffed Soft-Shell Crab, page 131

Gratin of Oysters and Mushrooms

1 pint oysters, fresh or frozen
¼ cup butter or margarine
½ cup green pepper, chopped
½ cup green onions, chopped
1 can (3 ounces) sliced mushrooms, drained
4 slices bacon, chopped, cooked and drained

½ teaspoon salt
½ teaspoon pepper
 Gratin Sauce
4 slices buttered toast, cut in fourths
¼ cup toasted bread crumbs

Thaw oysters if frozen. Preheat oven to 350 degrees. Remove any remaining shell particles; drain. Melt butter in saucepan and sauté green pepper and onions until tender. Add mushrooms, bacon, seasonings and oysters. Cook slowly for about 4 minutes. Combine oyster mixture with Gratin Sauce. Line a 9 x 9 x 1½-inch baking dish with buttered toast. Pour oyster mixture into the baking dish and sprinkle with crumbs. Bake at 350 degrees for about 8 minutes or until hot and bubbling. Serve at once. Yield: 6 servings.

Gratin Sauce

2 tablespoons butter or margarine
3 tablespoons all-purpose flour

1 cup milk
½ cup shredded Cheddar cheese

Melt 2 tablespoons butter in small saucepan over medium heat. Blend in flour to make smooth paste. Add milk gradually; stir constantly until mixture thickens. Add cheese. Cook on low heat, stirring constantly until cheese melts.

Oyster-Macaroni Cheese Bake

1 pint oysters, fresh or frozen
4 slices bacon
½ cup chopped green pepper
⅓ cup sliced green onions
1 can (10¾ ounces) condensed Cheddar cheese soup
1½ teaspoons salt

1 teaspoon prepared mustard
3 cups uncooked seashell macaroni
2 tablespoons diced pimiento
1 cup grated Cheddar cheese, divided

Thaw oysters if frozen. Preheat oven to 350 degrees. Drain oysters. Remove any remaining shell particles. In a 10-inch skillet, fry bacon until crisp. Reserving bacon drippings, remove bacon to absorbent paper; cool. Crumble bacon; set aside. Cook macaroni according to package directions; drain. Add green pepper and onions to reserved bacon drippings; cook until vegetables are tender but not brown. Stir in soup, salt and mustard; mix well. Remove from heat. Add cooked macaroni, crumbled bacon, oysters and pimiento; mix well. Spoon ½ of the mixture into a shallow 2-quart baking dish. Sprinkle with ½ of the cheese. Repeat, using remaining ingredients. Cover tightly. Bake at 350 degrees for 15 minutes. Uncover; continue baking until mixture is hot and bubbly, 15 to 20 minutes. Yield: 4 servings.

Oysters Casino

1 pint oysters, fresh or frozen
3 slices bacon, chopped
4 tablespoons chopped onion
2 tablespoons chopped green pepper
2 tablespoons chopped celery

1 teaspoon lemon juice
½ teaspoon salt
½ teaspoon Worcestershire sauce
⅛ teaspoon pepper
2 drops liquid hot pepper sauce

Thaw oysters if frozen. Drain. Remove any remaining pieces of shell particles. Place oysters in a well-greased 9 x 9 x 2-inch baking dish. Fry bacon until crisp. Add onion, green pepper and celery. Cook until vegetables are tender. Add lemon juice, salt, Worcestershire sauce, pepper and liquid hot pepper sauce; mix well. Spread bacon mixture over oysters. Bake in moderate oven, 350 degrees, for approximately 10 minutes or until oysters are done and edges curl. Yield: 6 servings. (**Photo, page 185**)

Oyster Fry

1 pint oysters, fresh or frozen
2 eggs, beaten
2 tablespoons milk
¼ teaspoon salt
⅓ cup all-purpose flour

2 cups soft bread crumbs
Vegetable oil for frying
Lime wedges (garnish)
Tartar sauce

Thaw oysters if frozen. Drain oysters. Remove any remaining shell particles. Beat together the eggs, milk and salt. Dip oysters into egg mixture, then lightly into flour. Dip into egg mixture once again, then coat with bread crumbs. Let stand 5 to 10 minutes before frying. To deep fry: Place oysters in a single layer in a fry basket. Deep-fry in hot vegetable oil, 360 degrees, for 2 to 3 minutes or until oysters are browned. Drain on absorbent paper. To pan fry: In a 12-inch skillet, place oysters in a single layer in hot oil. Fry at moderate heat for 2 to 3 minutes or until brown. Turn carefully; fry 2 to 3 minutes longer or until oysters are browned. Drain on absorbent paper. Serve with lime wedges and tartar sauce. Yield: 3 to 4 servings.

Tartar Sauce

1 cup mayonnaise or salad dressing
2 tablespoons chopped pickle
2 tablespoons chopped onion

2 tablespoons chopped parsley
2 tablespoons chopped olives

Combine all ingredients; chill. Yield: 1½ cups.

Try limes with your seafood instead of lemons: delicious and seedless.

Oyster-Mushroom Stuffing

1 pint oysters, fresh or frozen
1 pound mushrooms, coarsely chopped
1½ cups chopped celery with leaves
1 cup chopped onions
½ cup butter or margarine
2 cups soft bread cubes
¼ cup chopped parsley
2 tablespoons diced pimiento
2 teaspoons salt
1½ teaspoons poultry seasoning
¼ teaspoon pepper
2 eggs, beaten

Thaw oysters if frozen. Preheat oven to 350 degrees. Remove any remaining shell particles. Drain oysters, reserving liquor. In a 10-inch skillet, sauté mushrooms, celery and onions in butter until tender but not brown. Combine bread cubes, parsley, pimiento and seasonings. Add oysters, oyster liquor, vegetables and eggs to bread cube mixture; mix thoroughly. Makes approximately 9 cups stuffing. To serve as a side dish, place stuffing mixture in a well-greased 2-quart baking dish. Bake at 350 degrees for 25 to 30 minutes or until lightly brown. Yield: 6 servings.

Scalloped Oysters

1 pint oysters, fresh or frozen
¼ cup sliced celery
2 tablespoons minced onion
½ cup butter or margarine
2 cups finely crushed butter-flavored crackers
¾ cup milk
1 tablespoon minced parsley
1 teaspoon garlic juice
1 teaspoon lemon juice
1 teaspoon salt
⅛ teaspoon pepper
½ cup grated Cheddar cheese

Thaw oysters if frozen. Preheat oven to 350 degrees. Remove any remaining shell particles. Simmer oysters in their liquor until edges begin to curl. Remove from heat; drain. In a 10-inch skillet, sauté celery and onion in butter until tender but not brown. Add remaining ingredients, reserving ½ cup cracker crumbs and cheese. Pour mixture into a well-greased 1-quart shallow baking dish or individual ramekins. Combine remaining cracker crumbs and cheese. Sprinkle crumb mixture over casserole. Bake at 350 degrees for 15 to 20 minutes or until light golden brown. Yield: 3 to 4 servings.

Oysters with Salsa Verde

36 oysters, raw on the half-shell
4 slices bacon
¼ cup butter or margarine, melted
⅓ cup parsley, chopped

1 tablespoon lemon juice
⅓ cup bread crumbs
Salsa Verde
Rock salt

Preheat oven to 450 degrees. Wash unshucked oysters under cold running water to remove any foreign particles. Shuck oysters and wipe shells dry. Place oysters in deep half of shells. Arrange shells in a shallow pan that has been lined with rock salt. Cook bacon until crisp; remove bacon to absorbent paper, reserving bacon drippings. Crumble bacon when cooled. Add butter, crumbled bacon, parsley and lemon juice to reserved bacon drippings; stir well. Top each oyster with approximately 1 teaspoon of mixture and sprinkle with bread crumbs. Bake at 450 degrees for 10 to 12 minutes or until edges of oysters begin to curl. Serve with Salsa Verde. Yield: 6 servings.

Salsa Verde

1 cup chopped parsley
¼ cup chopped green onions
2 tablespoons capers
1 clove garlic, peeled and finely chopped

⅔ cup mayonnaise
2 tablespoons olive oil
1 tablespoon lemon juice
½ teaspoon prepared mustard

Combine parsley, green onions, capers and garlic in blender or food processor; blend until finely chopped. Add mayonnaise, olive oil, lemon juice and mustard; blend. Chill. Yield: 1¼ cups.

Smoky Oyster Kabobs

1 pint select oysters, fresh or frozen
⅓ cup olive oil
2 tablespoons dry vermouth
1 teaspoon chopped parsley
¼ teaspoon marjoram
¼ teaspoon thyme

⅛ teaspoon pepper
⅛ teaspoon garlic salt
1 large green pepper, cut into ½-inch pieces
½ pound fresh mushrooms
10 slices bacon, cut into thirds

Thaw oysters if frozen. Remove any remaining shell. Drain. Combine oil, vermouth, parsley and spices. Mix well. Add oysters, green pepper and mushrooms to marinade. Cover and refrigerate 1 hour. Wrap piece of bacon around each oyster and thread oysters and vegetables on four 12-inch skewers. Place kabobs in well-greased hinged wire grills. Cook about 4 inches from moderately hot coals for 5 to 7 minutes. Baste with sauce. Turn and cook for 5 to 7 minutes longer or until bacon is crisp. Yield: 4 servings.

Pompano Pouches

6 pan-dressed pompano or other pan-dressed fish (approximately ½ pound each), fresh or frozen
1½ teaspoons salt
⅛ teaspoon pepper
1 can (3 ounces) broiled-in-butter mushrooms, drained, chopped
½ cup dry white wine

¼ cup butter or margarine, melted
3 tablespoons finely chopped green onions
3 tablespoons lime juice
1 tablespoon chopped parsley
1 can (2½ ounces) button mushrooms, drained

Thaw fish if frozen. Preheat oven to 350 degrees. Clean, wash and dry fish. Sprinkle inside with salt and pepper. Cut 6 pieces of heavy-duty aluminum foil, 18 x 18 inches each; grease lightly. Place fish on foil. Combine remaining ingredients, except button mushrooms. Pour sauce over fish. Place 2 button mushrooms on each fish. Bring foil up over the fish and close all edges with tight double folds, making 6 packages. Bake at 350 degrees for 45 to 50 minutes or until fish flakes easily when tested with a fork. Yield: 6 servings.

Seafood Spanish Rice

1 pound skinless pompano (or other fish) fillets, fresh or frozen
½ cup chopped onion
½ cup chopped green pepper
½ clove garlic, minced
2 tablespoons butter or margarine
1 can (10¾ ounces) condensed tomato soup

1½ cups water
1½ cups quick cooking rice, uncooked
2 teaspoons Worcestershire sauce
4 whole cloves
1 teaspoon dry mustard
½ teaspoon salt
½ teaspoon pepper
Parsley (garnish)

Thaw fillets if frozen. Cut into 1-inch pieces. In a large skillet, cook onion, green pepper and garlic in butter until tender. Add remaining ingredients; mix well. Cook over low heat 10 to 12 minutes or until liquid is absorbed and fish flakes easily when tested with a fork. Remove cloves before serving. Garnish with parsley. Yield: 4 to 6 servings.

Kiev-Style Pompano

4 to 6 pan-dressed pompano or other pan dressed fish (approximately ½ pound each), fresh or frozen
1 teaspoon salt
⅛ teaspoon pepper
1 cup chopped parsley
¼ cup butter or margarine, softened

1 egg, beaten
¼ cup milk
1 teaspoon salt
¾ cup dry bread crumbs
½ cup grated Swiss cheese
3 tablespoons butter or margarine, melted

Thaw fish if frozen. Preheat oven to 500 degrees. Sprinkle inside and out with salt and pepper. Add parsley to butter and mix thoroughly. Spread inside of each fish with approximately one tablespoon parsley butter. Combine egg, milk and salt. Combine crumbs and cheese. Dip fish in egg mixture and roll in crumb mixture. Place on a well-greased 15½ x 12-inch baking sheet. Sprinkle remaining crumb mixture over top of fish. Drizzle with melted butter. Bake in an extremely hot oven, 500 degrees, for 15 to 20 minutes or until fish flakes easily when tested with a fork. Yield: 4 to 6 servings.

Stuffed Pompano Fillets

6 skinless pompano (or other fish) fillets (approximately 2 pounds), fresh or frozen
½ pound lean fish fillets, skinned, fresh or frozen, finely chopped
2 tablespoons butter or margarine
1 cup finely chopped onions
1 cup finely chopped pecans

1 teaspoon salt
1 egg, beaten
2 tablespoons milk
1 cup finely crushed butter-flavored crackers
1 tablespoon melted butter or margarine

Thaw fish if frozen. Preheat oven to 425 degrees. In large skillet, sauté onions in butter until tender. Add chopped fillets, pecans and salt. Cook and stir for 3 minutes or until fish flakes easily when tested with a fork. Remove from heat. Add egg, milk and cracker crumbs; mix well. Place 3 fillets in a well-greased 12 x 8 x 2-inch baking dish. Top each with ⅓ of the stuffing and then with remaining fillets. Secure fillets with wooden toothpicks or tie with string. Bake at 425 degrees basting occasionally with melted butter, for 25 to 30 minutes or until fish flakes easily when tested with a fork. Cut each stuffed fish in half to serve. Yield: 6 servings.

Redfish Antibes

2 pounds redfish (or other fish) fillets, skinned, fresh or frozen
1 tablespoon lemon juice
1 teaspoon salt
¼ teaspoon lemon-pepper seasoning
1½ cups sliced fresh mushrooms

½ cup chopped, roasted, salted hickory smoke-flavored almonds
3 tablespoons butter or margarine
2 tablespoons chopped parsley

Thaw fish if frozen. Preheat oven to 350 degrees. Place fish in a single layer in a well-greased 12 x 8 x 2-inch baking dish. Sprinkle with lemon juice, salt and lemon-pepper. Bake at 350 degrees for 10 to 12 minutes or until fish flakes easily when tested with a fork. Remove fish to a heated platter. Combine remaining ingredients in a 2-quart saucepan; cook over low heat for 5 to 7 minutes. Spoon hot mixture over fish. Yield: 6 servings.

Basil-Butter Fillets

2 pounds redfish (or other fish) fillets, skinned, fresh or frozen
¼ teaspoon salt
⅛ teaspoon pepper
4 tablespoons butter or margarine, melted

1 tablespoon soy sauce
1 tablespoon lemon juice
Basil Butter

Thaw fish if frozen. Sprinkle with salt and pepper. Place fillets in a single layer in a well-greased broiler pan. Combine butter, soy sauce and lemon juice. Brush half the sauce on top side of fish. Broil about 4 inches from source of heat for 4 to 5 minutes. Turn carefully and brush with remaining sauce. Broil 4 to 5 minutes longer or until fish flakes easily when tested with a fork. Top servings with equal amounts of Basil Butter. Yield: 6 servings.

Basil Butter

½ cup butter or margarine, softened

1 tablespoon dried basil

In blender, combine butter with basil; blend until well mixed. Yield: ½ cup.

Most fish are colorblind.

Rock Shrimp Atlantic

1½ pounds peeled, deveined rock
    shrimp, fresh or frozen
½ cup lime juice
½ cup lemon juice
1 cup all-purpose flour

¼ teaspoon liquid hot pepper sauce
2 tablespoons creole seasoning
Vegetable oil for deep frying

Thaw rock shrimp if frozen. Combine lime and lemon juices and liquid hot pepper sauce. Add rock shrimp to marinade; marinate for 1 to 2 minutes. Drain. Combine flour and creole seasoning. Coat rock shrimp with flour mixture. Fry in hot oil, 425 degrees, 45 seconds to 1 minute or until lightly browned. Drain on absorbent paper. Yield: 6 servings.

Fried Rock Shrimp Melt

1 pound peeled, deveined rock
    shrimp, fresh or frozen
¾-inch cube of Swiss or Monterey
    Jack cheese for each shrimp
3 green onions, sliced in ½-inch
    pieces

½ cup all-purpose flour
1 teaspoon salt
¼ teaspoon pepper
3 eggs, lightly beaten
1 cup dry bread crumbs
Vegetable oil for deep frying

Thaw rock shrimp if frozen. Mix flour, salt and pepper; set aside. Place one cube of cheese and one piece of onion into the curl of each shrimp. Secure with wooden toothpick through shrimp. Coat shrimp with flour mixture, dip into eggs, and then coat with bread crumbs. Fry shrimp at 350 degrees until golden brown—25 to 30 seconds. Yield: 8 servings.

Rock Shrimp and Linguine

1 pound peeled, deveined rock
  shrimp, fresh or frozen
1 cup sliced fresh mushrooms
¼ cup chopped green onions
1 clove garlic, crushed
⅓ cup butter or margarine
3 tablespoons all-purpose flour

1 teaspoon salt
¾ cup Rhine wine
2 cups half-and-half
⅓ cup chopped parsley
4 to 6 servings hot cooked linguine
Grated Parmesan cheese (optional)

Thaw rock shrimp if frozen. In 10-inch skillet sauté rock shrimp, mushrooms, green onions and garlic in butter over low heat for 1 to 2 minutes. Blend in flour and salt; mix well. Stir in wine and gradually add half-and-half, stirring constantly to form a smooth sauce. Add chopped parsley. Simmer for three minutes. Toss with linguine; sprinkle with Parmesan cheese, if desired. Yield: 4 to 6 servings.

Rock Shrimp Stir-Fry

1½ pounds peeled, deveined rock
  shrimp, fresh or frozen
2 tablespoons vegetable oil
½ cup thinly sliced green onions
2 cloves garlic, minced
1 teaspoon instant chicken bouillon
1 cup boiling water
1 teaspoon ground ginger

1 package (9 ounces) frozen French-
  style green beans, thawed
1 package (10 ounces) frozen
  chopped broccoli, thawed
1 can (4 ounces) sliced mushrooms,
  drained
1 tablespoon cornstarch
2 tablespoons soy sauce

Thaw shrimp if frozen. Heat oil in a 12-inch skillet. Add shrimp, onions and garlic; stir-fry 3 minutes. Remove shrimp. Add instant chicken bouillon and water; stir to dissolve. Add ginger, green beans, broccoli and mushrooms. Cover. Bring to boil; lower heat; simmer 6 minutes or until vegetables are tender-crisp. Combine cornstarch and soy sauce and stir into skillet. Add shrimp, stirring constantly until sauce thickens. Yield: 6 servings.

Delightful Dilled Shrimp

1½ pounds peeled, deveined, split rock shrimp tails, fresh or frozen
2 tablespoons salt
1 quart water
1 chicken bouillon cube
¼ cup hot water
2 tablespoons butter or margarine
½ teaspoon salt

¼ teaspoon onion salt
⅛ teaspoon white pepper
2 teaspoons cornstarch
1 tablespoon water
1 can (1 pound) cut green beans, drained
½ cup dairy sour cream
½ teaspoon dill weed

Thaw rock shrimp if frozen. Add salt to water and bring to a boil. Place shrimp in boiling water; cook 30 seconds. Drain. Rinse shrimp under cold running water for 1 to 2 minutes. Remove any remaining particles of sand vein. Dissolve bouillon cube in ¼ cup hot water. Melt butter in saucepan; add bouillon, salt, onion salt and white pepper. Add cornstarch to one tablespoon water; stir into bouillon mixture. Add green beans; heat. Add rock shrimp, sour cream and dill weed. Heat thoroughly, but do not boil. Yield: 6 servings.

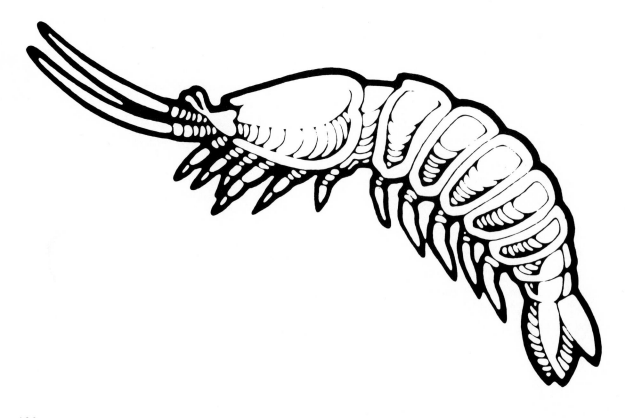

Oriental Scallops

2 pounds calico or bay scallops, fresh or frozen
1 package (7 ounces) frozen pea pods, thawed
¼ cup butter or margarine
2 tomatoes, cut into eighths
¼ cup water

2 tablespoons cornstarch
1 tablespoon soy sauce
½ teaspoon salt
⅛ teaspoon pepper
3 cups hot cooked rice
Soy sauce

Thaw scallops if frozen. Rinse with cold water to remove any shell particles; drain well. Cut large scallops in half crosswise. Drain pea pods. Melt butter in a 12-inch skillet. Add the scallops and cook over a low heat for 1 to 2 minutes, stirring often. Add pea pods and tomatoes. Combine water, cornstarch, soy sauce, salt and pepper. Add to scallop mixture and cook until thick, stirring constantly. Serve over rice with soy sauce. Yield: 6 servings.

Scallop Florentine Luncheon

1 pound cooked calico or bay scallops
¼ cup butter or margarine, melted
¼ cup all-purpose flour
½ teaspoon salt
¼ teaspoon white pepper

2 cups light cream
1 package (10 ounces) frozen chopped spinach
½ cup fresh sliced mushrooms
1 tablespoon prepared mustard
6 patty shells or toast points

Cook spinach according to package directions; drain. Melt butter in a 9-inch skillet; blend in flour, salt and pepper. Gradually add cream; cook until thickened, stirring constantly. Stir in scallops, spinach, mushrooms and mustard; heat thoroughly. Serve in patty shells or on toast points. Yield: 6 servings.

Cheese Almond Scallops

1 pound calico or bay scallops, fresh or frozen
½ cup water
½ cup dry white wine
¼ cup butter or margarine, melted
½ cup chopped green onions
½ pound small fresh mushrooms
3 tablespoons all-purpose flour
1 cup half-and-half
¾ cup shredded Swiss cheese
1 tablespoon catsup
½ teaspoon salt
½ teaspoon liquid hot pepper sauce
2 tablespoons coarsely chopped pimiento
Almond Rice

Thaw scallops if frozen. Cut large scallops in half. Combine water, wine and scallops in saucepan. Bring to the boiling point; reduce heat and simmer 3 to 4 minutes, depending on the size of the scallops. Drain scallops, reserving liquid. Keep scallops warm. Pour liquid into measuring cup and add enough water to equal 1 cup. In saucepan, sauté onions and mushrooms in butter until tender but not brown, stirring frequently. Blend in flour. Add reserved liquid and half-and-half; cook over moderate heat until thickened, stirring constantly. Stir in cheese, catsup, salt and liquid hot pepper sauce; heat. Fold in scallops and pimiento; heat through. Serve over Almond Rice. Yield: 6 servings.

Almond Rice

Prepare 6 servings of your favorite rice. Season and fold in ½ cup of toasted almonds.

Scallops have over thirty eyes—all of them blue.

Baked Stuffed Spiny Lobster, page 154

Crawfish Étouffée, page 132

Croaker Country Style, page 135

Manicotti Shrimp Marinara, page 201

Scallop Kabobs, page 191

Sweet and Sour Scallops

1 pound cooked scallops
1 medium onion, thinly sliced
1 small green pepper, cut into 1-inch
   squares
¼ cup melted butter, margarine or
   cooking oil
2 cans (8¼ ounces each) pineapple
   chunks in heavy syrup
½ cup white vinegar

¼ cup sugar
2 tablespoons cornstarch
1 tablespoon soy sauce
½ teaspoon dry mustard
¼ teaspoon salt
⅔ cup cherry tomato halves
3 cups hot cooked rice
½ cup toasted slivered almonds

Cut large scallops in half. Cook onion and green pepper in butter until tender but not brown. Drain pineapple and reserve syrup. Combine pineapple syrup, vinegar, sugar, cornstarch, soy sauce, dry mustard and salt; shake together until well blended; add to cooked vegetables. Cook, stirring constantly, until thick and clear. Gently stir in pineapple chunks, cherry tomatoes and scallops and heat thoroughly. Combine cooked rice and almonds. Serve sweet-and-sour mixture over Almond Rice (see page 184). Yield: 6 servings.

Basic Broiled Scallops

2 pounds calico or bay scallops, fresh
   or frozen
½ cup butter or margarine, melted
¾ to 1 teaspoon minced garlic

½ teaspoon salt
⅛ teaspoon white pepper
Paprika (garnish)

Thaw scallops if frozen. Rinse under cold running water to remove any remaining shell particles. Sauté garlic in butter over very low heat for 5 minutes or until tender but not brown. Place scallops in a single layer in a 12 x 8 x 2-inch baking dish; sprinkle with salt and pepper. Pour garlic butter over scallops; stir to coat scallops on all sides. Broil 4 inches from source of heat for 2 minutes; stir. Broil 2 minutes longer. Garnish with paprika. Serve immediately. Yield: 6 servings.

Seafood Festival Casserole

¾ pound bay or sea scallops, fresh or frozen
½ pound peeled, deveined shrimp, fresh or frozen
½ pound blue crab meat, fresh, frozen or pasteurized
6 tablespoons butter or margarine
¼ cup all-purpose flour
1 teaspoon salt

⅛ teaspoon pepper
1½ cups milk
2 tablespoons sherry
2 tablespoons butter or margarine
1½ cups soft, torn bread crumbs
¼ cup finely shredded Cheddar cheese
Paprika

Thaw seafood if frozen. Preheat oven to 350 degrees. Remove any remaining shell or cartilage from crab meat. If large scallops are used, cut in halves or quarters. Cook scallops and shrimp in 6 tablespoons butter about 1 to 2 minutes. Remove scallops and shrimp from skillet. Stir flour, salt and pepper into butter. Add milk; cook, stirring constantly until thick. Stir in sherry. Fold in crab meat, scallops and shrimp; heat. Spoon into individual baking shells or 1½-quart casserole dish. Melt remaining 2 tablespoons butter; remove from heat. Add bread crumbs and cheese; stir just until well blended. Sprinkle over seafood mixture. Bake in moderate oven, 350 degrees, about 15 minutes or until heated and crumbs are lightly toasted. Sprinkle with paprika. Yield: 6 servings.

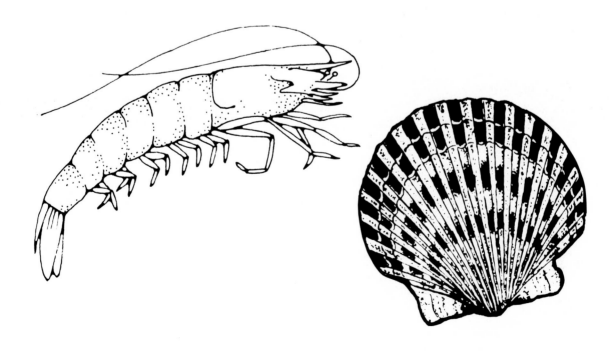

Scallop Kabobs

1 pound calico or bay scallops, fresh or frozen
2 cups cherry tomatoes
2 cups small fresh mushrooms
1 can (13½ ounces) pineapple chunks, drained
1 green pepper, cut into one-inch squares
¼ cup cooking oil
¼ cup lemon juice
¼ cup chopped parsley
¼ cup soy sauce
½ teaspoon salt
⅛ teaspoon pepper

Thaw scallops if frozen. Rinse scallops with cold running water to remove any remaining shell particles. Place tomatoes, mushrooms, pineapple, green pepper and scallops in a bowl. Combine oil, lemon juice, parsley, soy sauce, salt and pepper. Pour sauce over scallop mixture and let stand for 30 minutes, stirring occasionally. Using long skewers, alternate scallops, tomatoes, mushrooms, pineapple and green pepper until skewers are filled. Cook about 4 minutes over moderately hot coals. Baste with sauce. Turn and cook for 3 to 4 minutes longer. Yield: 6 servings. **(Photo, page 188)**

Backyard Scallops

1 pound bay or calico scallops, fresh or frozen
¼ cup vegetable oil
¼ cup lemon juice
1 teaspoon salt
⅛ teaspoon hickory liquid smoke
1 package (8 ounces) sliced bacon, partially cooked, cut into thirds
½ cup sesame seeds
Parsley (garnish)

Thaw scallops if frozen. Rinse with cold water to remove any shell. In a 2-quart bowl, combine oil with lemon juice, salt and liquid smoke; add scallops. Cover and chill 30 minutes, stirring occasionally. Remove scallops from marinade. Wrap each scallop with a piece of bacon and fasten with a wooden toothpick. Roll scallops in sesame seeds; place in well-greased hinged wire grill about 4 inches from moderately hot coals. Cook 2 to 4 minutes or until sesame seeds brown. Turn and cook 2 to 4 minutes longer or until scallops are tender. Yield: 4 servings.

Savory Baked Shark

2 pounds skinless shark (or other fish) steaks, fresh or frozen
2 teaspoons lemon juice
⅛ teaspoon pepper

6 slices bacon, chopped
½ cup soft bread crumbs
2 tablespoons chopped parsley
¾ cup thinly sliced onions

Thaw fish if frozen. Preheat oven to 350 degrees. Place fish in a single layer in a well-greased 12 x 8 x 2-inch baking dish. Sprinkle with lemon juice and pepper. Fry bacon until crisp. Remove bacon from drippings; drain and crumble. Combine bacon, bread crumbs and parsley. Cook onions in bacon drippings until tender. Spread onions over fish. Sprinkle crumb mixture over top of onions. Bake at 350 degrees for 25 to 30 minutes or until fish flakes easily when tested with a fork. Yield: 6 servings.

Garden-Baked Shark

1½ pounds shark (or other fish) fillets, fresh or frozen
½ teaspoon salt
¼ teaspoon pepper

1 can (16 ounces) mixed vegetables, drained
1 jar (12 ounces) home-style gravy with onion
Parsley (garnish)

Thaw fish if frozen. Preheat oven to 350 degrees. Skin fillets; cut into serving-sized portions. Place fish in a single layer in a well-greased 1½-quart shallow baking dish. Sprinkle with salt and pepper. In a 1-quart bowl, combine vegetables with gravy; spread over fish. Cover and bake at 350 degrees for 20 to 35 minutes or until fish flakes easily when tested with a fork. Garnish with parsley. Yield: 4 servings.

The fish in England's fish and chips is usually shark.

Curried Shark

1½ pounds fresh shark (or other fish) meat, cut into 1-inch chunks
2 tablespoons butter or margarine, melted
1 can (10¾ ounces) condensed cream of shrimp soup
1 can (10¾ ounces) condensed cream of mushroom soup
¾ cup dairy sour cream
1½ teaspoons curry powder
2 tablespoons chopped fresh parsley
Cooked rice, toast points or pastry shells

Sauté shark in margarine for 3 to 5 minutes over low heat, stirring frequently. Add soups and stir until well blended. Stir in sour cream, curry powder and parsley; mix thoroughly. Cover; simmer for 10 minutes or until fish flakes easily when tested with a fork. Serve immediately over cooked rice or toast points or in pastry shells. Yield: 4 to 6 servings.

Shark with Orange Butter

1½ pounds shark (or other fish) fillets, fresh or frozen
¾ teaspoon salt
¼ teaspoon pepper
3 tablespoons orange juice concentrate, undiluted
3 tablespoons butter or margarine, melted
Orange slices (garnish)
Parsley (garnish)

Thaw fish if frozen. Skin fillets; cut into serving-sized portions. Place fish in a single layer in a well-greased 1½-quart shallow baking dish. Sprinkle with salt and pepper. Combine orange juice and butter; pour over fish. Broil approximately 4 inches from source of heat 4 to 6 minutes. Turn fish and baste with orange butter. Broil 6 to 8 minutes longer or until fish flakes easily when tested with a fork. Garnish with orange slices and parsley. Yield: 4 servings.

Shark Casserole Crescent

2 cups cooked, flaked shark or other cooked, flaked fish
½ cup butter or margarine, melted
1½ cups sliced celery
1 cup chopped onions
2 chicken bouillon cubes, crushed
1 tablespoon chopped parsley
½ teaspoon salt

⅛ teaspoon pepper
1½ tablespoons cornstarch
2 cups milk
1 package (10 ounces) frozen mixed vegetables in butter sauce, thawed
1 can (8 ounces) refrigerated crescent rolls

Preheat oven to 350 degrees. In a 3-quart saucepan, add celery and onions to melted butter; add crushed bouillon. Cook mixture over medium heat until tender. Stir in parsley, salt and pepper. Combine cornstarch and milk; gradually stir into vegetable mixture. Cook over medium heat, stirring constantly, until sauce thickens, about 5 to 10 minutes. Add shark and mixed vegetables; stir until well blended. Pour into well-greased 11¾ x 8½ x 1¾-inch casserole dish. Gently unroll crescent rolls and place on top of casserole. Bake at 350 degrees for 20 minutes or until golden brown and casserole is bubbly. Yield: 6 servings.

Baked Shark with Mushrooms

1½ pounds shark (or other fish) fillets, fresh or frozen
½ teaspoon salt
¼ teaspoon pepper
1 cup sliced fresh mushrooms

¼ cup dry white wine
½ cup condensed cream of celery soup
1 cup grated sharp Cheddar cheese
Parsley (garnish)

Thaw fish if frozen. Preheat oven to 350 degrees. Skin fillets; cut into serving-sized portions. Place fish in a single layer in a well-greased 1½-quart shallow casserole. Sprinkle with salt and pepper. Combine mushrooms, soup and wine; spread over fish. Sprinkle with cheese. Cover and bake at 350 degrees for 20 to 25 minutes or until fish flakes easily when tested with a fork. Garnish with parsley. Yield: 4 servings.

Sicilian Fish Steaks

4 skinless shark or swordfish steaks, fresh or frozen
½ cup all-purpose flour
½ cup olive oil
1 cup chopped onions
1 clove garlic, finely minced
1 can (1 pound) tomatoes, chopped
¼ cup chopped black olives
1 tablespoon capers, drained
½ teaspoon sweet basil
½ teaspoon salt
¼ teaspoon pepper
Garlic-flavored croutons (garnish)

Thaw fish if frozen. Coat steaks in flour. Fry in oil on moderate heat 4 to 5 minutes or until brown. Turn carefully and cook 4 to 5 minutes longer or until fish flakes easily when tested with a fork. Place on serving dish and keep warm. In same oil, fry onions and garlic until onions are tender. Add tomatoes, olives, capers, basil, salt and pepper. Cook for 5 minutes. Spoon over fish and serve with croutons. Yield: 4 servings.

Tipsy Shark Steaks

2 pounds shark steaks or fillets, fresh or frozen
⅔ cup beer
⅓ cup cooking oil
1 teaspoon prepared mustard
1 teaspoon salt
¼ teaspoon garlic powder
¼ teaspoon pepper
2 tablespoons butter or margarine
½ teaspoon paprika
4 cups sliced onions
1 cup dairy sour cream, heated
½ teaspoon horseradish

Thaw fish if frozen. In a shallow dish combine beer, oil, mustard, salt, garlic powder and pepper. Add fish, cover, and marinate 30 minutes in the refrigerator. Remove fish from marinade and broil 4 inches from source of heat for 8 to 10 minutes or until fish flakes easily when tested with a fork. In a saucepan, melt butter and blend in paprika. Add onions and sauté until tender but not brown. Combine warm sour cream and horseradish. To serve, top each fish steak with onions and a spoonful of the sour cream mixture. Yield: 6 servings. (**Photo, page 165**)

Shark en Papillote

1½ pounds shark (or other fish) fillets, fresh or frozen
¾ teaspoon salt
¼ teaspoon pepper
⅓ cup butter or margarine, melted
2 tablespoons chopped parsley
1 tablespoon lemon juice
¾ teaspoon salt
½ teaspoon dill weed
2 tablespoons cooking oil
4 thin onion slices
1 cup thinly sliced carrots
1 package (6 ounces) sliced Swiss cheese

Thaw fish if frozen. Preheat oven to 400 degrees. Cut into serving-sized portions. Sprinkle fish with salt and pepper. Combine butter, parsley, lemon juice, salt and dill weed. Cut 4 pieces of parchment paper. (Note: Heavy-duty aluminum foil cut into 12-inch squares may be substituted for parchment paper.) Place fish, sauce and vegetables on half of the foil. To seal, fold foil over fish, making double folds into heart shapes about 10 x 12 inches each. Brush paper with oil. Place 1 teaspoon parsley butter on one half of each paper heart. Place fish in parsley butter. Separate onion slices into rings and place on fish. Top with ¼ cup carrot slices per portion. Pour remaining parsley butter over carrots, dividing evenly among four packages. Top each serving with a cheese slice. Fold other half of each paper heart over fillet to form individual cases. Seal, starting at the top of the heart, by turning edges up and folding, twisting the tip of the heart to hold case closed. Place cases on a baking pan. Bake in a hot oven, 400 degrees, for 35 to 40 minutes or until fish flakes easily when tested with a fork. To serve, cut cases open with a large "X" design on top; fold back each segment. Yield: 4 servings.

Shark have no bone, only cartilage.

Curried Shark with Rice Pilau

1½ pounds shark steaks, fresh or
 frozen
⅓ cup cooking oil
⅓ cup cider or apple juice

2 tablespoons chopped parsley
1 teaspoon curry powder
1 teaspoon salt
Rice Pilau

Thaw fish if frozen. Skin fish and cut into 1-inch cubes. Place cubes in a shallow baking dish. Combine remaining ingredients except Rice Pilau; mix thoroughly. Pour sauce over fish and let stand for 30 minutes, stirring occasionally. Remove fish, reserving sauce. Place fish on 6 skewers, approximately 7 inches each. Place on a well-greased broiler pan. Brush with sauce. Broil about 3 inches from source of heat for 3 to 4 minutes. Turn carefully and brush with remaining sauce. Broil 3 to 4 minutes longer. Serve over Rice Pilau. Yield: 6 servings.

Rice Pilau

1 cup uncooked rice
1 package (1⅜ ounces) onion soup
 mix

2 tablespoons cooking oil
2½ cups boiling water
¼ cup chopped parsley

Cook rice in oil until golden brown, stirring occasionally. Add soup mix and water; stir. Cover and bring to a boil. Reduce heat and simmer for 25 to 30 minutes or until liquid is absorbed. Add parsley. Yield: 6 servings.

Smothered Shrimp

1 pound peeled, deveined medium shrimp, fresh or frozen
1 large Spanish onion, coarsely chopped
1 green pepper, seeded and coarsely chopped
1 cup butter or margarine
1 can (8 ounces) tomato sauce
1 can (10¾ ounces) condensed cream of celery soup, undiluted
1 tablespoon lemon juice
1 teaspoon garlic juice
⅛ teaspoon Worcestershire sauce
⅛ teaspoon cayenne
3 cups cooked yellow rice

Thaw shrimp if frozen. Melt butter in a 10-inch skillet over medium heat. Sauté onions and green pepper until tender. Add tomato sauce and cook until mixture bubbles. Add soup, lemon juice, garlic juice, Worcestershire sauce and cayenne. Simmer 5 to 6 minutes, stirring occasionally. Add shrimp and cook for 10 to 12 minutes. Serve over rice. Yield: 6 servings.

Lemon Shrimp

1½ pounds peeled, deveined shrimp, fresh or frozen
3 cloves garlic, finely minced
¼ cup butter or margarine
1 package (10 ounces) snow peas, thawed
1 cup sliced fresh mushrooms
½ cup sliced green onions
¼ cup lemon juice
3 tablespoons chopped parsley
1½ teaspoons seasoned salt
½ teaspoon white pepper
3 cups hot cooked linguine noodles

Thaw shrimp if frozen. Cut large shrimp in half. In a large skillet cook garlic in butter until tender. Add shrimp, snow peas, mushrooms and onions, stirring for 5 to 6 minutes. Add lemon juice, parsley, seasoned salt and pepper; toss mixture and transfer to a heated serving dish. Serve with hot linguine. Yield: 4 to 6 servings.

Shrimp Ah-So

1½ pounds raw, peeled, deveined shrimp, fresh or frozen
2 tablespoons salt
1 quart water
2 tablespoons soy sauce
1 teaspoon cornstarch
½ teaspoon garlic powder
½ teaspoon ginger

1 can (1 pound) unpeeled apricot halves, cut in half
2 fresh kiwifruit, peeled and cut into wedges (optional)
2 cups hot cooked rice
½ cup toasted slivered almonds
½ cup chopped parsley
Soy sauce

Thaw shrimp if frozen. Add salt to water and bring to a boil. Place shrimp in boiling water and reduce heat. Cover and simmer 3 to 4 minutes. Drain shrimp. Rinse under cold running water for 1 to 2 minutes. Combine soy sauce, cornstarch, garlic powder and ginger; shake together until thoroughly mixed. Drain apricots, reserving liquid. Combine apricot liquid and soy sauce mixture in a 10-inch skillet. Cook over medium heat, stirring constantly, until thick and clear. Add shrimp, apricots and kiwifruit; cook over low heat for 1 to 2 minutes or until thoroughly heated. Combine hot rice, almonds and parsley. Serve shrimp mixture over Almond Rice (see page 184). Serve with additional soy sauce if desired. Yield: 6 servings. **(Photo, page 205)**

Louisiana Shrimp Boil

2 pounds large green headless shrimp, fresh or frozen
1½ ounces prepared shrimp boil
1 small onion, sliced
1 lemon, sliced

1 clove garlic, sliced
2 tablespoons salt
1½ quarts water
Dipping sauce

Thaw frozen shrimp but do not remove shells. Tie the shrimp boil, onion, lemon and garlic in a piece of cheesecloth. Place water in a 3-quart boiler. Add salt and the bag of seasoning. Cover and bring to a boil over high heat. Add shrimp and return to the boiling point. Reduce heat and simmer 5 minutes or until shrimp are tender. Drain. Serve with Peppy Seafood Sauce, Dill Sauce or Lemon-Butter Sauce (see pages 232, 234 and 181. Yield: 4 servings.

Shrimp and Carambola Dumplings

18 shrimp (21 to 25 count), peeled and deveined	2 Florida star fruit (carambola) Salt and pepper

Thaw shrimp if frozen. Wash, salt and pepper each one. Cut star fruit into 6 equal slices. Cut away skin; discard skin and end pieces. With a half-inch circular cutter, remove a small circle from center of each slice; reserve. Grill star fruit slices.

Mousse Mixture

1 pound peeled, deveined baby shrimp (150 count)	2 tablespoons Old Dutch Salad Dressing (or creamy or oil-based Italian dressing)
½ medium red pepper, seeded and poached	½ cup cooked white rice
½ medium green pepper, seeded and poached	½ teaspoon liquid hot pepper sauce Salt to taste
4 tablespoons heavy cream	Star fruit center from above
2 tablespoons butter	
2 tablespoons parsley	

Thaw shrimp if frozen. Preheat oven to 300 to 325 degrees. Combine all ingredients in container of a blender or food processor. Process until very smooth and sticky. Remove and divide into 18 equal balls. Take mousse and apply to outside of 18 shrimp (from above) about ½ inch thick and evenly around all but ½ inch of tail section. Refrigerate for approximately 20 minutes. Remove and stand each shrimp dumpling up in the center of a slice of star fruit. Place on buttered cookie sheet and bake approximately 10 minutes at 300 to 325 degrees. Remove and serve with Dill Mousseline. Yield: 6 servings.

Dill Mousseline Sauce

1 cup Hollandaise sauce	6 sprigs fresh dill
¼ cup heavy cream	

Whip heavy cream and combine carefully with warm hollandaise sauce. With kitchen shears snip dill into sauce. Stir and blend. Yield: 1¼ cups.

Manicotti Shrimp Marinara

¾ pound peeled, deveined shrimp, fresh or frozen
1 package (10 ounces) frozen chopped spinach
⅓ cup butter or margarine, melted
1½ teaspoons Worcestershire sauce
½ teaspoon celery salt
½ teaspoon salt
¼ teaspoon liquid hot pepper sauce
1½ cups chopped lettuce

½ cup chopped green onions and tops
½ cup chopped parsley
2 cloves garlic, peeled and minced
½ cup dry curd cottage cheese
1 egg, beaten
8 (4 ounces) manicotti shells
1 jar (32 ounces) thick spaghetti sauce
2 tablespoons Parmesan cheese

Thaw shrimp if frozen. Preheat oven to 350 degrees. Thaw spinach; drain. Melt butter in a medium-sized saucepan; blend in Worcestershire sauce, celery salt, salt and liquid hot pepper sauce. Add vegetables; simmer for 10 minutes or until tender. Add cottage cheese and egg to vegetable mixture. Prepare manicotti according to package directions. Stuff manicotti shells with equal amounts of vegetable mixture. Spread one cup spaghetti sauce in bottom of large casserole dish. Add stuffed manicotti shells to same dish and cover with additional cup of spaghetti sauce, spread evenly over shells. Cover casserole dish with aluminum foil, crimping it to edges of dish. Bake at 350 degrees for 30 minutes. Remove and uncover. Combine remaining spaghetti sauce and shrimp; spread mixture over casserole. Bake 7 to 10 minutes longer or until shrimp are opaque in the center when cut with a knife. Remove from oven; sprinkle Parmesan cheese over top of casserole. Yield: 8 servings. **(Photo, page 188)**

Smoked Butterfly Shrimp

2 pounds fresh jumbo shrimp, in shell

1½ cups butter-flavored cooking oil
Seafood seasoning or seasoned salt

Cut shrimp in butterfly fashion by running scissors along top, cutting through shell. Use a sharp knife to cut deep enough through flesh so shrimp will spread open, but leave shell attached on the underside. Remove sand vein and wash. Place on grill over low coals and wet hickory chips, shell side down. Brush generously with oil and sprinkle with seasoning or salt. Cook at moderately low temperature for 15 minutes, basting once or twice with oil. Turn shrimp over so meat is exposed to heat. Cook 4 to 5 minutes longer. Yield: 6 servings.

Florida Shrimp à la King

¾ pound cooked, peeled, deveined shrimp, fresh or frozen
½ cup sliced mushrooms
3 tablespoons chopped green pepper
3 tablespoons butter or margarine, melted

3 tablespoons all-purpose flour
½ teaspoon salt
⅛ teaspoon cayenne
1½ cups milk
2 tablespoons chopped pimiento
Patty shells or toast points

Cut large shrimp in half. In a 10-inch skillet, sauté mushrooms and green pepper in butter until tender; blend in flour and seasonings. Gradually add milk; cook until thickened, stirring constantly. Stir in pimiento and shrimp; heat. Serve in patty shells or on toast points. Yield: 6 servings.

Shrimp Miami

2 pounds large peeled, deveined shrimp, fresh or frozen
¼ cup olive or salad oil
1 teaspoon salt

½ teaspoon white pepper
¼ cup extra dry vermouth
2 tablespoons lemon juice

Thaw shrimp if frozen. Preheat electric skillet to 320 degrees. Add oil, salt, pepper and shrimp. Cook for 5 to 7 minutes, stirring constantly. Increase temperature to 420 degrees. Add vermouth and lemon juice. Cook one minute longer, stirring constantly. Drain. Serve hot or cold as an appetizer or entree. Yield: 6 servings.

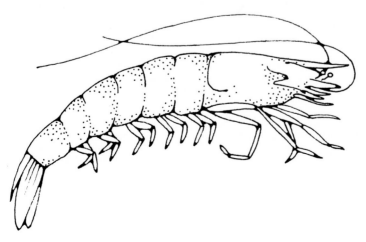

Shrimp Jambalaya

1 pound peeled, deveined shrimp, fresh or frozen
½ cup butter or margarine
1 cup chopped green onions and tops
1 cup chopped celery
½ cup chopped green pepper
2 cloves garlic, finely minced
1 package (8 ounces) sliced ham, cut into small pieces

1 can (28 ounces) chopped tomatoes and liquid
1 can (6 ounces) tomato paste
1 cup water
2 chicken bouillon cubes
½ teaspoon basil
½ teaspoon pepper
½ teaspoon liquid hot pepper sauce
1½ cups hot cooked rice

Thaw shrimp if frozen. Combine butter, onions, celery, green pepper, garlic and seasonings in 3-quart bowl. Cover and cook in microwave oven on high 12 minutes, stirring occasionally during cooking. Add ham, tomatoes, tomato paste, water and shrimp. Cover and cook on high 16 minutes, stirring occasionally during cooking. Place ¼ cup rice in each of 6 soup bowls. Fill bowls with jambalaya. Yield: 6 servings. **(Photo, page 167)**

Shrimp Ratatouille

1 pound peeled, deveined shrimp, fresh or frozen
¼ cup olive or salad oil
2 cloves garlic, finely chopped
2 small zucchini squash, unpared and thinly sliced
1 small eggplant, peeled and cut into 1-inch cubes
1 medium onion, thinly sliced

1 medium green pepper, seeded and cut into 1-inch pieces
1 cup sliced fresh mushrooms
1 can (1 pound) tomato wedges
1 can (8 ounces) tomato sauce
1½ teaspoons garlic salt
1 teaspoon crushed basil
1 teaspoon dried parsley
¼ teaspoon pepper

Thaw shrimp if frozen. Cut shrimp in half lengthwise. In large skillet, sauté zucchini, eggplant, onion, green pepper and mushrooms in oil for 10 minutes or until crisp-tender. Add shrimp, stirring frequently, for approximately 2 minutes. Add tomatoes, garlic salt, basil, parsley and pepper. Cover; simmer about 5 minutes or until shrimp are tender. Serve with rice or noodles. Yield: 6 servings.

Quick and Easy Shrimp

1 pound cooked, peeled, deveined shrimp, fresh or frozen
2 tablespoons butter or margarine, melted
1 medium green pepper, cut into strips
1 medium onion, sliced
1 clove garlic, peeled and minced

1 can (10¾ ounces) condensed tomato soup
⅓ cup water
2 teaspoons lemon juice
¼ teaspoon salt
⅛ teaspoon pepper
⅛ teaspoon liquid hot pepper sauce
3 cups cooked rice

Thaw shrimp if frozen. Cut large shrimp in half. In a 10-inch skillet, sauté green pepper, onion and garlic in butter until tender but not brown, stirring occasionally. Add soup, water, lemon juice, salt, pepper and liquid hot pepper sauce; simmer 8 to 10 minutes, stirring occasionally. Add shrimp; heat thoroughly. Serve over rice. Yield: 6 servings.

Broiled Marinated Shrimp

1½ pounds peeled, deveined shrimp, fresh or frozen
⅓ cup lemon juice
3 tablespoons olive oil
3 tablespoons chopped green onions and tops
2 cloves garlic, minced

2½ teaspoons creole seasoning
¼ teaspoon pepper
¼ teaspoon thyme leaves
½ cup butter or margarine
Chopped parsley (garnish)

Thaw shrimp if frozen. In a 2-quart bowl, combine first 9 ingredients. Cover; marinate in the refrigerator one hour, stirring occasionally. Drain shrimp, reserving marinade. Place shrimp in a single layer on a broiler pan. Broil 4 inches from source of heat 5 to 8 minutes (broiling time will vary with shrimp size) or until shrimp are pink and tender. Garnish with chopped parsley. In a 1-quart saucepan combine reserved marinade and butter; heat and serve with shrimp. Yield: 4 servings.

Broiled Swordfish with Macadamia Nut Butter, page 216

Parmesan-Stuffed Croaker, page 134

Company Crab, page 121

Heavenly Broiled Mullet, page 162

Rock Shrimp Wild Rice Casserole, page 182

Shrimp Kabobs with Fruity Glaze

2 pounds peeled, deveined large (14 to 15 per pound) shrimp, fresh or frozen, with tails left intact
18 lime or lemon wedges
½ cup apricot preserves
½ cup orange juice
½ cup lemon juice
¼ cup honey
1 tablespoon cornstarch

2 to 3 drops liquid hot pepper sauce
1 teaspoon chopped fresh or dried mint (optional)
Fruit kabobs—banana slices, orange wedges, fresh pineapple chunks and melon chunks (optional)
6 5-inch skewers

Thaw shrimp if frozen. Alternately thread lime or lemon wedges and shrimp on skewers. Cover shrimp tails with aluminum foil. Place kabobs on a tray; cover and refrigerate until ready to cook. In a 1-quart saucepan, combine preserves, orange and lemon juice, honey, cornstarch and liquid hot pepper sauce and cook over low heat; stir sauce until no cornstarch lumps remain. Cook until sauce thickens slightly, stirring constantly; simmer 3 to 4 minutes. Broil kakobs about 4 inches from moderate heat for 5 minutes on a well-greased rack of a grill (or in a well-greased baking pan in a conventional oven), basting occasionally with sauce and sprinkling with mint, if desired. Turn; cook 4 to 5 minutes longer, basting occasionally. Remove foil from shrimp tails. Serve with remaining sauce and favorite fresh fruit kabobs. Yield: 5 to 6 servings.

Batter-Fried Shrimp

1½ pounds peeled, deveined shrimp, fresh or frozen
½ cup vegetable oil
1 egg, beaten
1 cup all-purpose flour

½ cup milk
¾ teaspoon seasoned salt
¼ teaspoon salt
Vegetable oil for deep-frying

Thaw shrimp if frozen. Combine oil and egg; beat well. Add remaining ingredients; stir until well blended. Dip each shrimp in the batter, then deep-fry in hot oil, 350 degrees, for 30 to 60 seconds or until shrimp are golden brown. Remove with slotted spoon. Drain on absorbent paper. Serve immediately. Yield: 6 servings.

Creamy Shrimp with Spaghetti

1½ pounds cooked, peeled, deveined shrimp, fresh or frozen
¼ cup butter or margarine, melted
3 tablespoons all-purpose flour
½ teaspoon salt
2 cups milk
1 can (3 ounces) sliced mushrooms, undrained

⅓ cup sliced, pitted ripe or stuffed olives
1 tablespoon lemon juice
½ to ¾ teaspoon dill weed
4 to 6 servings hot cooked and seasoned spaghetti
Grated Parmesan cheese (optional)

Thaw shrimp if frozen. Melt butter in saucepan over medium heat; blend in flour and salt. Gradually add milk; cook, stirring constantly, until thickened. Add mushrooms, olives, lemon juice, dill weed and shrimp; stir carefully. Serve over spaghetti and sprinkle with Parmesan cheese, if desired. Yield: 4 to 6 servings.

Lemon-Garlic Broiled Shrimp

2 pounds peeled, deveined shrimp, fresh or frozen
2 cloves garlic, peeled and finely chopped
½ cup butter or margarine, melted

3 tablespoons lemon juice
½ teaspoon salt
⅛ teaspoon pepper
Chopped parsley (garnish)

Thaw shrimp if frozen. Sauté garlic in butter until tender but not brown. Remove from heat; add lemon juice, salt and pepper. Arrange shrimp in a single layer on a 15 x 10 x 1-inch baking pan. Pour sauce over shrimp. Broil about 4 inches from source of heat for 8 to 10 minutes, basting once during broiling. Garnish with parsley. Yield: 6 servings.

Shrimp-Stuffed Tomatoes

¾ pound cooked, peeled, deveined
  shrimp, fresh or frozen
6 large tomatoes
1 teaspoon salt
1 cup cooked rice
1 cup grated Cheddar cheese

1 egg, beaten
1 teaspoon salt
⅛ teaspoon pepper
1 tablespoon butter or margarine,
  melted
¼ cup bread crumbs

Thaw shrimp if frozen. Preheat oven to 350 degrees. Cut large shrimp in half. Wash tomatoes. Remove stem ends and centers; sprinkle with salt. Combine rice, cheese, egg, seasonings and shrimp. Stuff tomatoes with rice-shrimp mixture. Combine butter and bread crumbs; sprinkle over top of tomatoes. Place stuffed tomatoes in a well-greased baking dish. Bake at 350 degrees for 20 to 25 minutes or until tomatoes are tender. Yield: 6 servings.

Hurry Curry Shrimp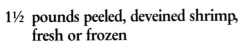

1½ pounds peeled, deveined shrimp,
  fresh or frozen
2 tablespoons butter or margarine,
  melted
1 can (10¾ ounces) condensed cream
  of shrimp soup

1 can (10¾ ounces) condensed cream
  of mushroom soup
¾ cup dairy sour cream
1½ teaspoons curry powder
2 tablespoons chopped parsley
Patty shells or toast points

Thaw shrimp if frozen. Melt butter in a 10-inch skillet. Add shrimp; cook over low heat for 3 to 5 minutes, stirring frequently. Add the soups and stir until well blended. Stir in sour cream, curry powder and parsley; mix well. Serve in patty shells or on toast points. Yield: 6 servings.

Make the job easier with a shrimp deveiner—the inexpensive plastic ones are the best.

Sweet and Sour Shrimp

1	pound cooked, peeled, deveined shrimp, fresh or frozen	1	tablespoon soy sauce
1½	cups apple juice	¼	teaspoon salt
½	cup diagonally sliced carrots	¼	cup apple juice
½	cup vinegar	2	tablespoons cornstarch
⅓	cup sugar	½	cup cubed green pepper
¼	catsup	¼	cup sliced green onion
2	tablespoons vegetable oil	2	cups hot cooked rice
		½	cup toasted slivered almonds

Thaw shrimp if frozen. In a large mixing bowl, combine 1½ cups apple juice, carrots, vinegar, sugar, catsup, cooking oil, soy sauce and salt. Stir until sugar is dissolved. Cover. Cook in microwave oven for 15 minutes or until carrots are cooked but still crunchy. Dissolve cornstarch in ¼ cup apple juice. Add cornstarch mixture, green pepper and green onion to carrot mixture. Cover and cook 2 minutes longer or until sauce has thickened. Add shrimp and cook 1 minute or until hot enough to serve. Add almonds to rice. Serve shrimp sauce over rice. Yield: 6 servings.

Smoked Shrimp Amandine

1½	pounds peeled, deveined shrimp, fresh or frozen	¼	teaspoon Worcestershire sauce
1	tablespoon lemon juice	½	cup butter or margarine, melted
1½	teaspoons salt	1	cup sliced almonds
⅛	teaspoon pepper	2	tablespoons chopped parsley (garnish)

Thaw shrimp if frozen. Combine shrimp, lemon juice, salt, pepper and Worcestershire sauce. Place shrimp in 6 well-greased individual aluminum disposable dishes. Sauté almonds in butter until golden brown. Spoon an equal amount of almond-butter mixture over each shrimp serving. Place the containers of shrimp on the rack inside the smoke oven (you may also use conventional oven). Cook in a very slow oven, 250 degrees, 20 to 25 minutes or until shrimp are pink and tender and have a golden smoke color. Garnish with chopped parsley. Yield: 6 servings.

Schooner Steaks Flamingo

2 pounds red snapper steaks, fresh
   or frozen
1 teaspoon salt
⅛ teaspoon pepper
1 cup grated Cheddar cheese

1 tablespoon prepared mustard
2 teaspoons horseradish
2 tablespoons chili sauce
¼ cup butter or margarine, melted

Thaw fish if frozen. Sprinkle both sides with salt and pepper. Combine cheese, mustard, horseradish and chili sauce. Place fish on a well-greased broiler pan about 2 inches from source of heat. Brush with butter and broil 5 to 8 minutes or until lightly brown. Turn carefully and brush other side with butter and broil 5 to 8 minutes longer or until fish flakes easily when tested with a fork. Place cheese mixture on top of fish. Return to broiler for 1 to 2 minutes or until cheese melts and browns. Yield: 6 servings.

Baked Fish

2 to 4 pounds dressed red snapper,
   fresh or frozen
4 thin slices onion
¼ cup butter or margarine, melted
1 teaspoon salt

⅛ teaspoon pepper
3 tablespoons orange juice
   concentrate, undiluted
1 tablespoon soy sauce

Thaw fish if frozen. Preheat oven to 350 degrees. Place fish in a well-greased baking pan. Make 3 diagonal cuts on fish and insert thin slices of onion. Melt butter, mix with salt, pepper, juice and soy sauce; brush over and under fish. Baste occasionally during cooking. Bake in moderate oven at 350 degrees for 20 to 30 minutes or until fish flakes easily when tested with a fork. Yield: 4 to 6 servings.

Snappers got their name in 1878 because of the swift way in which they strike their prey.

Greek Broiled Fish

2 pounds red snapper (or other fish) fillets, skinned, fresh or frozen
1 teaspoon salt
½ teaspoon pepper
2 tablespoons olive oil
3 tablespoons lemon juice
2 cloves garlic, finely minced

3 tablespoons olive oil
½ cup thinly sliced onion rings, cut into fourths
1½ cups chopped parsley
1 cup chopped fresh tomato
1 teaspoon lemon juice

Thaw fish if frozen. Pat dry with paper towels. Sprinkle fillets with salt and pepper. Place in a well-greased 15 x 10 x 1-inch baking pan. Combine 2 tablespoons olive oil, lemon juice and garlic; pour over fillets. Set aside. In a 1-quart saucepan, add 3 tablespoons olive oil and onion; cook until tender but not brown. Stir in parsley and tomatoes and cook just long enough to heat, about 1 minute. Stir in lemon juice. Set aside. Broil fillets about 4 inches from source of heat for 4 to 6 minutes. Turn carefully and baste fillets with pan drippings. Broil 4 to 6 minutes longer or until fish flakes easily when tested with a fork. Spread vegetable mixture evenly over fillets and serve. Yield: 6 servings.

Snapper Sauté

1 pound snapper (or other fish) fillets, fresh or frozen
1 cup sliced onions
1 cup thinly sliced carrots
1 large green pepper, seeded, cut into ¼-inch strips

¼ cup vegetable oil
2 large tomatoes, peeled and cut into wedges
1 teaspoon salt
½ teaspoon sweet basil
¼ teaspoon pepper

Thaw fish if frozen. Cut fillets into ½-inch pieces. Set aside. Sauté onions, carrots and green pepper in oil over medium heat for 10 minutes. Add fish, tomatoes, salt, basil and pepper; mix well. Cover, reduce heat and simmer 15 minutes. Yield: 6 servings.

Baked Stuffed Squid

2 pounds whole squid (approximately 8 medium or 14
 small), fresh or frozen
⅔ cup partially cooked rice
½ cup finely chopped onion
¼ cup chopped green pepper
¼ cup chopped parsley
1 teaspoon dried savory
½ teaspoon salt
¼ teaspoon garlic salt

⅛ teaspoon pepper
Chopped tentacles
1 can (1 pound) tomatoes
¾ cup white wine
½ cup chopped onion
1 tablespoon all-purpose flour
1 teaspoon salt
⅛ teaspoon pepper
⅛ teaspoon liquid hot pepper sauce
1 clove garlic, crushed

Thaw squid if frozen. Preheat oven to 375 degrees. Clean squid. Chop tentacles for stuffing. Combine rice, onion, green pepper, parsley, savory, garlic salt, salt, pepper and tentacles. Makes approximately 2 cups stuffing. Stuff squid loosely. Close opening with small skewer or wooden toothpick. Combine remaining ingredients and place in a well-greased 12 x 8 x 2-inch baking dish. Place squid in a single layer over the tomato mixture and cover with aluminum foil. Bake at 375 degrees for 30 minutes. Remove foil and bake uncovered at 300 degrees for additional 30 minutes. Yield: 4 servings.

Hearty Swordfish Steaks

2 pounds swordfish (or other fish)
 steaks, fresh or frozen
⅔ cup thinly sliced onion
1½ cups chopped fresh mushrooms
⅓ cup chopped tomato
¼ cup chopped green pepper
¼ cup chopped parsley

3 tablespoons diced pimiento
½ cup dry white wine
2 tablespoons lemon juice
1 teaspoon salt
¼ teaspoon dill weed
⅛ teaspoon pepper
Lemon or lime wedges

Thaw fish if frozen. Preheat oven to 350 degrees. Arrange onion slices in bottom of a well-greased 12 x 8 x 2-inch baking dish. Arrange steaks on top of onion slices. Combine remaining vegetables and spread over top of steaks. Combine wine, lemon juice and seasonings. Pour over vegetables. Bake at 350 degrees for 25 to 30 minutes or until fish flakes easily when tested with a fork. Serve with lemon or lime wedges. Yield: 6 servings.

Broiled Swordfish with Macadamia Nut Butter

2 pounds swordfish steaks, fresh or
  frozen
¼ cup all-purpose flour
2 teaspoons paprika
6 tablespoons butter or margarine,
  melted

1 cup macadamia nuts, coarsely
  chopped
1 tablespoon chopped parsley

Thaw fish if frozen. Combine flour and paprika; mix well. Roll steaks in flour
mixture. Place in a single layer on a well-greased 15 x 10 x 1-inch broiler pan. Drizzle
2 tablespoons melted butter over steaks. Broil about 4 inches from source of heat for
10 to 15 minutes or until fish flakes easily when tested with a fork. While steaks are
broiling, sauté macadamia nuts in remaining butter in skillet and allow to turn a
golden brown, stirring constantly. Remove from heat. Add parsley; mix. Pour over
steaks. Serve at once. Yield: 6 servings. **(Photo, page 206)**

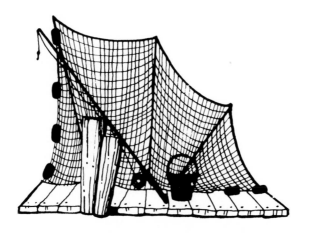

Fish with Spanish Sauce

2 pounds of skinless tilefish (or other fish) fillets, fresh or frozen
¼ cup olive oil
3 garlic cloves, finely chopped or crushed
1 large onion, coarsely chopped
1 medium green pepper, coarsely chopped
1 can (16 ounces) tomatoes, drained

1 can (8 ounces) tomato sauce
Juice of 1 lime
1 bay leaf
1 teaspoon oregano
¾ teaspoon salt
¼ teaspoon pepper
¼ cup bread crumbs
2 tablespoons butter or margarine

Thaw fish if frozen. Preheat oven to 450 degrees. In a 2-quart saucepan, heat olive oil and cook garlic, onion and green pepper until tender-crisp but not browned. Stir in tomatoes, tomato sauce, lime juice, bay leaf, Worcestershire sauce and oregano. Add salt and pepper. Simmer, stirring occasionally, until slightly thickened and well blended, about 45 to 50 minutes. Rinse fillets and pat dry. Place on a lightly oiled, foil-lined baking pan. Cover with sauce and bake at 450 degrees for 10 minutes. Sprinkle with crumbs and dot with butter. Bake 8 to 10 minutes more or until fish flakes easily when tested with a fork and top is lightly browned. Serve with rice. Yield: 4 to 6 servings.

Tangy Glazed Tilefish

2 pounds tilefish (or other fish) fillets, fresh or frozen
⅓ cup butter or margarine, melted
⅓ cup catsup
⅓ cup frozen lemonade concentrate, thawed, undiluted

1 tablespoon prepared mustard
½ teaspoon salt
½ teaspoon garlic salt
1 large bay leaf, crumbled

Thaw fish if frozen. Cut fillets into serving-sized portions. Place fish in a single layer in a 12 x 8 x 2-inch baking dish. Combine remaining ingredients; mix well. Pour over fish; turn to coat evenly. Cover. Marinate in refrigerator at least 30 minutes. Arrange fish, skin side up, on a well-greased 15 x 10 x 1-inch broiler pan. Brush with sauce. Broil about 4 inches from source of heat for 3 to 5 minutes. Turn carefully; brush with sauce. Broil 4 to 5 minutes longer or until fish flakes easily when tested with a fork. Yield: 6 servings.

Fish Fingers with Creamy Vegetable Sauce

1½ pounds tilefish (or other fish) fillets, fresh or frozen
½ teaspoon salt

4 slices bacon, cut in half
Creamy Vegetable Sauce

Thaw fish if frozen. Cut fillets into 8 equal fingers approximately 1 x 3 inches. Sprinkle with salt. Wrap a half-slice of bacon around each finger and secure with a wooden toothpick. Place on a broiler pan about 4 inches from the source of heat and broil for 4 to 6 minutes. Turn carefully and broil 4 to 6 minutes longer or until bacon is crisp and the fish flakes easily when tested with a fork. Place fish fingers on a warm platter and cover with Creamy Vegetable Sauce. Yield: 4 servings. **(Photo, page 148)**

Creamy Vegetable Sauce

2 tablespoons butter or margarine
½ cup finely chopped green pepper
¼ cup finely chopped celery
2 tablespoons finely chopped onion
2 tablespoons grated carrot
2 tablespoons all-purpose flour

½ teaspoon salt
½ teaspoon basil leaves
¼ teaspoon tarragon leaves
1 cup milk
½ cup plain yogurt
1 tablespoon all-purpose flour

In a medium saucepan, melt butter. Cook green pepper, celery, onion and carrot until tender but not brown. Reduce heat; stir 2 tablespoons flour, salt, basil and tarragon into vegetable mixture. Add milk all at once; cook, stirring constantly until thick and bubbly. Stir remaining tablespoon of flour into yogurt; add to sauce. Cook and stir until heated thoroughly. Yield: 1½ cups.

Tilefish Alsacienne

2 pounds tilefish fillets, skinned and deboned, fresh or frozen, cut into 1-inch fingers
1 egg, beaten
½ cup all-purpose flour
Vegetable oil for frying
1 small cabbage
1 tablespoon lemon juice
½ cup water
4 tablespoons butter or margarine
2 tablespoons red or rosé wine (optional)
1 teaspoon salt
½ teaspoon pepper
Cheese Sauce

Thaw fish if frozen. Roll in beaten egg, then flour; fry in 1-inch of oil at 360 degrees for 10 to 12 minutes or until fish flakes easily when tested with a fork. Drain on absorbent paper. Cut cabbage in quarters and remove the stalk. Shred very fine; soak in lemon juice and water for 30 minutes. Drain. In a large skillet melt butter. Add wine, salt, pepper and cabbage. Simmer covered until crisp-tender, about 12 to 15 minutes. Arrange cabbage on bottom of dish; place fish fingers on top and cover with Cheese Sauce. Yield: 6 servings.

Cheese Sauce

2 tablespoons butter or margarine
1 tablespoon all-purpose flour
½ teaspoon salt
¼ teaspoon pepper
1 cup milk
½ cup grated Cheddar cheese

Melt butter in saucepan. Add flour, salt and pepper. Pour in the milk and stir until thick and bubbly. Remove from heat. Add grated cheese, stirring until cheese melts. Serve immediately while warm. Yield: 1¼ cups.

Fish à la Pepper

1½ pounds tilefish (or other fish) fillets, fresh or frozen
½ cup boiling water
½ teaspoon instant chicken broth
1 teaspoon garlic salt
½ teaspoon lemon-pepper seasoning
2 tablespoons vegetable oil

¼ cup tomato sauce
1 teaspoon capers
½ medium green pepper, seeded, cut into rings
½ medium red pepper, seeded, cut into rings

Thaw fish if frozen; cut into 4-inch pieces. Dissolve instant chicken broth in water. Sprinkle fish with garlic salt and lemon-pepper. Cook fish in oil in a 12-inch nonstick skillet over moderate heat for 5 minutes, turning often. Add broth, tomato sauce and capers to fish. Reduce heat; cover and simmer 10 minutes. Top with pepper rings and cook uncovered 5 minutes longer or until fish flakes easily when tested with a fork and peppers are tender. Yield: 4 servings.

Cider-Baked Trout

1½ pounds skinned sea trout (or other fish) fillets, fresh or frozen
¼ teaspoon salt
1 cup apple cider
½ cup water
2 tablespoons butter or margarine
1 tablespoon minced green onion

1½ tablespoons all-purpose flour
2 tablespoons half-and-half
½ teaspoon lemon juice
½ teaspoon seasoned salt
¼ teaspoon pepper
1 tablespoon chopped fresh parsley (garnish)

Thaw fish if frozen. Preheat oven to 350 degrees. Place fillets in greased 13 x 9 x 2-inch baking dish. Sprinkle with salt. Combine apple cider and water; pour over fillets. Cover with foil. Bake at 350 degrees for 10 to 12 minutes or until fish flakes easily when tested with a fork. Remove to a serving platter and keep warm. Strain cooking liquid and set aside. In a small saucepan melt butter and cook onion until tender but not brown. Blend in flour; cook 1 minute, stirring constantly. Add reserved liquid gradually. Cook over medium heat, stirring constantly, until thickened. Stir in remaining ingredients, reserving parsley for garnishing; heat through. Spoon sauce over fillets. Sprinkle with chopped parsley. Yield: 4 servings.

Trout Wellington

2 sea trout fillets (½ pound each),
 fresh or frozen
1 teaspoon salt
½ teaspoon pepper
1 tablespoon lemon juice

1 can (8 ounces) refrigerated
 crescent rolls
Crab Stuffing
Egg yolk for glazing
Water

Thaw fish if frozen. Preheat oven to 425 degrees. Season fillets with salt, pepper and lemon juice. Set aside. Make crab stuffing. Separate crescent roll dough into 2 portions. On a lightly floured board, roll out each portion of dough and cut to form fish shapes. First fish-shaped dough assembly should measure 2 inches longer and 1 inch wider than fillet. Cut second fish-shape 2 inches longer and 3 inches wider than fillet. Set aside. Spread a thin layer of stuffing on the first fish-shaped dough assembly. Lay fillet on this and spread ½ of crab stuffing on top of the fillet. Layer with remaining fillet; cover top and sides with remaining stuffing. Place second dough assembly on top; pinch edges together to seal. Use scrap dough to make fins, eyes and gill openings. With a round half-inch cutter, form scale impressions. Brush with egg yolk and water mixture. Place in a floured baking pan and refrigerate 1 hour. Remove to a greased shallow baking pan. Cook at 425 degrees for 10 minutes; reduce heat to 350 degrees and bake 10 minutes or until fish crust is brown and fish flakes easily when tested with a fork. Serve warm with vegetables or fruit. Yield: 4 servings.

Crab Stuffing

½ pound crab meat, fresh, frozen or
 pasteurized
1 egg white
⅓ cup whipping cream
½ cup coarsely chopped celery

½ cup bread crumbs
¼ cup melted butter
1 teaspoon lemon-pepper seasoning

Thaw crab if frozen. Remove any remaining shell particles. Place all ingredients in a processor and mince to form a smooth spread. If mixture is too thick, add more cream.

Sea Trout with Niçoise Dressing

1½ pounds sea trout (or other fish)
   fillets, fresh or frozen
2 teaspoons lemon juice
¼ teaspoon salt
   Niçoise Dressing

Salad greens
6 cherry tomatoes, cut in halves
Parsley (garnish)
French bread

Thaw fish if frozen; pat dry. Preheat oven to 425 degrees. Cut fish into serving-sized portions. Brush both sides of fish with lemon juice; sprinkle with salt. Place fish skin side down in a well-greased 13 x 9-inch baking pan. Bake at 425 degrees for 10 to 15 minutes or until fish flakes easily when tested with a fork. Remove fish from oven; drain. Prepare Niçoise Dressing and spoon over warm baked fish. Chill 1 hour. Wash salad greens; shred and arrange on a large serving platter. Reserving dressing, carefully remove chilled fish and place with tomatoes on salad greens. Garnish with parsley. Spoon reserved dressing over all. Serve with French bread. Yield: 4 servings.

Niçoise Dressing

½ cup olive oil
3 tablespoons wine vinegar
2 tablespoons capers
3 cloves garlic, minced
1 thinly sliced green onion (white part only)

1 teaspoon parsley flakes
½ teaspoon dried basil
¼ teaspoon salt
⅛ teaspoon white pepper

Combine all ingredients in shaker or jar with a tight-fitting lid; shake well. Spoon Niçoise Dressing over warm baked fish. Yield: ¾ cups.

Sea Trout Sesame

1½ pounds skinned sea trout (or other fish) fillets, fresh or frozen
¾ cup dairy sour cream
¼ cup grated Parmesan cheese
1 tablespoon lemon juice
1 tablespoon grated onion

1 teaspoon garlic salt
⅛ teaspoon white pepper
1 cup fresh bread crumbs
½ cup sesame seeds
Vegetable oil

Thaw fish if frozen; pat dry. Preheat oven to 400 degrees. Cut into serving-sized portions. In a mixing bowl, combine sour cream, Parmesan cheese, lemon juice, grated onion, garlic salt and pepper. In a separate bowl, mix bread crumbs and sesame seeds. Dip both sides of fillets in sour cream mixture; coat with bread crumb-sesame seed mixture. Place fillets on a well-greased shallow baking pan. Drizzle top of fillets lightly with vegetable oil. Bake at 400 degrees for 20 to 25 minutes or until coating is golden brown and fish flakes easily when tested with a fork. Yield: 4 servings.

Quick Barbecued Fish

1½ pounds sea trout (or other fish) fillets, skinned, fresh or frozen
⅓ cup barbecue sauce

1 can (3 ounces) French-fried onions, chopped, or 1½ cups crushed barbecued potato chips

Thaw fish if frozen. Cut fillets into 4 serving-sized portions. Dip fish in barbecue sauce. Place fillets in a single layer on a platter with thick portions to the outside edge of dish. Sprinkle with crushed onions or chips. Cook in microwave oven, uncovered, on high 6 to 8 minutes, rotating the platter after 3 minutes. Yield: 4 servings.

Sea Trout with Pecan Rice

2 pounds sea trout (or other fish) fillets, fresh or frozen
½ cup all-purpose cornmeal
1 teaspoon salt
¼ teaspoon pepper
¼ cup vegetable oil
½ cup finely chopped pecans
Pecan Rice
Lime wedges (garnish)

Thaw fish if frozen. Preheat oven to 400 degrees. Skin fillets and cut into serving-sized portions. Combine cornmeal, salt and pepper. Roll in cornmeal mixture. Place on a well-greased 15 x 10 x 1-inch baking pan. Pour oil evenly over fillets. Bake in a hot oven, 400 degrees, for 20 to 25 minutes or until fish flakes easily when tested with a fork. Sprinkle pecans over fillets 2 to 3 minutes before end of cooking time. Serve with Pecan Rice. Garnish with lime wedges. Yield: 6 servings. **(Photo, page 128)**

Pecan Rice

1 cup uncooked brown rice
¼ cup finely chopped onion
2 tablespoons butter or margarine
½ cup finely chopped pecans
2 tablespoons minced parsley
¼ teaspoon basil
¼ teaspoon ground ginger
¼ teaspoon salt
¼ teaspoon pepper

Prepare rice according to package directions. In a 1½-quart saucepan, cook onion in butter until tender but not brown. Add hot cooked rice, pecans, parsley, basil, ginger, salt and pepper; mix well. Serve with fish. Yield: 6 servings.

Planked Trout with Potatoes Duchesse

1 4-pound sea trout, dressed with head and tail on, fresh or frozen
8 tablespoons butter, melted
1 fresh whole lemon
Salt and pepper

Potatoes Duchesse
Fresh parsley sprigs (garnish)
1 lemon cut lengthwise into wedges (garnish)

Thaw fish if frozen. Preheat oven to 450 degrees. Rinse trout under cool running tap water and pat dry with paper towel. Season inside and out with salt, pepper and juice of ½ lemon. Place 4 tablespoons butter inside the trout and use skewers and string to close the cavity. Grease the inside of a baking pan large enough to hold the trout. Place the fish in the pan and brush with 2 tablespoons melted butter. Bake 20 minutes at 450 degrees. Remove from oven and carefully transfer to the center of an oak plank large enough to hold the fish comfortably. Remove skin from fish body, leaving head and tail on. Brush with juice of ½ lemon and 2 tablespoons melted butter. Using a pastry bag fitted with a large star tip, pipe the Potatoes Duchesse in separate rosettes around the trout. Brush with melted butter and broil 2 to 3 minutes to brown lightly. Serve at once. Garnish with parsley sprigs and lemon wedges. Yield: 4 servings.

Potatoes Duchesse

6 medium boiling potatoes, peeled and quartered
1 tablespoon salt
2 egg yolks
3 tablespoons butter, melted

2 tablespoons heavy cream
½ teaspoon white pepper
½ teaspoon salt
⅛ teaspoon nutmeg

Cook potatoes and 1 tablespoon salt in boiling water until potatoes are done. Drain immediately. Beat until fluffy. In a separate bowl, mix together 2 egg yolks, butter, heavy cream and seasonings. Slowly pour into puréed potatoes, beating gently. Do not allow potatoes to become too thin as they will need to be firm to make the rosettes.

Seafood Lasagna

1 pound sea trout fillets, fresh or frozen

½ pound cooked, deveined medium shrimp, fresh or frozen

8 ounces lasagna noodles

1½ cups prepared Italian sauce

15 ounces low-fat ricotta cheese

2 tablespoons grated Parmesan cheese

Thaw seafood if frozen. Preheat oven to 400 degrees. Poach fillets and drain. (To poach: Bring small amount of water in skillet to boiling point. Reduce heat and place fillets in single layer in skillet. Simmer until fish flakes easily when tested with a fork, taking care to retain shape of fillets.) Cook lasagna noodles according to package directions. Line bottom of a shallow 2-quart oblong well-greased baking dish with ⅓ of noodles. Carefully place sea trout over noodles, cover with ⅓ of sauce and half of ricotta cheese. Add another layer of lasagna noodles. Place shrimp over noodles and spread an additional ⅓ of sauce. Top with remaining ricotta cheese. Add another layer of noodles. Spread remaining sauce over noodles. Sprinkle with Parmesan cheese. Bake at 400 degrees for 10 to 15 minutes or until heated thoroughly. Yield: 8 servings.

The age of a fish is determined by growth rings on its scales, like the rings of a tree trunk.

Honey-Almond Tuna Steaks

1½ pounds yellowfin tuna steaks, fresh or frozen
3 tablespoons lime juice
2 tablespoons vegetable oil
2 tablespoons honey
2 tablespoons soy sauce
¼ teaspoon ginger
¼ teaspoon cinnamon
⅓ cup slivered almonds

Thaw steaks if frozen. Place fish in a single layer in a shallow dish. Combine lime juice, oil, honey, soy sauce, ginger and cinnamon. Pour mixture over steaks and cover. Marinate in refrigerator 1 to 2 hours, turning once. Remove steaks, reserving marinade for basting. Place on a well-greased broiling pan. Broil about 4 inches from source of heat for 3 minutes; baste steaks and broil 2 minutes longer. Turn and baste. Cook 3 minutes, baste; place slivered almonds on top of steaks. Cook 1 to 2 minutes longer or until tuna has a slightly pink center. Yield: 4 servings.

Polynesian Yellowfin Tuna Steaks

2 pounds yellowfin tuna steaks, fresh or frozen
⅓ cup soy sauce
1 can (8 ounces) unsweetened crushed pineapple
2 tablespoons catsup
2 tablespoons vegetable oil
2 tablespoons finely chopped parsley
1 tablespoon lemon juice
1 clove garlic, finely chopped
½ teaspoon oregano
½ teaspoon pepper

Thaw steaks if frozen. Cut steaks into serving-sized portions. Place fish in single layer in a shallow dish. Combine all remaining ingredients. Pour sauce over fish and marinate in refrigerator for one hour, turning once. Remove fish, reserving marinade for basting; place fish on a well-greased broiler pan. Broil about 4 inches from source of heat for 3 to 4 minutes. Turn carefully and baste with remaining marinade. Broil an additional 3 minutes longer or until tuna has a slightly pink center. Yield: 6 servings.

Jiffy Broiled Yellowfin Tuna

2 pounds yellowfin tuna steaks,
  fresh or frozen
2 tablespoons vegetable oil
2 tablespoons soy sauce
2 tablespoons Worcestershire sauce

1 teaspoon paprika
½ teaspoon chili powder
½ teaspoon garlic powder
⅛ teaspoon liquid hot pepper sauce
Lemon wedges (garnish)

Thaw steaks if frozen. Place steaks in single layer on a well-greased broiler pan. Combine remaining ingredients except lemon wedges to make sauce. Pour sauce over steaks. Broil about 4 inches from source of heat for 3 to 4 minutes. Turn carefully and baste with sauce. Broil 3 to 4 minutes longer or until tuna has a slightly pink center. Yield: 6 servings.

Oriental Yellowfin Tuna

½ pound cooked, flaked yellowfin
  tuna
1 cup chicken broth
1 tablespoon soy sauce
½ teaspoon ginger
⅛ teaspoon black pepper
2 tablespoons cornstarch
1 tablespoon vegetable oil
2 cups celery, cut diagonally

1½ cups red onions, sliced
1 can (8 ounces) bean sprouts,
  drained
1 can (6 ounces) bamboo shoots,
  drained
1 can (4 ounces) sliced mushrooms,
  drained
2 cups cooked rice

Mix chicken broth, soy sauce, ginger and pepper. Stir in cornstarch until dissolved. Heat oil in frying pan or wok over highest heat. When hot, toss in celery and onions; stir-fry 1 minute. Add bean sprouts, bamboo shoots and mushrooms. Stir broth mixture and add to vegetables. Stir and cook just until sauce is thickened. Add tuna and stir until sauce is clear. Serve over rice. Yield: 4 servings.

Sailor's Yellowfin Tuna

2 pounds yellowfin tuna steaks,
  fresh or frozen
3 cups water
¾ cup lemon juice
1 cup chicken broth
⅓ cup sugar
⅓ cup lemon juice
2 tablespoons water
1 tablespoon dry sherry

1½ teaspoons soy sauce
2 tablespoons cornstarch
1 bag (10 ounces) fresh spinach,
  coarsely shredded
½ teaspoon salt
¼ teaspoon white pepper
½ cup all-purpose flour
Vegetable oil
Lemon wedges

Thaw fish if frozen. Combine 3 cups water and ¾ cup lemon juice. Place steaks in shallow baking dish and marinate in lemon juice mixture in refrigerator for 30 minutes. In a 1-quart saucepan, combine chicken broth, sugar, ⅓ cup lemon juice, 2 tablespoons water, sherry, soy sauce and cornstarch; mix well. Cook over medium heat, stirring constantly, until smooth and thick. Keep warm. Place fresh spinach evenly on serving platter. Remove fish from marinade and dry. Sprinkle with salt and pepper. Dredge steaks in flour. Place in heavy frypan which contains about ⅛ inch of oil, hot but not smoking. Fry at moderate heat for 2 to 3 minutes. Turn carefully and cook 2 to 3 minutes longer or until tuna has a slightly pink center. Drain on absorbent paper. Arrange fish on spinach. Pour hot lemon sauce over fish and spinach. Garnish with lemon wedges. Yield: 6 servings.

Charcoal-Grilled Tuna Steaks

2 pounds yellowfin tuna steaks,
  fresh or frozen
½ cup vegetable oil
¼ cup lemon juice
2 teaspoons salt

½ teaspoon Worcestershire sauce
¼ teaspoon white pepper
⅛ teaspoon liquid hot pepper sauce
Paprika

Thaw steaks if frozen. Cut into serving-sized portions and place in a well-greased hinged wire grill. Combine remaining ingredients, except paprika. Baste fish with sauce and sprinkle with paprika. Cook about 4 inches from moderately hot coals for 5 to 6 minutes. Turn, baste with sauce and sprinkle with paprika; cook for 4 to 5 minutes longer or until tuna has a slightly pink center. Yield: 6 servings.

SAUCES

Lemon-Caper Sauce

½ cup mayonnaise or salad dressing
1 tablespoon drained capers
1 tablespoon lemon juice

½ teaspoon Worcestershire sauce
2 drops liquid hot pepper sauce

Combine all ingredients and chill. Yield: ⅔ cup.

Peppy Seafood Sauce

½ cup chili sauce
½ cup catsup
3 tablespoons lemon juice
1 tablespoon horseradish
1 tablespoon mayonnaise or salad dressing

1 teaspoon Worcestershire sauce
½ teaspoon grated onion
¼ teaspoon salt
3 drops liquid hot pepper sauce
⅛ teaspoon pepper

Combine all ingredients and chill thoroughly. Yield: 1½ cups.

Lemon Cream Sauce

½ cup dairy sour cream
1 tablespoon lemon juice
1 tablespoon chopped parsley

1 teaspoon horseradish
¼ teaspoon salt

Combine all ingredients and chill. Yield: ⅔ cup.

Cool Blender Sauce

1 egg
1 teaspoon salt
1 teaspoon sugar
1 teaspoon prepared mustard
2 drops liquid hot pepper sauce
⅛ teaspoon pepper
1 teaspoon instant minced onion

3 tablespoons lemon juice
¾ cup mayonnaise
¾ cup salad oil
⅓ cup chopped parsley
1 clove garlic, minced
1 tablespoon horseradish

Put into blender the first nine ingredients. Cover, blend a few seconds, uncover, add oil slowly, keeping motor running. Blend until thick and smooth. Add parsley, garlic and horseradish and blend until smooth. Yield: 2¼ cups.

Cocktail Sauce

1½ cups catsup
1 tablespoon lemon juice
1 tablespoon Worcestershire sauce
2 tablespoons horseradish

1½ teaspoons sugar
¼ teaspoon salt
⅛ teaspoon liquid hot pepper sauce
⅛ teaspoon pepper

Combine all ingredients and chill. Yield: 1¾ cups.

Cucumber Sauce

1 tablespoon butter or margarine
1 tablespoon all-purpose flour
½ cup milk
1 cup finely diced, peeled cucumbers, drained

½ cup mayonnaise
2 tablespoons lemon or lime juice
½ teaspoon salt
¼ teaspoon paprika
⅛ teaspoon pepper

Melt butter and blend in flour, add milk. Cook over medium heat until thick, stirring constantly. Remove from heat, add remaining ingredients and chill. Yield: 2¼ cups.

Dill Sauce

¾ cup mayonnaise or salad dressing
½ cup dairy sour cream
½ teaspoon dill weed

½ teaspoon sugar
½ teaspoon salt
⅛ teaspoon pepper

Combine all ingredients. Mix thoroughly. Chill. Yield: 1¼ cups.

Sour Cream Sauce

⅓ sour cream
4 teaspoons white wine
1 teaspoon lemon juice

¼ teaspoon salt
¼ teaspoon dill weed

Combine all ingredients and mix thoroughly. Chill at least 1 hour to blend flavors. Yield: ½ cup.

Piquant Sauce

⅓ cup dairy sour cream
2 tablespoons French dressing

1 teaspoon lemon juice

Combine all ingredients and mix thoroughly. Chill. Yield: ½ cup.

Sweet and Sour Sauce

½ cup catsup
⅓ cup orange marmalade
3 tablespoons red wine vinegar
1 tablespoon soy sauce

1 tablespoon lemon juice
2 teaspoons dry mustard
1 teaspoon horseradish
¼ teaspoon curry powder

In a saucepan mix all ingredients together and heat until hot and bubbly. Serve warm. Yield: 1 cup.

Cranberry-Orange Sauce

⅓ cup sugar
2 teaspoons cornstarch
½ cup orange juice

½ cup water
1 cup raw cranberries
2 teaspoons grated orange rind

Combine sugar and cornstarch in a 2-quart saucepan and mix. Add orange juice and water; cook, stirring constantly, until mixture comes to a boil. Add cranberries and cook 5 minutes or until skins on cranberries pop, stirring occasionally. Fold in orange rind. Yield: 1¼ cups.

Plantation Hot Sauce

½ cup honey
½ cup prepared mustard
½ cup cider vinegar
¼ cup Worcestershire sauce

2 teaspoons liquid hot pepper sauce
1 teaspoon salt
1 tablespoon chopped parsley

Blend honey and prepared mustard; stir in remaining ingredients. Heat to boiling. Yield: 1½ cups.

White Sauce

2 tablespoons butter or margarine
2 tablespoons all-purpose flour
¼ teaspoon salt

⅛ teaspoon pepper
1 cup milk

Melt butter in saucepan. Stir in flour, salt and pepper. Add milk and cook until thickened and smooth, stirring constantly. Yield: 1 cup.

Cheddar-Tomato Sauce

4 slices bacon, chopped
½ cup chopped onion
½ cup chopped green pepper
1 can (10½ ounces) condensed tomato soup

1 cup grated sharp Cheddar cheese
¼ cup milk
1 teaspoon Worcestershire sauce
½ teaspoon prepared mustard
⅛ teaspoon pepper

Fry bacon until crisp. Drain bacon, leaving 1 tablespoon of bacon drippings. Add onion and green pepper and cook until tender. Add remaining ingredients. Heat until cheese melts, stirring constantly. Yield: 2½ cups.

Hasty Horseradish Sauce

½ cup horseradish sauce

¼ cup mayonnaise or salad dressing

In a 1-quart saucepan, combine ingredients; heat, stirring constantly. Do not boil. Yield: ¾ cup.

Mustard Sauce I

2 tablespoons dry mustard
½ teaspoon cornstarch
¼ teaspoon salt

¼ cup water
¼ cup light corn syrup
1 teaspoon vinegar

Blend mustard, cornstarch, salt and 2 tablespoons water until smooth. Stir in remaining ingredients. Bring to a boil; remove from heat and cool. Yield: ½ cup. Eat with care — it's hot!

Mustard Sauce II

2 teaspoons butter or margarine
½ cup dairy sour cream
1½ tablespoons prepared mustard

½ teaspoon parsley flakes
⅛ teaspoon salt

Melt butter and add remaining ingredients. Heat at a very low temperature, just until warm, stirring occasionally. Do not boil. Yield: ⅔ cup.

Spicy Sauce

½ cup hot barbecue sauce

¼ cup pineapple preserves

In a ½-quart saucepan, combine ingredients and bring to a boil, stirring constantly. Yield: ¾ cup.

Macadamia Nut Sauce

1 cup macadamia nuts, coarsely
   chopped

½ cup butter or margarine, melted
1 tablespoon chopped parsley

Brown nuts in butter. Add parsley. Yield: 1 cup.

Sweet and Sour Sauce

1 cup apple juice, divided
¼ cup vinegar
3 tablespoons sugar
2 tablespoons catsup
1 tablespoon grated onion

1 tablespoon butter
2 teaspoons soy sauce
⅛ teaspoon salt
2 tablespoons cornstarch

Combine ¾ cup apple juice, vinegar, sugar, catsup, onion, butter, soy sauce and salt in a saucepan and bring to a boiling point. Dissolve cornstarch in remaining ¼ cup apple juice. Add gradually to hot sauce and cook until thickened, stirring constantly. Yield: 1½ cups.

Lemon Relish

½ cup dairy sour cream
¼ cup crushed pineapple, drained
2 tablespoons finely chopped green pepper
1 tablespoon finely chopped onion

1 tablespoon light brown sugar
1½ teaspoons grated lemon peel
¼ teaspoon dry mustard
¼ teaspoon celery salt
⅛ teaspoon ground cloves

Combine all ingredients. Chill. Yield: 1 cup.

Tartar Sauce

½ cup mayonnaise
1 tablespoon minced onion
1 tablespoon minced pickles

1 tablespoon minced parsley
1 tablespoon minced olives

Mix all ingredients thoroughly and chill. Yield: ¾ cup.

Tartar Sauce Supreme

⅓ cup mayonnaise
2 tablespoons milk
2 tablespoons chopped sweet pickle

2 tablespoons chopped toasted almonds
½ teaspoon salt

Combine all ingredients and chill. Yield: ⅔ cup.

Cranberry Tartar Sauce

½ cup mayonnaise or salad dressing
¼ cup diced jellied cranberry sauce
1 tablespoon chopped onion

1 tablespoon chopped sweet pickle
1 tablespoon chopped parsley
1 tablespoon chopped olives

Mix thoroughly and chill. Yield: 1 cup.

Horseradish Cream Sauce

½ cup dairy sour cream
3 tablespoons mayonnaise
2 tablespoons Dijon mustard
2 teaspoons grated onion
2 teaspoons lemon juice

2 teaspoons cream-style prepared horseradish
½ teaspoon garlic powder
¼ teaspoon cayenne

Combine all ingredients and mix thoroughly. Chill. Yield: 1 cup.

Louis Dressing

½ cup mayonnaise or salad dressing
2 tablespoons chili sauce
2 tablespoons chopped green onions and tops
2 tablespoons chopped green pepper
1 hard-cooked egg, chopped

1 tablespoon chopped pimiento-stuffed olives
½ teaspoon lemon juice
⅛ teaspoon salt
⅛ teaspoon pepper

Combine all ingredients and chill. Yield: 1½ cups.

Deluxe Dressing

¾ cup mayonnaise or salad dressing
¼ cup catsup

1½ teaspoons lemon juice
½ teaspoon chili powder

Combine all ingredients and mix thoroughly. Chill. Yield: 1 cup.

Rémoulade Dressing

1 cup mayonnaise or salad dressing
¼ cup chopped onion
¼ cup chopped pickle
1 hard-cooked egg, chopped

1 tablespoon lime juice
1 teaspoon capers, chopped
½ teaspoon liquid hot pepper sauce

Combine all ingredients and mix thoroughly. Chill. Yield: 1½ cups.

Green Goddess Dressing

½ cup mayonnaise or salad dressing
¼ cup dairy sour cream
2 tablespoons chopped chives
2 tablespoons chopped parsley

1 tablespoon lemon juice
½ teaspoon Worcestershire sauce
¼ teaspoon finely chopped garlic

Combine all ingredients in blender; process 10-15 seconds. Chill. Yield: 1 cup.

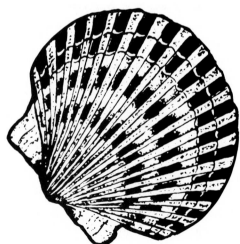

Avocado Cream Sauce

½ cup mashed avocado
⅓ cup dairy sour cream
2 tablespoons lemon juice
½ teaspoon sugar

¼ teaspoon chili powder
¼ teaspoon salt
¼ teaspoon liquid hot pepper sauce
1 clove garlic, crushed

Combine all ingredients and mix by hand or in blender until smooth. Chill.
Yield: 1 cup.

Orange Cream Sauce

¼ cup whipping cream
2 tablespoons orange juice

1 tablespoon mayonnaise or salad dressing

Whip cream. Blend mayonnaise and orange juice; fold into whipped cream.
Yield: ⅔ cup.

Honey-Celery Seed Dressing

½ cup honey
½ cup cider or red wine vinegar
⅓ cup salad oil
3 tablespoons sugar

¾ teaspoon dry mustard
½ teaspoon paprika
½ teaspoon celery seed
½ teaspoon salt

Combine ingredients; mix well and chill. Yield: 1⅓ cups.

Orange Barbecue Sauce

½ cup orange juice
⅓ cup catsup
3 tablespoons brown sugar
2 tablespoons lemon juice

1 tablespoon instant minced onion
1 tablespoon soy sauce
¼ teaspoon salt

In a ½-quart saucepan, combine all ingredients and heat. Yield: 1 cup.

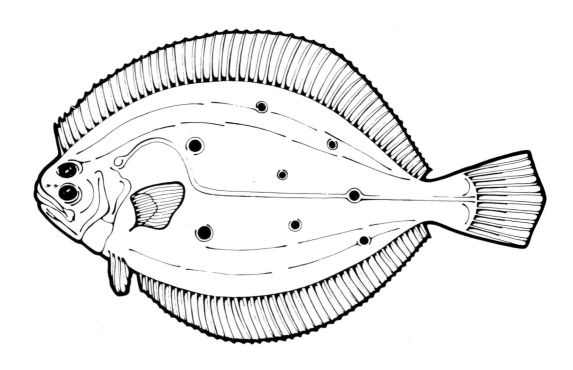

A Brief History of Southeastern Fishing

Most of us are familiar with the Bible's commercial fishermen who were asked to lay down their nets and become "fishers of men." They are part of a long tradition of fishing as a way of life, and that tradition, greatly enhanced by technology, was part of what European settlers brought to America with them.

Historians familiar with St. Augustine, Pensacola and other coastal areas of the Gulf of Mexico and the South Atlantic Ocean would be quick to add that the European fishermen landed in a world already populated by a fishing people. Native Americans were adept at harvesting both fish and shellfish. Indian

Key West Upper Harbor, circa 1900

mounds being examined today contain oyster, clam and mussel shells and bones from various types of fish. Certain spears and traps recovered from these sites have been identified as tools for harvesting seafood from the warm, unpolluted waters of the South.

Influenced by these two segments of fishing history, early settlers of the United States were as enthusiastic about seafood as today's consumers. One of our most illustrious founding fathers, Benjamin Franklin, operated several retail fish markets in Philadelphia. The power of the British king to grant fishing rights to the New World explorers of his choice was an important economic tool during our country's formative years. Salted fish transported on sailing vessels from the colonies to Europe was quite a profitable trade.

The transition from those earliest days to today's modern and safe fishing vessels has been eventful. Many historians consider Fernandina Beach, Florida, as the birthplace of the shrimping industry. Small steam and "one-lung" gasoline engines powered small wooden craft leaving the fish houses of Fernandina Beach for the long voyage of several miles along the unpopulated beaches of northeast Florida.

Finding markets for shrimp was difficult in the beginning. The many bars along the coast proved to be the first good customers. Old-timers who remember those days report that bar owners would be sure to put plenty of salt on their shrimp so that the

Pinching heads off shrimp, 1947

246

Letting out shrimp net, 1947

patrons would drink more beer. For fishermen, this scheme was a real boost because the next step was buying more shrimp to salt down. Today, the first bar owner who salted his shrimp is also recognized as one of the earliest marketing geniuses of the seafood industry.

From such small beginnings, the shrimping industry has become the most valuable of all seafood enterprises, producing nearly 400 million pounds of shrimp worth in excess of a billion dollars at the dock level. After value is added through processing and distribution, the shrimp industry is worth three to five billion dollars to the U.S. economy —not bad for a little critter first utilized in a small Florida town.

With shrimp, as with all fisheries, a clean and healthy environment is

Oysters, 1957

Oyster shuckers, 1909

essential to maintaining a plentiful supply of the product.

Southern oysters got their start as commercial creatures in another small Florida town, Apalachicola. In its heyday, this small port town had as many as twenty-five four-masted schooners anchored in the bay to pick up cotton for shipment to Europe. The cotton merchants looked forward to their stay in Apalachicola because they were able to partake of the town's raw oysters.

By the turn of the century, the oyster industry was thriving, and sailing ships with young oyster shuckers would go into the bay and spend several nights shucking oysters

Oyster boat, 1909

Women doing crab, 1956

Crawfish man, 1958

for shipment to northern markets. Because three rivers flow into the Apalachicola, it is perfect for growing oysters. The bay is shallow with the salinity needed to produce a mature oyster in less than eighteen months. Compare this with the two and one-half years of the growth cycle in some northern climes, and it is easy to understand why this relatively small bay system can produce so astoundingly.

For most of the species found in the South, Louisiana has by far the most extensive potential for fish and shellfish production because of extensive uninhabited marsh area. The Carolinas and Virginia can also boast about their seafood industry. Sea scallops, flounder, crabs and oysters make Virginia a dominant force, and the shrimp, crab, whiting, and flounder found in the Carolinas are truly outstanding. Low-country Carolina cooking is known throughout the world. They have a saying in South Carolina that people must never put "she-crab" soup on their foreheads because their tongues will beat their brains out trying to get to the soup. It's that good.

While Mississippi and Alabama have relatively short coastlines, the

Sorting calico scallops

Catch on a snapper boat, circa 1920

Snapper boat Washakie *in Pensacola harbor, circa 1920*

Brunswick fleet, 1921

seafood harvested in their area is outstanding. The oysters, shrimp and fish from these two states often find their way into distinctive local recipes.

One of the historical photos in *Southern Seafood Classics* features six men, one sailboat, two skiffs, one tin shed and a hog. This is one of our earliest disposal systems at work. The men would clean the fish and let the viscera drip into the water, where it would either sink and be eaten by the crabs or float to where the hog was standing. The hog would devour the remains and gain weight at the same time. Chances are that their particular system would not be permitted today, but in the old days, it was not only efficient but also inexpensive.

Few people today realize exactly how far the seafood industry in this country has come. The men and women from all the coastal towns in the South are responsible for making an enormous variety of seafood products available to their fellow citizens throughout the United States. As you try the recipes in this cookbook, think for just a moment about what it took to put the seafood on your table. Conjure up a scene of small boats, of sailboats, of immigrants trying to settle a new land and provide a living for their families. Think of the untold opportunities of which they took advantage while turning their dreams into realities for the future. Think also of the new and continuing opportunities that await today's fishermen in the deeper parts of the Gulf and the South Atlantic. Then you can understand that you are participating in a history that is long and proud.

Coastal traders, circa 1900

Southeastern

◆ Gulf Coast ◆

SPECIES	Jan.	Feb.	March	Apr.	May	June	July	Aug.	Sept.	Oct.	Nov.	Dec.
Black Sea Bass	●	●	●									●
Bluefish	●							●	●	●	●	●
Croaker						●	●	●	●	●		
Flounder									●	●	●	●
Grouper			●	●	●	●	●	●	●			
King Mackerel	●	●	●									
Mullet								●	●	●	●	●
Pompano	●	●	●	●	●						●	●
Redfish	●	●						●	●	●	●	●
Red Snapper					●	●	●	●	●	●	●	●
Sea Trout	●	●							●	●	●	●
Shark			●	●	●	●	●	●	●			
Sheepshead	●	●	●	●								●
Spanish Mackerel	●	●	●	●							●	●
Swordfish	●	●	●	●	●							●
Tilefish				●	●	●	●	●	●	●		
Blue Crab				●	●	●	●	●	●	●		
Clams												
Oysters	●	●	●	●	●				●	●	●	●
Rock Shrimp	●						●	●	●	●	●	●
Scallops												
Shrimp	●	●	●	●	●	●	●	●	●	●	●	●
Spiny Lobster	●	●	●					●	●	●	●	●
Stone Crab Claws	●	●	●	●	◖					◖	●	●

Lack of symbol indicates limited availability of fresh seafood.   Symbols indicate months of greater availability of fresh seafood.   Most products available all year in the frozen form.

Seafood Availability

◆ Atlantic Coast ◆

SPECIES	Jan.	Feb.	March	Apr.	May	June	July	Aug.	Sept.	Oct.	Nov.	Dec.
Black Sea Bass	●	●	●	●	●	●	●	●				
Bluefish	●	●	●	●								
Croaker					●	●	●	●	●	●		
Flounder										●	●	●
Grouper		●	●	●	●	●	●					
King Mackerel	●	●	●	●	●							
Mullet								●	●	●	●	●
Pompano	●	●	●								●	●
Redfish	●	●	●							●	●	●
Red Snapper			●	●	●	●	●					
Sea Trout	●	●	●	●								●
Shark		●	●	●	●	●						
Sheepshead									●	●	●	●
Spanish Mackerel	●	●	●									●
Swordfish			●	●	●	●	●					
Tilefish					●	●	●	●	●	●	●	●
Blue Crab				●	●	●	●	●	●	●		
Clams	●	●	●	●	●	●	●	●	●	●	●	●
Oysters	●	●	●	●	●				●	●	●	●
Rock Shrimp	●	●	●							●	●	●
Scallops					●	●	●	●	●	●	●	
Shrimp	●					●	●	●	●	●	●	●
Spiny Lobster	●	●	●					●	●	●	●	●
Stone Crab Claws	●	●	●	●	◖					◖	●	●

Mullet

135 Calories
19 Grams Protein
6 Grams Fat
1 Gram Carbohydrate

Red Snapper

104 Calories
20 Grams Protein
3 Grams Fat
0 Carbohydrate

Flounder

86 Calories
19 Grams Protein
1 Gram Fat
0 Carbohydrate

Red Drum

85 Calories
19 Grams Protein
1 Gram Fat
0 Carbohydrate

Sea Trout

88 Calories
17 Grams Protein
2 Grams Fat
0 Carbohydrate

Yellowfin Tuna

123 Calories
24 Grams Protein
4 Grams Fat
0 Carbohydrate

Preparation tips for low-calorie, low-fat cooking: Instead of frying, bake or broil seafood with small amounts of butter, margarine or salad dressing used for flavoring. One tablespoon of butter or margarine adds 108 calories. Poaching in water, white wine or fish stock adds variety without calories. Use 1/4 cup liquid per pound of seafood for poaching and be sure not to overcook.

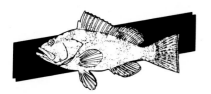 *Grouper*

88 Calories
20 Grams Protein
1 Gram Fat
0 Carbohydrate

 *Crab*

78 Calories
16 Grams Protein
1 Gram Fat
1 Gram Carbohydrate

 *Shrimp*

80 Calories
19 Grams Protein
0 Fat
0 Carbohydrate

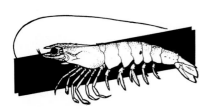 *Oysters*

72 Calories
8 Grams Protein
2 Grams Fat
5 Grams Carbohydrate

 *Clams*

54 Calories
9 Grams Protein
1 Gram Fat
3 Grams Carbohydrate

 *Scallops*

79 Calories
16 Grams Protein
1 Gram Fat
2 Grams Carbohydrate

Eating two fish meals per week is recommended because the oil in fish is a major source of eicosapentenoic acid (EPA). The oil in fish may be helpful in reducing coronary heart disease.

Nutrition data based on servings of 3½ ounces raw seafood.

Seafood and Sensible Nutrition

Americans are just beginning to recognize that seafood and good health are a natural combination. In 1986 Americans consumed a record amount of seafood—14.7 pounds per person. That figure represents an increase of 8.5 percent over 1985 figures, and a 20 percent increase is expected before the end of the century.

Why this sudden wave of interest in seafood? One answer is fish oil, the form of fat found in seafood. In the late 1970s population studies suggested that Greenland Eskimos, who dine heavily on seafood, were not plagued by heart attacks in spite of their high fat and cholesterol intake. Researchers speculated this low incidence of heart disease was primarily due to a component of fish oil known as omega-3 fatty acids.

No one is suggesting that Americans adopt the traditional Eskimo cuisine, but researchers do agree that consumers can benefit from eating more seafood not only because of recent findings related to fish oil but also because of seafood's more familiar nutritional attributes.

Getting Back to Basics with Seafood

For years, people have recognized seafood as an excellent source of top-quality protein, vitamins and minerals. This still holds true today. Ounce for ounce, the amount of protein in seafood is comparable to the amount in beef and chicken. Seafood offers the essential amino acids (building blocks of protein) that our bodies cannot manufacture and which, therefore, must be obtained through the diet. In addition, the protein in fish is easy to digest because there is a higher ratio of muscle protein to connective tissue. This quality offers a clinical advantage to persons who may require a low-bulk diet for certain digestive disorders.

Seafood is also a good source of certain vitamins—most notably vitamin B_6, vitamin B_{12} and niacin. Generally, these vitamins participate in various chemical processes related to fat, protein and energy metabolism. Also, some species, especially fattier fish, provide moderate amounts of the fat-soluble vitamins A and D.

Seafood is a source of essential minerals, such as phosphorous, selenium, iodine and fluoride. More specifically, shellfish offer substantial amounts of copper and zinc, with oysters containing ten to twenty times the amount of zinc found in other shellfish.

Iron is a mineral that receives extra attention because many consumers, especially children and pre-menopausal women, have difficulty getting enough iron to meet their needs. Although seafood is not commonly mentioned as a source of iron, some types of shellfish surpass red meat in their iron content. Generally, mollusks (those shellfish that live on the ocean floor, such as oysters, scallops and clams) are rich in iron. In fact, eight medium oysters provide about half the U.S. required daily allowance for iron.

Adequate calcium intake is also a concern, especially with increasing interest in and research on osteoperosis. While most seafoods contain relatively low levels of this mineral, small canned fish that have soft, edible bones are excellent sources of calcium. Canned salmon and sardines are examples of fish that can add calcium to the diet.

Health-conscious consumers are also mindful of sodium, a mineral found in excessive amounts in the average American diet. It is estimated that a healthy person needs only 1,100 to 3,300 milligrams of sodium per day to maintain good health. However, many Americans commonly consume five thousand to seven thousand milligrams each day. Sodium intake is strongly linked to hypertension, although a cause-effect relationship is not clear. Also, studies suggest that some people are more sensitive to dietary sodium than others. Generally, health professionals agree that it is sensible to limit sodium intake in a moderate way through prudent food selection.

Contrary to what many believe, fresh, unprocessed seafood contains only small amounts of sodium, even though it comes from the ocean's salty waters. Most fresh finfish contain sixty to one hundred milligrams of sodium per three and one-half ounces of fish, while shellfish rank slightly higher with two hundred to four hundred milligrams for three and one-half ounces of the edible portion of the fish. Sodium is added to seafoods during various processing methods, so canned, frozen and seafood-based imitation products can be higher in sodium than the fresh product. Rinsing canned seafood cuts down on sodium. A study showed that a three-minute rinse of canned water-packed tuna decreased the sodium content by 80 percent, leaving only 62 milligrams of sodium for three and one-half ounces of tuna. Also, people on a sodium-restricted diet should rely more on fresh, unprocessed seafood and cook with spices and salt-free seasonings.

Getting to the Heart of the Matter

In addition to these more familiar nutritional qualities, seafood's other healthful attributes are drawing more attention, especially with so many people trying to make healthy changes in their lifelong eating habits. Fat, fish oil, calories and cholesterol are all diet-heart issues that are bringing seafood into the spotlight.

Fat: Back in the 1920s Americans derived approximately 32 percent of their calories from fat. Over the years, that figure has changed dramatically. Surveys now estimate that fat comprises an average of 40 percent of our calories. Many experts advise Americans to cut back, and what better way to do that than by eating more seafood? Ounce for ounce, most species are much lower in fat than many other foods in today's "typical" American diet.

Fish range between 1 and 15 percent total fat content, and most shellfish contain less than 2 percent fat. Ground beef ranges between 15 and 30 percent fat, cheddar cheese is about 33 percent fat and peanut butter is over 50 percent fat. Clearly, seafood, including the "fatty" fish, is a much leaner choice than many other foods in our diet.

The fat content of a single species may vary dramatically as a result of biological and environmental factors. For example, in preparation for migration and spawning, the fat composition of a mullet may increase from 5 percent in spring to over 15 percent during the winter months. Fat content fluctuates more in fattier fish than leaner fish.

Also remember, not all fat is created equal. Over the past fifteen years, Americans have been told to replace **saturated fats** (the solid fat found in most animal products) with **polyunsaturated** alternatives in order to lower their risk for heart disease. Until now, the focus has been on using vegetable oils instead of fats such as butter and lard. Today, however, we are becoming aware of one simple but important long-known fact: compared to most other animal products, seafood is not only lower in total fat but also contains a high proportion of polyunsaturated fat. So, by substituting seafood in the diet, many people can substantially lower their intake of total fat, saturated fat and calories.

Fish oil: Because the fat in seafood is mostly unsaturated, it is present as oil rather than solid fat. Within the past ten years, the research on fish oil and its health-related benefits has quickly gained momentum. Specifically, researchers have been studying the polyunsaturated building blocks, the **omega-3 fatty acids**, that make up fish oil. The omega-3 name refers to the molecules' chemical structure. Studies indicate that these fatty acids affect certain cells and processes in a way that may help reduce the risk of heart disease and alleviate the symptoms of other disorders.

The link between the Greenland Eskimos' high intake of seafood and their low incidence of heart disease initiated further research on omega-3 fatty acids, including both population and laboratory studies. So far, the results emerging from these studies are encouraging. The most consistent effects that researchers have noted are a drop in serum triglycerides (fats in the blood) and an increase in bleeding time, both of which are beneficial in terms of reduced risk for heart disease. As far as other parameters are concerned (such as serum cholesterol and lipoprotein levels), scientists have noted beneficial effects, but not consistently. The results of their studies vary, based on the health status of the individuals, the subjects' initial blood levels of triglycerides (fat) and cholesterol, the amount and form of fish oil given, and the length of administration. In other words, no two studies are alike, so it is difficult to look at the data as a whole and draw firm conclusions.

Although they are enthusiastic, many researchers and health professionals are quick to note that they have just started putting the puzzle together and agree that it is too early to recommend general supplementation with concentrated fish oil products. Likewise, no one can claim that popping a few capsules will take the place of a healthy diet and lifestyle.

While it is true that higher fat fish generally contain more omega-3 fatty acids, all seafoods, including shellfish, are a source of omega-3s. Species in Southeastern waters that contain substantial amounts of these special fatty acids include bluefish, king mackerel and pompano.

Calories: Calorie counting has almost become a national pastime, with many Americans engaged in that seemingly endless battle to lose an extra ten pounds. What's more, one out of every five Americans is significantly overweight, and each year the rate of adolescent obesity climbs higher. Obesity is linked to many other disorders including heart disease, diabetes, high blood pressure, back problems and gall bladder disease. Likewise, obese people risk more complications during surgery and pregnancy. Because calories are such an important issue, it's good to know that seafood is exceptionally low in calories. A five-ounce portion of seafood (uncooked) will have anywhere from 130 to 230 calories, depending on its fat content. Those same five ounces of ground beef (80 percent lean) have four hundred calories. What better tasting way to cut out calories?

Cholesterol: Although researchers still are not sure about the degree to which cholesterol in the diet affects cholesterol in the blood, most agree that consumers need to decrease their cholesterol intake to one hundred milligrams of cholesterol for every one thousand calories, with a maximum intake of three hundred milligrams of cholesterol per day. In a conscious effort to follow this advice, many Americans deprive themselves of their favorite seafood sensations for fear that they may contain too much cholesterol. However, note that one medium oyster contains about nine milligrams of cholesterol, while an egg yolk has about 270 milligrams.

Obviously, not all shellfish are high in cholesterol, as many people think. There are two distinct groups of shellfish: the mollusks (clams, oysters, scallops and mussels) and the crustaceans (shrimp, crab, lobster and crayfish). As a group, crustaceans are generally higher in cholesterol, while the mollusks rate much lower on the scale, having only half to one-third the cholesterol of foods such as beef and poultry.

Some cholesterol values are much lower than previously thought. Fifteen years ago when researchers first measured what they thought was cholesterol in shellfish, they were actually measuring a whole group of related compounds known as sterols. Today, however, new analytical methods can distinguish cholesterol from its chemical relatives, so certain values, especially for some mollusks, are much lower than previously

thought. Also keep in mind that any cholesterol values are *approximate*. Cholesterol content within a species can vary up to forty milligrams depending on the season, location, spawning, how recently the animal shed its shell, etc. In addition, remember that cholesterol is not the same thing as fat, even though cholesterol's molecular structure is classified as a type of fat (or lipid). In food, the cholesterol content is considered separately from the fat content.

Also, there is no such thing as "good" or "bad" cholesterol in foods. While the amount of cholesterol will vary, the basic chemical structure is the same. The terms "good" and "bad" cholesterol were originally used to describe different protein-cholesterol complexes in the bloodstream. HDL-C (high density lipoprotein-cholesterol) is sometimes referred to as the "good guy" because when blood cholesterol is measured, a higher HDL-C fraction is associated with a lower risk for heart disease. Conversely, LDL-C (low density lipoprotein-cholesterol) was thought of as "bad cholesterol" since more LDL-C suggests a higher risk of heart disease. Other factors such as total serum cholesterol, smoking habits, heredity, exercise, etc., also help predict a person's risk for heart disease.

If you are trying to keep your cholesterol intake below three hundred milligrams per day, as encouraged by the American Heart Association, a three and one-half ounce serving of lobster will provide about one-third of the day's allotment. Eight medium shrimp (count thirty to thirty-five per pound) have only half the cholesterol of one medium egg yolk. It's easy then to include shellfish on the day's menu provided that you're careful about other dietary sources of cholesterol. Neither should seafood be judged by cholesterol content alone. When it comes to eating right, total fat and saturated fat are just as important to consider. All varieties of shellfish contain less than 4 percent fat, while most have less than 2 percent fat, which is mostly unsaturated.

Recipe Renovation with Nutritious Seafood

You are ready to make some healthy changes in your eating habits. But are you afraid that some of your favorite seafood recipes overdo it on the cholesterol, fat and calories? Don't worry. All it takes is a little recipe renovation:

• Take a look at each ingredient. Is it a keeper or can it be thrown out entirely? You can often do without the added salt that many recipes call for. Also some casseroles work well without the crunchy toppings that are often listed in the recipe.

• Can you cut down on the amount of some ingredients? You'll save one hundred calories by using one tablespoon of oil instead of two. Instead of whole almonds try using a smaller amount of sliced almonds and sprinkle them sparingly.

• Try substituting with lighter alternatives. Use low-fat yogurt instead of sour cream. Rather than dipping fish in whole eggs before breading, use only egg white or skim milk. Instead of nuts, try a crunchy alternative like water chestnuts or celery.

• Many new low-fat, low-calorie substitutes have appeared on the market, which make substitutions even easier. Mayonnaise, cottage cheese, margarine, yogurt and cheddar cheese are all examples of ingredients that are now available with less fat and fewer calories than the original products.

• Prepare mixed dishes that combine seafood with vegetables, grains and pasta. This is a good way to stretch a small portion of seafood, and you can actually decrease the amount of fat and cholesterol per serving.

• To keep from overestimating, measure ingredients when necessary, especially fats and oils.

• Instead of relying on heavy sauces for flavor, prepare fish with spices and flavorful vegetables such as basil, curry, onions, peppers, garlic and ginger.

• Bake, broil, grill and steam seafood instead of frying. Also, oven frying is a healthier alternative than deep-fat frying.

Got the picture? Recipe renovation might involve a little trial and error as well as some initial tastebud adjustment, but give yourself a chance. You'll be doing your health a favor.

Health Tips

PREPARATION

One rule for cooking fish is to cook it 10 minutes per 1 inch of thickness. (To determine thickness, measure thickest part of fish with a ruler.) Double cooking time for frozen fish. The 10-minute rule applies for all cooking methods except microwaving.

Remember, fish cooks quickly. Fish is done when the flesh becomes opaque and the fish flakes easily with a fork. Over-cooking tends to toughen and dry out the flesh.

Poaching, steaming, baking, broiling, sautéing and microwaving are excellent low-fat cooking methods. Select any of these methods to keep the calorie and fat content of your seafood dishes low.

If you need to limit your sodium intake, request that salt not be added to your meal during preparation.

STEAMING

Place seafood on a steaming rack set 2 inches above boiling liquid in a deep pot. Season as desired. Cover tightly. Reduce heat and steam until done. Mollusks, such as mussels and clams, and other seafoods are excellent when steamed.

BAKING

Place seafood in a baking dish. Add sauce or topping to keep moist. Cover and bake at 400 degrees until done. Suggested sauce: 1 tablespoon melted polyunsaturated margarine, 1 tablespoon lemon juice, ¼ teaspoon onion powder and ½ teaspoon dried basil. Makes enough for one pound of fish.

BROILING

Place seafood on a broiler pan. Brush with a small amount of melted polyunsaturated margarine and lemon juice. Flavor with herbs and spices, such as pepper and dill weed. Broil 4 to 5 inches from heat source without turning. Cook until done.

POACHING

Estimate amount of liquid needed to barely cover a single layer of fish in a saucepan or skillet. Suggested liquids include skim milk, water or wine. Season liquid with chopped carrots, celery, onions and peppercorns. Bring seasoned liquid to a boil. Cover and simmer about 10 minutes. Add fish. Simmer until done. Poaching is an easy method of preparing fish for the beginning cook.

SAUTÉING

Heat a small amount of polyunsaturated margarine or boil with liquid, such as white wine, in a skillet. Add chopped mushrooms, green onions, lemon juice and seafood to liquid. Sauté over medium high heat until done.

MICROWAVING

Place seafood in a nonmetal dish and cover with plastic wrap. Cook approximately three minutes per pound or follow manufacturer's directions.

DINING OUT

To maintain a "heart healthy" meal plan away from home, follow these tips:

APPETIZERS

Fresh seafood items, such as oysters on the half-shell, make excellent choices for appetizers. Choose fresh fruits and vegetables or seafood cocktails with lemon wedges. Avoid paté, creamed soups, caviar, fried hors d'oeuvres or dips that are high in fat.

SOUPS

Choose cioppino, vegetable or bean soup. Broths and consommés are higher in sodium. Cream soups may be high in fat.

SALADS

Order fresh green salads with seafood or fresh fruit. Limit shrimp and cheese. Omit hard-boiled eggs, bacon or imitation bacon bits. Order vinegar and oil-based or diet dressings on the side.

ENTREES

Request that seafoods be poached, steamed, stir-fried, broiled or baked. Try flavoring with a squeeze of lemon. Avoid deep-fried foods or foods prepared with butter, breading, rich cream or cheese sauces. If the serving size is large, ask the waiter to package half a portion to take home.

HERBS AND SPICES

Herbs and spices can be combined in creative ways to make seafood recipes more flavorful. Instead of using your salt shaker, try cooking fish with herbs or spices to enhance its flavor. If unfamiliar with cooking with herbs and spices, start by combining ¼ teaspoon of 1 or 2 herbs or spices per pound of seafood.

Allspice	Dill weed	Paprika
Sweet basil	Fennel seed	Parsley
Bay leaf	Marjoram	Rosemary

Cayenne	Mustard	Saffron
Chervil	Nutmeg	Tarragon
Dill seed	Oregano	Thyme

Celery seed or leaves
Curry Powder
Garlic powder

Other seasonings: garlic, lemon and wine
Suggested combinations include:
Basil, marjoram and oregano
Garlic powder and lemon
Parsley and tarragon

Seafood Smoking Chart

Size and Shape	Quantity for 4 Servings	Marinating Time in Brine*	Cooking Temperature	Cooking Time
Butterfly fillets (1 pound each before filleting)	4 pounds	30 minutes	150°-175° 200° 250°	1½ hours 45 minutes 30 minutes
Fillets or steaks (½-inch thick)	1½ pounds	30 minutes	150°-175° 200° 250°	1 hour 30 minutes 20 minutes
Fillets or steaks (¾-inch thick)	1½ pounds	45 minutes	150°-175° 200° 250°	1½ hours 30-45 minutes 30 minutes
Fillets or steaks (1-inch thick)	1½ pounds	45 minutes	150° 200° 250°	1¾ hours 30-45 minutes 30 minutes
Fillets or steaks (1½ inches thick)	2½ pounds	1 hour	150°-175° 200° 250°	2 hours 1¼ hours 45-50 minutes
Pan-dressed	2½ pounds	30 minutes	150°-175° 200° 250°	2 hours 1¼ hours 45-50 minutes

*To brine fish: Thaw fish if frozen. Combine 1 gallon cold water and 1 cup salt; stir until dissolved. Marinate fish in brine in refrigerator for specified time before smoking. Rinse fish thoroughly in cold water and dry carefully after brining.

Timetable for Cooking Fish

METHOD OF COOKING	MARKET FORM	AMOUNT FOR 6	COOKING TEMPERATURE	APPROXIMATE COOKING TIME (minutes)
Baking	Dressed Pan-dressed Fillets or steaks Frozen fried fish portions Frozen fried fish sticks	3 pounds 3 pounds 2 pounds 12 portions (2½ to 3 oz. each) 24 sticks (¾ to 1¼ oz. each)	350° 350° 350° 400° 400°	45 to 60 25 to 30 20 to 25 15 to 20 15 to 20
Broiling	Pan-dressed Fillets or steaks Frozen fried fish portions Frozen fried fish sticks	3 pounds 2 pounds 12 portions (2½ to 3 oz. each) 24 sticks (¾ to 1¼ oz. each)		10 to 16* 10 to 15 10 to 15 10 to 15
Charcoal Broiling	Pan-dressed Fillets or steaks Frozen fried fish portions Frozen fried fish sticks	3 pounds 2 pounds 12 portions (2½ to 3 oz. each) 24 sticks (¾ to 1¼ oz. each)	Moderate Moderate Moderate Moderate	10 to 16* 10 to 16* 8 to 10* 8 to 10*
Deep-Fat Frying	Pan-dressed Fillets or steaks Frozen raw breaded fish portions	3 pounds 2 pounds 12 portions (2½ to 3 oz. each)	350° 350° 350°	3 to 5 3 to 5 3 to 5
Oven-Frying	Pan-dressed Fillets or steaks	3 pounds 2 pounds	500° 500°	15 to 20 10 to 15
Pan-Frying	Pan-dressed Fillets or steaks Frozen raw breaded or frozen fried fish portions Frozen fried fish sticks	3 pounds 2 pounds 12 portions (2½ to 3 oz. each) 24 sticks (¾ to 1¼ oz. each)	Moderate Moderate Moderate Moderate	8 to 10* 8 to 10* 8 to 10* 8 to 10*
Poaching	Fillets or steaks	2 pounds	Simmer	5 to 10
Steaming	Fillets or steaks	1½ pounds	Boil	5 to 10

*Turn once during cooking.

INDEX